AT THE
STRANGERS' GATE

AT THE
STRANGERS' GATE

Arrivals in New York

ADAM GOPNIK

ALFRED A. KNOPF
New York Toronto
2017

THIS IS A BORZOI BOOK
PUBLISHED BY ALFRED A. KNOPF
AND ALFRED A. KNOPF CANADA

www.aaknopf.com
www.penguinrandomhouse.ca

Knopf, Borzoi Books, and the colophon are registered trademarks
of Penguin Random House Ltd.
Knopf Canada and the colophon are trademarks
of Penguin Random House Canada Limited.

Permissions to reprint previously published material may be found
following the acknowledgments.

Library of Congress Cataloging-in-Publication Data
Names: Gopnik, Adam, author.
Title: At the strangers' gate : arrivals in New York / Adam Gopnik.
Description: First edition. | New York : Knopf, 2017. | "This is a Borzoi book."
Identifiers: LCCN 2017016651 | ISBN 9781400041800 (hardback) |
ISBN 9781101947500 (ebook)
Subjects: LCSH: New York (N.Y.)—Description and travel. | Gopnik, Adam—
Family. | Gopnik, Adam—Friends and associates. | New York (N.Y.)—
Biography. | New York (N.Y.)—Social life and customs—20th century. |
BISAC: BIOGRAPHY & AUTOBIOGRAPHY / Personal Memoirs. |
BIOGRAPHY & AUTOBIOGRAPHY / Artists, Architects, Photographers. |
LITERARY CRITICISM / Books & Reading.
Classification: LCC F128.55 .G669 2017 | DDC 974.7/1042—dc23
LC record available at https://lccn.loc.gov/2017016651

Library and Archives Canada Cataloguing in Publication
Gopnik, Adam, author
At the strangers' gate : arrivals in New York / Adam Gopnik.
Issued in print and electronic formats.
ISBN 978-0-676-97828-5   eBook ISBN 978-0-7352-7313-9
1. Gopnik, Adam—Homes and haunts—New York (State)—New York.
2. Gopnik, Adam—Family. 3. New York (N.Y.)—Description and travel.
4. New York (N.Y.)—Biography. 5. New York (N.Y.)—Social life and customs—
20th century. I. Title.
F128.55.G66 2017   917.47'10443   C2017-901087-5

Jacket photo by Blake Gopnik
Jacket design by Chip Kidd

Manufactured in the United States of America
First Edition

This one is only for

MARTHA

*First, last, love, life, ever, always,
awake, or (quite often in this book) asleep.*

Contents

Part One THE BLUE ROOM

1 The Blue Room and the Big Store   3
2 The First Fall   20
3 Food Fight   39
4 My First Job   49
5 Seeing Theo   57
6 The Simple Logic of Summer Shirts   84
7 Men Making Pictures of Women Wearing Clothes   108

Part Two THE BIG STORE

8 SoHo, 1983   133
9 Writing   193
10 Sleeping and Talking   211
11 Wanderings   225
   Epilogue   250

   Acknowledgments   255

Part One

THE BLUE ROOM

The Blue Room and the Big Store

A Bus to the City, a Train to a Wedding

On the morning I was to be married in New York, I went to a bookstore, as I always did in moments of crisis or bliss—until all the bookstores closed and you had to seek some comfort or inspiration somewhere in the ether, like a monk. There I found what I hoped would serve as an epigraph for our approaching wedding. It was from the eighteenth-century Japanese poet Issa, the most humorous and tender of haiku makers, and it ran simply:

> *The world of dew is*
> *a world of dew,*
> *but even so . . .*

I grasped it at once, or thought I did, in all its pregnant simplicity, its simple bow and implicit enormity. Life passes, and it's difficult, but within it, pleasures and epiphanies arise—you marry the prettiest girl you've ever met in the greatest city on earth. Don't kid yourself—but maybe you can kid yourself a bit. (Years later, when I was writing "Talk of the Town" for *The New Yorker,* I would interview one of The Andrews Sisters about Bing Crosby: "You couldn't kid him a lot," she said warily. "But you could kid him a *little*." It depended on the angle that he wore his hat. Life, it occurred to me, is like Bing Crosby, its moods indicated by the pressures of the time, like that hat. That morning, the hat was on at just the right angle.)

Years later still, when she was pregnant, Martha, the girl I married that morning, made me promise not to go to a bookstore while she was in labor. As it happened, the labor was drawn out, and, wanting to avoid an argument with the obnoxious obstetrician, I took a break during hour six, and did end up in a bookstore around the corner from the hospital. It was a good move. Martha was so panicked by my absence—with the constant noise of ambulances arriving at the emergency entrance nearby, she easily imagined some tragic-karmic accident—that she dilated. I arrived just in time for the birth of our son, and carrying a wonderful copy of Santayana's *The Sense of Beauty*, which, I swear, I really did intend to read aloud to her, if things had gone on any longer.

But that, as I said, was years later—actually, only a few, as older people reckon these things, but at the time, what would stretch to a decade seemed a lifetime. It *was* a lifetime.

When I say "married in New York" I know that it might sound rather like top hats and morning coats and a ceremony at St. Thomas Episcopal. In fact, on a bleak December day, we would take the 5 train to City Hall, with a license and blood test results in hand, and submit to a minute-and-a-half-long ceremony administered by an official who looked a bit like Don Ameche in his guise as host of *International Circus* from my childhood. And so, after approximately forty-five further seconds of obligation and vows, we took the subway back to the nine-by-eleven basement room where we were beginning our life, a place that we had dubbed "the Blue Room," in honor of an old Rodgers & Hart song that I was insane enough to remember, and that Martha was insane enough to accept as a guide to living. The song was about a couple who choose a "blue room," a single studio where they can start their life: "Not like a ballroom, / A small room, / A hall room . . ." Away from everyone else, in the smallest studio in Manhattan, they were happy.

The subway trip downtown was, in a way, only an extension of a trip south we had begun a few months before in Canada, getting on a bus marked "New York City," like something out of a 1940s musical. My father saw us off. Fathers are supposed to give advice to young men and women leaving the provinces for the metropolis. D'Artagnan's father in *The Three Musketeers* tells him to fight duels with everyone once he gets to Paris—sensible advice for a guy with a sword who knows how to use it. When Sky Masterson—you know, the hero of *Guys and Dolls*—leaves Colorado for New York, *his* father tells him that if a guy in the big city shows you a brand-new deck of cards, seal unbroken, and wants to bet that when he opens it the jack of hearts will leap out and squirt cider in your ear, don't take that bet: the jack *will* leap out and start to squirt. That is to say, in the big city, nobody makes an apparently crazy bet if the deck isn't already gaffed. (This is, of course, a corollary to the famous advice that if you're sitting at a card table and can't figure out who the sucker is, you're the sucker.)

My father's advice when I left Canada for New York was simple: "Never underestimate the other person's insecurity." This was excellent counsel, and what trouble I would get into came mostly from forgetting it. Everyone, even the apparently powerful, is struggling inside with a raging fear of being unloved, or at least unappreciated, an emotion only magnified by the enormity of the city. Thinking it over decades later, I suspect my father was getting at the real point of Sky Masterson's dad's advice about not taking the bet on the squirting jacks, or its corollary, anyway: everybody at the table may be a sucker. The guy with the gaffed deck is playing with a gaffed deck because he doesn't think he can win with one that isn't. Even the wise guys are most often suckers inside, or feel like it. That's what makes them insecure. It is the dapper and self-contained card sharp who is the illusion of the card table—or the city.

My father spoke in the summer of 1980. I arrived in New York that August, and the next ten years of my life were big ones. But I was twenty when I got here, so they would have been big for me if I had spent them at a recording station in the Arctic Circle. With the special energy that we have when we first arrive in a new place, Martha and I diligently explored all the odd corners of the city. We inspected what seemed like every navigable inch of Central Park, going in and out of all the gates that Olmsted and Vaux had named, poetically, when they designed it, with the Strangers' Gate, up at 106th and Central Park West, having for us a special resonance. We were strangers, and we had arrived, and we dreamt of becoming citizens.

＝＝＝

Almost forty years on, the eighties in New York seem momentous in the larger life of the world, too. Forty years is the natural gestation time of nostalgia, the interval it takes for a past period to become a lost time, and, sometimes, a golden age. There's a simple reason to explain why. Everybody's shocking first intimation of the setting sun—which takes about forty years to happen—inspires a look back at the sun rising, and its imagined light makes everything from then look golden. Though pop culture is most often performed by the young, the directors and programmers and gatekeepers— the suits who control and create the conditions, who make the calls and choose the players—are, and always have been, largely forty-somethings. The four-decade interval brings us back roughly to a point when they were becoming aware of themselves. Forty years ago is the potently fascinating time when we were just arriving, when our parents were youthful and in love, the Edenic period preceding the fallen state recorded in our actual memories.

Yet the eighties, though once again a set subject, still bear more disapproval than it seems quite fair to load on any past time. Their light shines in retrospect more brassy yellow than truly gold and generous. The time gets summed up in a phrase no one actually said: Greed is good. Greed *was*, perhaps, more unapologetic at the time than it had ever been before. It was not so much that we experienced capitalism with the gloves off as capitalism without guilt, or, to put it another way, without a conscience. A lot of people got rich and had no shame about it, along the way remaking the city in their image.

Still, the truth is that no period or place belongs to the neat summaries of popular history. Moods don't change so readily; lives aren't lived in such neatly determined packages. We live as much in defiance of the popular themes as in thrall to them. The headlines are of no help when we're making up our own epitaphs. When I think of the eighties I can recall one or two shimmering nights when rich men did rule, but I recall more mornings when having a pair of sneakers and a Walkman seemed to mark one most as a lover of his time. History and experience still are measured out on separate cutting boards. We know that, exactly, by how badly they fit each other. When we put on our period clothes, so to speak, the pants puddle and the waist tugs and the jacket won't quite button up. The adjustments that have to be made are the proof of how off the measurements are in memory. I used to tell my readers, during the part of the eighties I spent giving anonymous advice as a fashion copywriter, that God is in the details, or that a love for the details is what takes the place of God. I said this to the readers of a men's fashion magazine, who must have been startled to find such chewy aphoristic atheism in its pages—or, rather, not "readers," since they were, as intended, too busy looking at the pants. The zippers of experience and the broad cut of history never quite fit.

Still, something did change then. Not human nature, perhaps, something more like the national character. In the eighties in New York all the bounds of money began to loosen. At the same time, most of the certainties that rich people once had about sex and life and marriage and roles that people played came to an end. Most notions of equality dissolved, but so did most notions of gentility. The tandem effect is still baffling to a lot of people, who thought it had all along been the gentility perpetuating the inequalities, instead of the other way round. In 1961, Lenny Bruce was arrested and martyred for saying "cocksucker" in a nightclub in California. By the time Ronald Reagan was President, anyone could say "cocksucker" in any nightclub in California; or, rather, by the time you could say "cocksucker" in any nightclub in California, Ronald Reagan was President. Sorting out the contradictions—or at least living within them tolerably—is part of the work of getting the era.

Why, in a city ruled by brutal materialism, did things seem increasingly unreal? One answer was that the buying and selling had become so abstract that only unreal signs could represent them. Money had always meant a lot. Now some thought that money meant *everything*, that only money had weight in the world. Others thought that now money *meant* everything. Not just that everything had been pushed aside for the pursuit of money but that even what remained as art or music had no way of getting itself expressed except *through* money—or some fluid that represented it. Jeff Koons's art was like this. Money wasn't just its subject. Money was its essence—or was supposed to be. The cold, dead hand of the commodity was not to be juiced or colored or mocked or made to look religious—"iconic," to use that awful word—as it had in the age of Warhol. It was all there was. Money had pushed every other value aside. Money was indistinguishable from art. Koons's silver bunny was the demon of our time: once a plaything, now encased in bullion, ridiculous and sinister and cold. Money had made itself into art.

This was false, of course. As long as mortality exists, money will be mocked. You really *can't* take it with you. There were plenty of things that money couldn't mean. (Jeff Koons, encountered one time on the street, wept for a son taken from him, whom no amount could summon back or replace; later, I would also see the critic Robert Hughes, Koons's bête noire, weep on the same street for his own lost son.) But those things led a more furtive or vestigial life.

I had the sense of another divide taking shape, one harder to see but just as important. To myself, I called it "The Blue Room and the Big Store," and even thought already then of writing a book with that title. The world was getting blowsier and bigger and harder to capture; the counter-life was taking place in smaller and smaller rooms. It took place in stranger and stranger subcultures, in more bizarre and eccentric existences, lived more marginally than before. This made for a kind of broken disjunction between public life and private experience.

Within that divide, we were still an ambitious generation. Ambition seemed admirable and also plausible, in a way that it no longer quite does to many. We accepted an astonishing amount of absurdity in our living conditions and appetites—our *Girls* tiny apartments—in pursuit of our ambitions, but on the whole we expected them to be realized. Today the young live less absurd lives, but have more chastened ambitions. Adequacy seems, bitterly, enough. Watching Lena Dunham's series about twenty-somethings in Brooklyn now, I am startled to see the protagonist, Hannah, getting exactly the same job at the same men's magazine that I had gotten in 1983. But where we saw such jobs—absurdly, but even so—as an obvious step on the ladder to writerly fame, Hannah feels trapped and miserable. The people in the cubicles around hers also seem trapped. There's more room to breathe, but less room to maneuver. "We just want things to be adequate," remarked a smart and admired but slightly resigned member of the editorial staff on the magazine where I happily ended up, following the journey described in these pages. She meant that the old arcs of ambition and aspiration seemed unpersuasive. We tolerated woeful inadequacy in sure and certain hope, as the Anglican prayer for the dead would have it, of eventual deliverance. When I go to the homes of the twenty-somethings now, I sense that they live on higher floors, but have lower ceilings.

I was certainly ambitious to accomplish things, though if you had asked me, on the bus going south, to define what the things were I was ambitious to do—well, what strikes me now is how circuitous it all was. I wanted to become some odd amalgam of E. B. White and Lorenz Hart, writing wry essays with one hand and witty lyrics with the other, while supervising a sort of salon of like-minded people—while Martha and I shared a townhouse out of *The House on East 88th Street*, with lots of children and a Christmas tree that went floor to ceiling. And maybe an alligator, too.

But what I had actually undertaken to do was to spend four years studying academic art history in an extremely demanding and competitive graduate school. Though one part of me pretended that I was just serving time and using their fellowship money while I waited for the other, niftier stuff, the truth was that my naturally competitive instincts made me want to triumph there, too. So I thought that I would, in the spare time taken from literature and the musical theater, nimbly repair the dusty study of old pictures, which I had decided relied too much on musty archival research. I would reform art history by writing evocative treatises on the true nature of, say, Renaissance art while simultaneously pursuing all the other, larger ambitions.

What puzzles me now is that I did not see the sheer *cumbersomeness* of this life plan: going to graduate school while trying to write pieces for magazines while hoping to become a composer—basically, doing one thing full-time and another part-time in order eventually to do something else entirely. (But, then, I realize I still do more or less the same thing now; I just do it in an environment where it's declared useful rather than wasteful.) If there is one thing I've learned, it's that ambition shouldn't be pursued circuitously at all, but in a straight line: see that thing out there and then chase it. Straight lines are worthy of their good publicity: they really are the shortest routes between two points. But circuitous ambitions at least lead you around in their own wide circles. It does take you longer to get where you're going, but you take a wide route while you do. I wasted years of time being ambitious about things that were not my ambition, but I met a lot of entrancing people doing it. And meanwhile all the ambitions really came together, as a single task, around the only thing I have ever been any good at: putting the right set of words in their one possible order. I was pursuing that in a straight line at least.

Straight lines or curved, one might almost say that ours was the last ambitious generation—but that would be too typically ambitious a statement. In the mid-eighties, our friends were young novelists and artists, and their books were published and their pictures hanged and their prices advanced, and their advances grew,

and though the intelligent among them knew that we were clinging, by the very edge of our fingernails, to the half-inch ledge on
the crumbling façade of a building already condemned and under
demolition—still, the view from up there looked fine for the
moment. The old equations of ambition and energy and success still
held, or seemed to.

═══

So we arrived in New York and, staying for a time at a discount hotel
in midtown, carefully spending fellowship money, we went to an
apartment broker on East Eighty-sixth Street, and for a week looked
at tiny one-bedrooms in Yorkville. (I was going to go to school at
Seventy-eighth and Fifth; Martha was beginning at Columbia.)
Martha liked none of them, and the exasperated broker at last sent
us to go look at a studio on Eighty-seventh Street near First Avenue.
I think now perhaps he was hoping that, seeing something like this
one, we would also see sense, and stop hoping for too much, settle
for one of the others we'd already seen. This one, you see, was a
nine-by-eleven room in a basement. It defined impossibility.

But he didn't know how crazy we were. Or how entrapped in
our particular folie à deux, in which impossibility became a form
of idealization. This tiny studio looked out on the back of a church
with a stained-glass window on leaded backgrounds. From it, we
could walk to the Metropolitan Museum. It was just a shoebox, but
we felt it was a romantic shoebox. (The rent was about the same as
it was in all the tiny apartments we looked at. Three hundred and
seventy-nine dollars a month. Four hundred was our top.) We were
so enraptured with the idea of our escaping and intertwining that
everything unappealing about the place was transposed into the key
of irresistible. *"We'll have a blue room, / A new room, / For two room,
/ Where ev'ry day's a holiday / Because you're married to me. . . ."*

Like all romantic illusions, this one got debunked pretty quickly:
by mice and cockroaches and other, less mobile kinds of squalor.
But the point of a romantic illusion is not that it is an illusion but
that it is romantic. The romance renews the illusion. I reinhabit it

as I write. No one really surrenders an illusion in the face of a fact. We prefer the illusion to the fact. The more facts you invoke, in fact, the stronger the illusion becomes. All faith is immune to all facts to the contrary, or else we would not have such hearty faiths and such oft-resisted facts. If your faith is in life's poetry, as ours was, a tiny room inadequate by any human standard and designed to make life borderline impossible looks appealing. The less possible it becomes, the more beautiful the illusion looks. Such illusions—call them delusions; I won't argue now—grow under the pressure of absurdity as champagne grapes sweeten under the stress of cold ground. We learn in life through the process of replacing one illusion with a slightly roomier one. We don't learn about rooms by learning that you can't live in a room. You just make the room your life. Then you find another. You hope it's bigger. You hope it's rooms.

———

We are on a subway, going to City Hall, together, as we were on the bus before. Who were we, the boy and girl on the bus and then the train? My inadequacy as hero of the city or even the story is the subject of these pages. Heroes declare their inadequacy to be heroes by the act of writing: to explain is to excuse. Every story is an apology for something. But the heroine, or anyway distaff-side talker, Alice to my Ralph, is another story, and deserves—or anyway demands—a page or two of her own.

Martha was already who she would become, and to say that is to begin to describe her. To write about someone who has been your companion, lover, partner, and cosigner—ending as the CEO and CFO of a tiny money-losing venture with two extremely well-paid employees with great educational benefits—for almost forty years is difficult, while to write lovingly, not to say amorously, of your wife is considered very bad form. Uxoriousness may be admirable in life, but it's dubious in prose. I have tried to understand why this is, and the simple reason is that it seems at once oddly boastful and untrue. The lounge singer who winks at his wife and says, "That beautiful lady has been with me for forty years," is, we feel sure, actually winking at the coat check girl. Too much wife wooing is dubious because the subject is listening, hovering around the margin of the page. Sigh for a lost love and the world sighs with you; sigh for a current spouse and the world doesn't know which way to look. But what can I do?

At eighteen, she was the prettiest girl I had ever seen, and that she should have found me appealing remains the great event, and mystery, of my life. Her prettiness, however old-fashioned the word, is uncontroversial, I'm told. She was and would become many other things as well, a feminist and a filmmaker, but it would be a lie to say that the prettiness was not the first thing I noticed about her, as it would be the steadiest thing I would keep about her.

We met before college. I was five years out of high school—I had graduated, God help me, at fourteen—and she was still in it. She had grown up with her Icelandic mother and her sister, Julia, who was the one who gave the party where we met, in a gracious stone house with a garden on the outskirts of Montreal—a "suburb," I should say, but in winter especially it felt more like a frontier outpost than a subdivision. It was like entering a three-woman convent. They shared a mannered, melodious way of speaking. Oddly, though I assume she still speaks that way now, I can hear it only in memory. They liked mock clichés, or clichés used in a mocking way—"She's a woman *truly* at the crossroads" or "It was *quite* the soirée"—which they repeated with mischievous smiles. The accent was part drawl unique to Montreal English-speakers, and part lilt by way of Iceland. A simple sentence I heard her say on the night we met—"We all went to the lecture, but it was a bit of a catastrophe!"—became a study in melodic extension: "We all went to the lec-shure—but it was a bit of a cat-aaaas-trophe." They loved old-fashioned expressions, which they used with ironic delight. "We were truly *ensconced* at the hotel" or "By then, the *hurly-burly* was a thing of the past . . ." or "Let us do this deed while the fit is upon us. . . ." They loved planning elaborate social occasions—teas and brunches and "at homes"—but were equally wary of guests who would not leave. "If we invite Caroline, she'll stay talking all after*noon*," Julia would

say to Martha conspiratorially. "So you say that you have to finish a paper and I'll say that I'll call her a taxi—if we let her walk
to the bus, she'll stand by the door for *hours*." They planned their
escape from the social occasions they were planning with even more
delight than they planned the occasions themselves.

Beautiful and passionate, she had made love to a series of suitors
in the basement of that same house—the mother was Nordic, after
all, and pleased at least to know where her daughter was—with an
enthusiasm (and resourcefulness) that belied her china doll aspect.
That aspect, her mother knew, was an illusion maintained by sleep
and energy and maternal care, and there was at most a three-hour
window before the girl's stamina collapsed. Her mother was sure
she was even more fragile than she was. And so she encouraged her
in the habit of being a marathon sleeper.

She certainly slept more than anyone I have ever known. I would
call at eleven in the morning on a Saturday and she would be sleeping. Twelve noon . . . still asleep. To this day, her normal serving of
sleep is ten solid hours, and eleven is not unknown. But later, when
children arrived, and for twenty years it meant getting up in the
middle of the night and then early in the morning, she would do it
uncomplainingly. She was as fragile as her mother feared, but more
resilient than her mother knew. The gracility and the resilience both
became my companions.

The resilience had come, I learned soon enough, from having her
soul pulled so taut with longing. She longed for London streets. She
longed for Paris parks. (Later, she would find out that the London
streets were mostly imaginary, though the Paris parks were real.)
She longed for a life bigger and brighter and more engaged than the
one she knew in the pretty, reliable winter world of Montreal.

We had both grown up in Montreal, going to school and then
college in its still-thriving—what would once have been called its
"bustling"—*centre-ville*, its center city. Montreal seemed dream-
like then, even to those who were awake in it. Thirty years behind
American cities, it was still a sweet place to live. There was a thriving downtown, unscarred by social change. To shop mooningly

at Ogilvy's department store, still Scottish in feel, with the same Christmas windows for a quarter-century, was to feel oneself in touch with the old Empire. To have lunch—as she loved to do—at Eaton's, in its ninth-floor re-creation of the dining room of the SS *Île de France*, was to inhabit the kind of happy, bourgeois civilization that had already been atomized in "safe" cities elsewhere. It was more like Fitzgerald's St. Paul at the turn of the century than like the now despoiled Philadelphia where I had been born. You could spend a night on rue Saint-Denis, which, though not Parisian, was French, or go to any of the thriving Hungarian cafés and enjoy something more than a tourist's taste of an older, Middle European culture. It was sweet to spend a summer night at La Ronde, the amusement park, or a winter morning skiing on Mount Royal. There was a gentleness to Montreal then, which was, I suppose, largely inseparable from its provincialism. (This was true provincialism, the kind born of a language group secluded from a larger world; later, the Québécois provincialism was extended, as much by indifference as benevolence, to the sub-provincialisms, Jewish and Hungarian and Haitian, that it superintended.) Montreal was what I can only call a naïve city—it had a naïveté of tone, an earnestness of spirit, which I still recognize in things that began there, like the Cirque du Soleil. What they share is not having soured on the simpler kinds of pleasure. Even those of us who dreamed of a larger horizon and more varied flavors sensed how sweet it was to live there. But it was also a small place, and we wanted out. Now sweetness seems to me so much rarer than spaciousness as to be relished above all things. But I didn't know that then.

That I became her flock of birds to get out is odd and lucky. Someone once called her in print the most innately polite person she had ever met, and the truth is that in each of us natural sociability had been overlaid with Canadian politeness, and hers with a further coat of Icelandic courtesy, producing a veneer of politeness so extreme that many took it for disingenuousness—which of course, in another way, it was.

Ambitious and erotically alive, startlingly experienced for an eighteen-year-old, she loved expressing her capacity for passion. There's a photograph from our wedding day—our second ceremonial wedding day, the following summer in Montreal—in which she is reaching right over the Mies chair in my parents' living room to kiss me, her face buried in mine, with the contortion of my body registering a surprise I felt then and still feel, on occasion. *I don't deserve her,* I thought. *You don't deserve her,* her mother thought. *No one deserves me,* I think she thought—and, thinking that, decided that she might as well make herself a gift to one of the undeserving, if he came with a destination.

She was above all stylish, a prodigy of fashion, really. She had a clothes philosophy and an unerring eye for what looked right—to wear the right thing was to become another kind of person. She loved clothes as no one I have ever known. This was not frivolous, and even less was it superficial. Someone who took such trouble to pull herself together—the one right T-shirt could take days of shopping—had decided to face the world with joy. Had decided to outface the world. (Years later, when Richard Avedon became our adoptive father, they could talk for hours about angles and hems, sharing a faith in fashion that sounded silly if made too articulate, but was sublime if lived as laughter.)

"You're making me sound like an airheaded clothes horse," she said a moment ago. It wasn't just clothes, she urges me to point out, right now, hovering above my keyboard: she loved "beautiful things" of all kinds. Okay. But what was astonishing to my teenage mind was that each beautiful thing was for her nestled in a kind of web of invisible wires, each tugging on scenes from old musicals and chapters from old books, from *Mary Poppins* to novels by Virginia Woolf, so that a Wedgwood plate or a tartan robe pulled with it, toward it, entire worlds of feeling that she longed for. My own family had a taste for beauty, God knows, but it tended toward things whose beauty was self-contained—my parents collected minimal art, planks and slabs of heavily lacquered wood—or else was a function of the thing's newness, my family being true believers in the myth of the avant-garde. If it was strange and new it was beautiful.

For her, it was by being *not* strange and *not* new that things earned their beauty. They were familiar, but familiar not from a middle-class life in Canada; rather, from an imaginary life glimpsed in books and movie theaters, which she was determined to get to. Ever since she was small, she had been following the invisible wires that tugged on things from their point of origin, the places she longed for. The things also longed for their original homes, and if one simply followed them religiously enough, one might get there, too. The invisible wires all led away from Montreal, sweet though it was, away from family, loving though they might be, away from home. The invisible wires all led elsewhere.

We decided that we believed in what we called "poetry," which meant anything except rhymed or metered verse. It meant an attitude toward life that didn't take practicalities too seriously. It was materialistic without being at all realistic—though now I know that materialism without realism is a ticket to the poor house, or a life of debt. We would walk through the department stores of Montreal, and choose suits and plates and chairs. The moment we became a couple (all the other coupling stuff aside) came when, looking in a store window on Sherbrooke Street, she said, "What's the most beautiful thing in the window?" ("That girl," I would answer, peering at her reflection, her bitter-almond eyes smiling in a queenly way at the compliment, not unwelcome for being entirely expected.) We *always* agreed on the most beautiful thing in the window: it was Georg Jensen china—or lavender cotton socks, or red-tattersall shirts, or a subtle plaid.

She had a proprietary vocabulary for clothes and objects, whether her own or not: something might fall short by being too "costumey," or too clownish—too much "like a minor operation in Buffalo," or "like a birthday in a kibbutz." My clothes were all of the above. I was still effectively dressed by my mother, whose tastes ran toward the avant-garde delight in garish colors. Once, on a bus, when we were first dating, Martha couldn't help herself, and with her jaw uncharacteristically clenched, she tore off a harlequin bow tie that I was innocently wearing with a red velvet bolero jacket. Clothes figured that prominently in her emotional life.

Not that she was superficial. She loved literature and poetry, instructing me on the greatness of Alice Munro (at a time when I was still pretending that my favorite writer was Julio Cortázar, an obscure South American postmodernist—Borges must have seemed too common) long before most people recognized it; Canada's future Nobel laureate was known then as a short-story writer for girls and women. But material things were her immediate daily means of poetic expression; to wear the wrong one, or cherish the wrong object, meant to follow the wrong thread to the wrong place. Every outfit suggested a scene: a walk on the beach, a rainy morning in London, an afternoon in Paris, where she had never yet been, making the chance of eventually taking her there the closest thing I held to a trump card in my measly hand.

So, New York. For most of the first half of the decade, we would live in that basement room, and see other basement dwellers and tenementarians come out, like cockroaches, in the evenings to look for pizza and walk the streets in shorts and sneakers, a new uniform. For the second half, we lived in a bigger room, a small loft, filled with rats and mice, the walls unaccountably bleeding treacle and our neighbors full of strange aspirations. They were mostly artists, who in those years believed in SoHo as an avant-garde quarter as thoroughly and as unreflectively as their predecessors had in Montparnasse. That they were all on a lease that was shorter, and more narrowly ruled by the brutalities of the real-estate market, was not a vision available to any of us, except as an abstraction that ultimately governed life, though not, we thought, our lives. (Back then, a Saturday morning in SoHo had rules and rituals as fixed as any potlatch of the First Nations. Now no one remembers their absurdities, except a few lone survivors who, like me, remember their beauties.)

Two arcs are traced here: First is the one by which a couple of lovers from Canada become a New York couple, New York citizens, within New York circles, learning to replace the poetry of aspiration with the prose of experience. The other, small by most standards but big to me, since sentences are all that writers have to live by: my own transit from someone who wrote in the manner of a graduate student—contentious "but" after the next pugnacious "yet"—to someone who told stories, or at least tried to, and, perhaps crucially, could make his living by the attempt. That journey cost me more in sweat and perplexity than I now like to recall, but—no, *and*—it was worth it, at least inasmuch as anyone's life is worth recalling in shape. My life was a struggle to move from "but"s to "and"s; from the contestatory cliché of academic struggle to the inclusive habits of storytelling. So I ask the reader to grant this writer a few implicit "and"s. The form is not "memoirs" but *mémoires*, fables from a time about a few people inside it. It takes us from a twoness that for three years was nearly complete, to a set of connections: that's how we build a life. The world can never be as convincing as a couple is. But a couple is too insulated to remain a world. Somehow we found our way through the first marriage that people make, two people bound together by desire and laughter and ambition—the first marriage, before children come, and desire becomes duty, laughter loyalty, and ambition a grimmer kind of responsibility.

A bus and then a train. We are on a bus heading south, we are on a train on our way to City Hall. We took the bus from Hyannis to New York City, and now the subway to City Hall, keys clutched in our hands, an absurd but (narrowly!) potent idea of poetic existence in our hearts. *"The world of dew"?* The world was dew, I thought, though, as I looked around the 5 train, it really didn't seem that dewy. The truth was that dew was one thing you couldn't find in Manhattan if you looked high and low. But you could find the world. I looked at the pretty girl in white wool across from me. I knew that I loved her. I thought she loved me. Life was beginning. The dew could wait. The dew would have to wait.

2

The First Fall

lost my pants on my first morning in New York, and have been looking for them ever since. To lose one's pants is, I suppose, the simplest and purest of burlesque acts, just what always happens to clowns and baggy-pants comedians—although, in point of physical fact, my trousers never really got to the floor-clinging stage, having got lost before I could ever put them on in public. And it didn't happen truly on the first morning, though it feels that way. More like the first month. Still, I have been walking with my pants at my spiritual, or anyway narrative, ankles ever since. I *feel* them there, or, rather, not there.

They were, you see, the lower, and lesser, half of a suit in which Martha and I intended to armor ourselves against the chances and difficulties of our first New York winter. In August 1980, as I have said, we searched for and then rented the world's smallest apartment on First Avenue and Eighty-seventh Street—it was a single nine-by-eleven room, and I am not exaggerating. We chose it from an admittedly grim set of possibilities, because of its "view." It was in the basement of a modern building, but if you craned your neck up from the window, you could see, across the way, the stained-glass windows of the morning chapel-house of the Church of the Holy Trinity. That gave tone to our basement.

These days, couples newly arriving in New York are sent out into the outer boroughs, where they slowly ooze out work and love, like a spreading stain. In those days, young couples were placed in drawers inside the big buildings in "good" neighborhoods of Manhattan. Then they shut the drawers. In these tiny drawers we were forgotten, like embarrassing costume jewelry. It was as if a whole generation were living in the hidden remnant spaces of the great remaining buildings.

I often asked myself why, in movies of the early sixties, Young Couples Like Ourselves arriving in New York always ended up in top-floor apartments. The running joke—of films like *Barefoot in the Park* and *Sunday in New York*, and wasn't there *Barefoot on Sunday* and *Love in the Park;* the titles were as transitive as the tales— was always about the huffing and puffing of in-laws or the telephone installer as they climbed to the top of the stairs. Our generation, by contrast, were lodged in "garden" apartments up and down First and Second Avenues—basement flats that look out on the airshaft—or else in studios like ours.

Back then, the reason seemed to me one of essentially spiritual difference—the early sixties was a time of aspiration, upward, where hope lay somewhere on the roof. ("Up on the Roof" was an anthem of that aspiration.) Our generation plunged downward, either ambitiously toward the punk clubs on the Bowery, or just into the basement of the building.

The truth was simpler, and more terrifying: the honeymooners of the sixties had never actually given up their fifth-floor walk-ups. The mythical part of the Jane Fonda–and–Robert Redford movies was that they ever get out of the first apartment. The reality was that if they didn't move sideways, out to the suburbs, they didn't move at all. Years later, I read Neil Simon's dour but immensely entertaining memoir of his early years, in which he reveals that the fifth-floor one-room apartment, with the fold-out bed and improvised bathtub, in which he installed his *Barefoot* couple for the stage version, was modeled on the place he and his first wife still occupied when their first child was born. They were able to move out only after . . . the success of *Barefoot in the Park.* So, if you planned to have an extra room for the baby, you had better become the most successful Broadway playwright of the age.

New York real estate already raced ahead of all but the truly rich. A game of musical chairs was played, with music and no chairs. People mostly just sheltered in place, adding a loft bed high above as the child arrived, or having ingenious shaggy carpenters build hidden storage or renovate bathrooms. When we eventually managed a paint job, the painter assured us that it would "really open the place up." Of course, nothing, aside from an explosion, could have managed to do so, but that didn't matter.

This was typical of the faith of the permanently situated—we were all stowaways aboard the ship *Manhattan,* and glad if our little barrels or stolen sleeping places under the tarps of the lifeboats could be made one touch cozier. We had the basement apartments because the fifth-floor walk-ups were still occupied by the couples who had moved in twenty years before. No one ever moved out. They merely adjusted.

=====

The suit was but one more bulwark of poetry and against normalcy, for fantasy and against realism. It was a way of accepting fate without accepting it. Martha had her one beautiful dress, a lovely white Ports cashmere number; and so, for symmetry's sake, we decided to take our fellowship money to Barneys and use some of it, even waste it, on one perfect suit. So we went and bought a Ted Lapidus inky-blue suit—that was Martha's name for its color—to be our shield in the city. This one perfect suit would get us through life. It wasn't the first suit we would have chosen. We bought it because it was a suit and on sale. It had a yoked back, and, as Martha admits now, she had never really believed in yoked backs, nor did she entirely believe even in inky blue.

But it was a good suit. And there was another reason, too, that this suit suited. Ted Lapidus had designed the white suit John Lennon wears on the cover of *Abbey Road*. The blessing of the Beatles was upon that label. This was still a big blessing at the time. Though the Beatles had broken up and dispersed ten years before, they had never stopped being the big full moon that hung over our generation, just too young to have seen them at their height, mere ten-year-olds when they were there in 1966 and 1967. That made it possible to believe in them fully. Their music was full of melodies, melodies that seemed to have been found more than made; and melodies are the one thing the world wants most from art.

I wanted to make melodies, too. My life plan, as I say, was to write songs for shows. I thought you could do so just by strumming the guitar long enough until the words came to you. This was not a very good plan. But we did have a more direct path, we thought: we knew someone who'd once had dinner with the sister of a close friend of Art Garfunkel's psychotherapist. Something like that. Anyway, I made a tape for her. That was enough. Our acquaintance would go down the line and get the tape to Art. And in between, I would write jokes for comedians. It seemed like a plan for life.

Am I being too tender about our own lost selves? I can just hear that accusation murmured in those same margins where spectators see spouses as they really are, and I think—if we can't be tender about our own longings, knowing that even at their best they take a disillusioned turn, then what is the sense of living? If we can't regard our own yearnings with a longing for the time when we first felt them, then there is not much more to life than consuming things, settling scores, and growing old and bitter. Tenderness toward one's lost self is sentimental; tenderness toward one's lost longings is just life.

═══

So: poetry and one good suit. It was a kind of Scott Fitzgerald recipe for managing in New York. Once we laid claim to this tiny basement apartment as our New York home, infusing it with "poetry" was harder than it seemed. For one thing, it was already infested with cockroaches. We hadn't seen them in the daylight, when we first looked at it; we didn't meet them until we tried to spend our first night there. And there were many kinds and varieties of cockroaches. Really, it was kind of an entomological laboratory. There were little well-organized German cockroaches; and there were the Asian cockroaches as well, busy and enterprising. And there were those enormous American cockroaches, then called water bugs, who resembled wasps displaced from their natural habitat. They would just remain immobile and horrible in the middle of the tiny room, all elbows and haunches and condescension—just standing there, taking up space.

Cockroaches have largely fled New York now, having been replaced by their sinister near relation, the bedbug. But do bedbugs come in so many kinds? They seem to have the spirit of this later time, instead: they are there to aggravate and annoy but not really to terrify. They deprive the young of a feeling of adequacy, inflicting some welts, but without pointing them toward the abyss: we have *got* to get out of here, is what you feel about an invasion of roaches, agents of psychological warfare. (I'm told that cockroaches, after having been devastated by the weaponizing of boric acid, are coming back, or that they come in waves only to recede again, like boy bands or realist painting.) But then our room was a melting pot of insects, really, like something out of an old thirties cartoon, the insects dancing all night to a bass guitar made of an overturned bucket and mop. And so we put a piece of plywood against the baseboard, just alongside the foldout bed, in an attempt to keep the cockroaches from coming into the apartment, because we were Canadians, and thought that this would keep them out. We were politely asking them not to enter. A piece of plywood this big would surely be a sufficient shield against the entire population of New York City bugs.

How did the neighbors cope? I'm not sure. We were interested only in each other. Watching Martha dress and undress casually every morning and night held me dry-mouthed and rapt. A suitably colorful klatch of eccentrics was what the old movies would have supplied. But such types must have all been up on the higher floors. Right behind us on the basement level was the superintendent, Mr. Fernandez, who lived with his wife and their boy, Herman, whom they yelled at routinely—Martha, who had never heard anyone raise a voice, much less yell at a child, was horrified—and then an airline stewardess and (sometimes) her boyfriend, who would come home drunk every few weeks, bellowing, "Mary! Mary! Open up." Once, locked out, after buzzing furiously on their intercom, he climbed up the cast-iron railing that divided us from them, reaching the window of the first-floor neighbor's apartment, which he entered, allowing him to come downstairs and pound on Mary's door for more direct petition. She opened to him, finally. It was a building filled with love, in all its strange kinds.

So we had a piece of plywood to keep us safe and a poetic outlook to elevate us and one great suit to be our talisman. In those days, young couples starting out went to furniture stores where you could buy piney things in need of painting. Before the suit, then, would come raw pine and something from "Dixie Foam"—a store by that name on the Lower East Side cut hunks of foam rubber into shapes to serve as furniture. (They've since moved to Brooklyn, of course.) We had them make us a foldout bed in a sort of gray-beige velvet—Martha called it "graige"—which we kept shut up by day, unfolded by night. When we dressed it, night after night, we followed an order that I will doubtless still be recalling on my own last bed: fitted contour sheet bought on Orchard Street, a candy-striped "comforter" that had come from God knows where, a soft wool Hudson's Bay blanket, and finally, topping it all, an old red sleeping bag of dubious provenance, which we'd slipped into a white duvet cover. Martha, who said that the sleeping bag had belonged to "an old boyfriend," was disturbingly vague about when it had come into her possession, why it was full-sized, and what had happened to make it hers. In the morning, as I made coffee on the little stove,

Martha, neat in all things, would roll up each layer of warmth, and the room would go back to looking like a doll's house with a modern sofa in it.

We spent a month decorating that place, no larger than a refrigerator, albeit a refrigerator with a window. In the years since, we would have a loft in SoHo, apartments in Paris, a co-op on a better New York block, but we have never spent so much time decorating a place as we did that nine-by-eleven room. We had no money to spend on anything, and no space to put anything in if we had had money to spend. But we spent hours in Conran's, days on the sixth floor of Bloomingdale's, frowning and worrying our way through the possibilities. There was a man—an out-of-work actor, I suppose—who gave demonstrations of SilverStone pots and pans, a kind of nonstick cookware new at the time. He was terrific, flipping crêpes up and over in the perfectly smooth gray pans and crying out, "Hi-ho, SilverStone!" We would go back day after day to watch him and imagine owning one of the pans. He began to give us the same quizzical look that Ellis Larkins, the great and elegant jazz pianist had when we'd sat at a little table at the Carnegie Tavern to hear him and nursed a Perrier each all night while we did: we were enthusiastic fans of performers, but not big spenders on entertainment.

I think of that month, of September 1980, and I smell the distinctive sweet and slightly burnt smell of crêpe batter striking a nonstick surface, with Bloomingdale's all around us. Shopping at department stores seemed an eternal sort of thing, but it was changing—it had changed and was about to change again. The material basis of middle-class aspirations was in flux. Nowadays, Bloomingdale's is just another department store, busy and pleasing, but in those years it had a meaning and a feeling all its own—one that seemed to sum up a different kind of consumerism just then coming into being. It was a department store culture very much unlike the one we knew in Montreal, which was still ruled by the old middle-class hierarchies of expensiveness. In Montreal, well-off people wore furs and shopped at Holt Renfrew's and liked looking comfortable—"affluent" was an Anglo-Montrealer word as much as "hygienic" was a Toronto one. The basic idea that dungarees were in the basement, cloth coats on two, and the fur salon on the top floor still ruled.

Something different was happening in New York, another kind of mix-up. It was already exemplified by the then new idea of "designer jeans." This was, as I would learn more fully later, a classic capitalist switcheroo of the kind that the economist Thorstein Veblen had analyzed a century before: by making the thing with low status into the thing with the most status, you could create a state of perpetual unease in your customers, and the turmoil over what to buy would keep mass consumerism alive. The department store didn't exist to fill its customers' needs. It existed to make the customer unsure of what he, or she, needed. It was the principle of the squirting cider, the sucker's bet, combined with my dad's dictum that insecurities are the one modern universal. He had meant insecurities about academic relationships, I think, but it extended to insecurities about social position. Manhattan was a kind of black hole of insecurity, where so many insecurities had collapsed one onto another to form a mass so dense no serenity of any kind could ever escape its gravity.

E. B. White writes somewhere about having more or less lived in Grand Central Terminal during his early years in New York in the 1920s. We lived at Bloomingdale's in the same way. In those days, Bloomingdale's ("like no other store in the world") even had its own foreign policy: every year it would "feature" some new country— China, Israel, and the Philippines are ones I recall—and present its goods as the latest thing. Years later, doing a documentary about department stores in New York, I met Marvin Traub, the CEO of Bloomingdale's in that heyday—before he lost the store, to, of all ignominious fates, a Canadian tycoon, who, arriving from the north, like us, ruined it. Before that, I discovered, each of the new territories Traub had colonized, even if each was presented as though a serendipitous accident, was calculated and planned to the profitable penny. The surprisingly affordable frozen yogurt had been sought and found abroad, and was produced at a loss in order to draw in the customers. What looked like an overcharge of abundance was actually a big accounting ledger, with dollars in and dollars out neatly balanced: frozen yogurt and designer jeans and Indonesian wicker driving more sales of socks and stockings and face lotions, where the real profits were. What looked like Oz was a neatly laid-out trap for spending, as cynically designed as a Las Vegas casino, which I suppose looks like Oz, too, if that's your idea of emerald.

The simple act of shopping itself was undergoing an alteration that, though it was taking place before our eyes—or exactly *because* it was taking place before our eyes—was harder to see. In a world where real estate was already impossibly expensive, with everyone stuck in smaller and smaller places, the lures and dangles held out by materialism became other things. This was the process that would produce, by the end of the decade, giant muffins and oversized suits as substitutes for an American abundance that no one under forty could any longer afford—an abundance that had to be worn or eaten, since it could not be owned and lived in. In place of real apartments, you got objects and entertainments that were a hyper-puffed imitation of old-fashioned abundance. ("A dim parody of middle-class life," Martha, with her keen eye, would scorn some apartment we might look at, or visit, with its tiny cubbies for bedrooms and one pointless wall of exposed brick.)

"Premium" ice cream was the first small offering to the dispossessed. Häagen-Dazs is now one more standard item in the supermarket freezer. But at the 87 Deli across the street from the Blue Room, it was new to us. Invented in the Bronx by a brilliant ice cream visionary named Reuben Mattus, who saw that the day of the gummy old ice creams had passed, it carried an imaginary Danish origin, a meaningless pseudo-Danish name, and a map of Scandinavia with a little star marking its non-place of non-birth. (He had the best of motives for locating his real ice cream in this imagined place: the Danes had saved Jews.) It had a butterfat content twice as high as in Sealtest or Breyers, and so soon gave birth to other fake-Scandinavian ice creams, like Frusen Glädjé, which was sold in a domed, white plastic container.

The inventor had spotted the vulnerable point in the change of generations. What we really wanted was not so much flavor or novelty or variety as simple richness, in compensation for the riches we didn't have. It was a pun played on the palate. It was also the first of the consolation prizes that our generation would learn to accept. The apartments got smaller and the ice cream got fattier. Eating premium ice cream in a tiny space with roaches was almost the same as living in a reasonable amount of room. That was how capitalism, in its intuitively adaptive way and through the force of natural selection exerted by our changing needs, produced the product perfectly suited to our circumstance. We bought it. We ate it. (Häagen-Dazs was sold by its founder, complete with made-up name and map, to Pillsbury in 1983, another sign of corporate things to come.)

ATM machines were another new event of the period, which carried a similar meaning. Countless little glass money-dispensing rooms, entered into by cool cards, right out of *The Man from U.N.C.L.E.*, became a new architectural feature of the city. The idea of the cash machine, which now seems either self-evident or dated, seemed exciting then. Cautiously withdrawing thirty-five dollars at a time from our tiny fund, and doing it first at the Chase machine on Third Avenue but soon at cash machines all over town—Chemical Bank! Manufacturers Hanover!—we came into a different daily relation to money than our parents had done. My grandparents had belonged to a check-cashing generation, proud to be engaged in it. To have an institution as large as an American bank in effect endorse their signature on a little bit of paper as equivalent to money meant to be taken seriously as a citizen. My parents, in turn, were credit-card cultists—they loved having them, signing them, showing them, using them. For those who came of age in the boom times after the Second World War, the whole notion of credit, of sharing in a limitless improving future—of being trusted to buy now and pay later since later would be so much richer than now—had some of the same significance that the notion of being trusted with checks had for my grandparents.

We in turn, generationally, had regressed, I realized, back into a cash economy—we used checks just to pay the utilities. The machines were one more instrument of that infantilization; we went to the machines for something that felt, at least, like our allowance. But the little glass rooms and the mysterious mechanisms they contained were one more way to make our permanent adolescence seem almost glamorous: the code, the room, the machine's deep internal rumblings as it consulted the great chain of other machines, and then the sudden appearance of the actual money. It was one more consolation for our regression. (Later in the decade, the glass rooms became shelter for the homeless, and so doubled in meaning: you had to see, or pretend not to see, the helpless in their misery as you got your money, and so they became home to shame as well as cash, and oversaw their interaction.)

═══

The formula typically used to describe these two poles of life was public squalor and private affluence. Really, it was more like public squalor and private intensity, both realities ever present and conditioning your experience. You went from the surreally seedy subway to Fragonard at the Frick, and from the still-unmanicured lawns of the park to the mall and roller-skating civilization along the mall. Now the city is far more homogenous, safer, and more consistent, either from the inside out or from the outside in. But the extravagance of opposites that governed our first months is lost. The Blue Room was smaller than you could imagine; the big store, the world outside, bigger than you ever expected it to be. (Now, cynics say, we have remodeled the outer world in the image of our own comfort. But we couldn't then.)

In most places in the city the outside was terrible and the inside wonderful. In the subway, the outsides of the cars were wonderful and their insides terrible. The subways were still covered in what years later I would learn to call "wild style" graffiti, and the cars as they arrived in the stations seemed fluorescent and beautifully psychedelic—as wild as Frank Stella's constructed exotic birds. But their insides were sordid and angry, covered with cranky random "tags," an assault of scratched-in names and indelible black scribbles. The discrepancy of styles—which to the MTA was, of course, no discrepancy at all: vandalism inside, vandalism out—seemed to our unargumentative eyes part of the larger doubleness of the still-wonderful city. The subway was a parable of New York life, turned inside out: beautiful in passing, it was alarming within. It would take until the end of the decade for the cars to be cleaned, but by then even the vandals would be gentrified; the graffiti artists would have names and reputations and European collectors, even as their work was successfully eliminated from the trains. "It's not what that homeboy is saying to my face that bothers me," the artist called A-One would tell me at the end of the decade at a dinner party in SoHo. "It's what he's saying to Sotheby's."

I had persuaded myself, with some misconceived gallantry, that it was unsafe for Martha to be coming home late at night from the cutting room on Ninth Avenue and Forty-fifth Street, where she was an apprentice, syncing documentary films all day. But I was not being *entirely* hysterical. They had found a dead body in a dumpster on her first day at work. Nowadays, people long for such excitements—you could sell condos to the new generation of hipsters if you promised them a dead body in the basement dumpster—but in those days there were still a few too many corpses for comfort. Today's dead body might produce tomorrow's, and you should guide your girlfriend home in safety to be sure she would not become it.

Though now the subway is as crowded at ten at night as it is in the high afternoon, in those days the subway rolled mostly empty, with its windows down, and the hot stale air rushing inside (little air conditioning yet, and one entered the few air-conditioned cars with a shock of ice-cream-like delight). A few lines still had seats covered with lacquered straw, and real straps to hang from, across from the open windows. Grim-faced kids strolled back and forth between cars, in search of something—I used to joke that they must be looking for the dining car. (Martha would laugh at that. The honeymoon is really not erotic but comic: however long your spouse continues to laugh at the same jokes, until her face begins to twist in a grimace of mordant "here it comes" irony.) I even wrote Martha a song, called

"God Bless the IRT": *"God bless the IRT / Brings my baby back to me / God bless the downtown train / Brings her to my arms again. / Someday we'll ride in cabs / Bathe in tubs of Häagen-Dazs /Till then the IRT was all that / Brings her safe to me."* (Okay, it was an off rhyme—"Dazs" and "cabs"—but, I still think, a resourceful one, and true to its time.)

———

Sometime in that first fall, I discovered toggle bolts. There was a hardware store right around the corner, run by the Weinstein brothers, and they patiently diagrammed the workings of the toggle bolts with the same slightly bemused look of "Is this level of ignorance really possible?" that art historians might wear explaining to first-year students that famous pictures were usually displayed in frames. The toggle bolt is a weird little device, the hardware equivalent of a cockroach and just as essential in New York apartments. "Ya drill a hole in the wall, ya know, into the Sheetrock—your walls aren't made of cement or granite or anything, ya see?" one Weinstein brother would explain dubiously, demonstrating how it worked. "And then these pop out"—on the other side of the wall, the toggle's two little wings spread out in an instant, just like a cockroach's. "They hold it in there, so you can hang your shelves or whatever."

I bought a drill, and spent days drilling holes and then popping in the toggle bolts. They made a wonderful "plop!" sound as, invisibly, they opened in the space behind the wall. It was a lovely *2001: A Space Odyssey* slow-motion docking sound. The ash smell of the burning holes and then the plop of the toggle bolt . . . It's probably the closest I've ever come to understanding the appeal of semi-automatic weapons.

We hung the glass shelving all around the apartment and put our books out. The glass shelves looked light and beautiful, as the sun glinted through the venetian blinds and caught them. I quickly discovered, though, that the least touch on any of the shelves would make them all tremble, sympathetically, as during an earthquake. I straightened one slightly, or intended to, and the toggle bolts gave way, just bending right down and coming out of the wall, since (I realize now) the little wings weren't anchored to anything but the flimsy drywall. Then the shelf slid off the bracket, sending the books piling down onto the next shelf. I could easily imagine one fallen shelf bringing down the next, like an old casino building being imploded.

We had locked ourselves into a small, cantilevered, explosive cage. The entire room was booby-trapped; or, rather, a booby had made a trap out of the entire room. If a single glass shelf above the bed were to fall, the ensuing crash seemed likely to end with our being shredded as we slept. It was like living inside a hand grenade, with the pin pulled. We would lie in our unfolded bed at night, one eye scanning the baseboard for the cockroaches, the other on the glass shelves, waiting for signs of an avalanche. What lovemaking we did we did discreetly, for fear of agitating all the glass. We lived and breathed as lightly as possible. I suppose it would have been a one-day story in the *New York Post:* "Glass Warfare: Newlyweds Die in Uptown Basement." Then the super would have swept us out, sent another couple in, and shut the drawer on them, in turn.

═══

All of this is what that one good suit was going to protect us from. I thought of it often, even while it was away at the tailor's. Its neat dark blue wool, so filled with poetry, would distinguish us; its suave stylishness set us apart from the pavement just outside our window. I don't think I've really described the suit adequately. It was a simple two-button suit, cinched at the waist in a way that struck us both as "classic"—a quiet word we liked, applied to suits. Navy blue was a color we both had doubts about. It could look "ordinary," Martha's word, in a way that black did not. But if the navy blue crowded into black, backed into black, was that not in itself a sort of superior condition? Just as all art aspires to the condition of music, we reasoned, then all navy blue aspires to the condition of black—and wasn't the business of aspiring the thing you wanted everything in your life to indicate? We wanted a wool that *yearned* a little. The suit was itself another toggle bolt; its two legs and arms would insert themselves through the dubious drywall of our new life and cling tight, anchoring our existence.

Martha had gone back to Montreal to collect our few things when I took the Ted Lapidus suit to a tailor. (I am short, and all my pants have to be hemmed.) Those days, if you lived on the Far East Side in Yorkville, as we did, you lived in a genuine neighborhood. Eighty-sixth Street was lined with German restaurants, so much that the Ideal Restaurant at 5:00 p.m. looked like a George Grosz engraving, pale and obese Middle Europeans dining on fat and starch. There were streets filled with the smell of Hungarian paprika, and a restaurant that specialized in curried goat. And so there were tailors of every imaginable ethnic affiliation, too: Greek tailors and Jewish tailors, Korean tailors and Chinese tailors, each sewing in the window of his storefront, a strange New York form of street theater. I took the suit to a Greek tailor, and as he measured me I knew that life was going to be okay, because, despite the cockroaches, despite the tininess of our room, despite our absolute lack of funds, despite the urban blight that threatened to blight us, too, I had a suit. *I had a suit*. A suit that now would fit.

About a week later, when I had been told the suit would be ready, I went back to collect it from the tailor, my heart full. I tried it on. It was everything I had ever hoped a suit could be. "It fits nice!" the tailor said, which he wasn't, I decided, obliged to do. He slid the suit reverently into a garment bag, I threw it over my shoulder, and I walked it back to our tiny basement apartment, where I unzipped it just to feast my eyes once more at this deliverance, the garment that would keep me safe and in poetic elevation from the cockroaches and the subway and the world around me.

As I unbuttoned and parted the jacket, I realized . . . that the pants were gone. They were . . . gone! Gone completely, gone away—just not there! I knew that the pants *had* been there when I left the tailor's. Then I looked again at the garment bag—and I realized it had no bottom. It was a New York garment bag: a vinyl envelope over a slippery hanger, with no bottom to hold things in. It was as gaffed as

Sky Masterson's imaginary deck of cards. The pants, I realized, had slid right off the smooth plastic hanger and were sitting somewhere out there on the street. They were gone. Gone for good. I knew it at once.

The truth is that fish don't really have a theory of water. That's the truth about fish being out of water; they know two states: fine and "Oh my God!" That's all fish really know about water, and that was all I knew at that moment. The trousers were gone and the suit was ruined. I ran back to the Greek tailor and he said words that I will never forget as long as I live, because they were so perfectly elegiac: "It used to fit nice. It used to fit really nice."

That use of the past tense sealed the fate of those pants somehow. And when the moment of irretrievable loss takes place, the feeling, no matter how trivial the object, no matter how small the thing lost, that moment—when the vase breaks, when the trousers are gone, when the car crashes, when the ship begins to go down—induces the same feeling in the pit of your stomach, that sudden sick feeling of no turning back, of life altered forever. The value of the things lost differs; the lurch of irretrievable loss is always the same.

I ran up and down First Avenue for hours. It was just when homeless people were beginning to appear on the streets in New York, and I eyed every homeless man I saw, sure that he had taken my size-29 trousers and was wearing them. I still do that, gaze turning sidelong, to this day.

I called Martha in Montreal, even though calling long distance was still a reasonably big deal. "Darling," I said, "I've lost the trousers. I lost the pants of my suit!" And she said, "Oh my God, oh no," because only she knew the depth of the loss that this was for us. And then she said something very strange. She said, "Have you looked in the park?" and I realized that she had a kind of theory that all lost things—like the Island of Misfit Toys—were sort of immediately, magically displaced into Central Park.

I began scouring the streets of Manhattan looking for my lost pants, from First Avenue to Seventy-ninth Street and back down. I had in those days a strong synesthetic association with the numbered streets on the Far East Side. The eighties were yellow-gold. The seventies were red. The sixties, rich people's country, were cooler green, and the fifties gray-blue. The map of colors overlays the map of memories as I search for my lost trousers, peering into gutters and looking for what might be now a crumpled ball of blue fabric, yet still be retrievable as pants.

I walked and searched for hours, past the point of rational hope of recovery. The streets seemed darkened and transformed. What had only hours ago seemed the jaunty stage set of a musical, storefronts scented with Hungarian paprika, now seemed hostile and vertiginous and barbed, like the set of a German Expressionist film rising up in angular facets. No one cared that I had lost my pants. They'd been washed away in the great nothingness of the city. Every wire had been cut, and they fell not just to the ground but out of the imaginative realm that gave them meaning in our minds. In Montreal, a pair of pants having slipped from a hanger would have lain there on the ground, on Sherbrooke Street or Mountain Street, unavoidable. People would have stepped around them. Someone would have picked them up and put them on a fence. There would have been a whole *"What is this?"* thing. Here there was no *thing* at all, just the vast flowing current of people and filth and objects that somehow moved up and down First Avenue, carrying my pants along inexorably with them, as though toward a waterfall somewhere around the Queensboro Bridge. I had imagined living in a Scott Fitzgerald story, and now here I was in something out of Gogol, where a poor clerk searches the dark streets for his briefcase or overcoat or nose. And I knew that this loss was real and that I would spend the rest of my life in New York searching for my lost trousers.

A month later, John Lennon was murdered outside his New York apartment, and that, too, changed the contours of possibility, and darkened the colors of New York life. His love and ingenuous appreciation of the city—so tourist-like—had not been able to protect him from its lethality. (I remember weeping into the *New York Post*. In the Blue Room there was no corner to put anything away in—everything loomed immense, and the *Post* headline about

Lennon worst of all.) Our basic sense of life's essential salubrious-
ness had been damaged. There was no safety in Ted Lapidus suits.
The Beatles had represented the good fortune of three generations:
the generation their own age, who had grown up with them; those
right behind them, like us, who had been educated by them; and
those just ahead, who had been rejuvenated by them. Their essential
lesson was one of optimism. Now that optimism would be impossible to sustain. The only turn to make was inward, while looking
outward, another form of the poles that I was already beginning to
sense, though only just beginning, would govern our experience.
There were two worlds, sharply opposed worlds of comfort and
death, the hearth and the street. I was, as I say, beginning to sense
this, though it would be years before I really grasped it. The space
between sensing things and grasping them, between trying them
on and really *wearing* them, is large, and includes most of what we
mean by wisdom. It was exactly the experience I had been deprived
of when I lost my pants.

It was later that month, on December 19, the anniversary of our
first night together, that Martha and I got on the subway—she
wearing her beautiful white dress and I the jacket from that beautiful broken suit, paired with an old pair of jeans, a hole in the knee—
and went down to City Hall, where we got married, with those lines
from Issa in my pocket: *"The world of dew is / a world of dew, / but
even so."*

And no matter how many suits I've bought since, I'm still missing the pants. I have shopped for and altered and owned many suits,
gray and black and double-breasted—though never again navy
blue—and many of them from Barneys. But the truth is, in life we
buy one suit that is then replaced, again and again. If the first suit
has lost its trousers, you never really get them back. Buying your
first suit is a little like losing your virginity: you get many revis-
its, but not a redo. You get to try again, but you don't get to try it
over. It happened as it happened, and no amount of improvement
can improve it.

And so I still feel that I walk through the world without trousers, no matter where I go or how many years have gone by. They fell, somewhere, to the ground, like an unknown soldier. I've never recovered them. Because the truth is that what we learn in New York is that a piece of plywood will never protect you from the wild, and that suit trousers, once lost, are lost forever. The city makes you the opposite of the emperor with the new clothes. He walked around unclothed, and everyone noticed but him. In New York, you walk around naked from the waist down for decades, and nobody knows but you.

3

Food Fight

When, in later decades, I would indicate to people the size of the apartment that Martha and I lived in for those three years, they'd always ask the natural question: How did you go on together at all? How come you didn't get furious with each other, or come to hate each other? From a non-, or anti-, romantic angle, the apartment had the look of one of those experiments that bad social scientists run with underpaid student volunteers: how long before they go crazy when forced to live together in a space not big enough for one person, let alone two?

We didn't fight, though. One reason we didn't fight was that the studio *was* so small, so small that you could never get sufficient perspective for the fighting to happen. In order to really have a quarrel, you have to sort of step back three steps and eye the other person darkly. There just was no room for that. We were on top of each other, not in that sense—well, in that sense, too, at times—but we were also *colliding* with each other all the time. I don't have any mental image of Martha from those years, except as a kind of Cubist painting, noses and eyes and ears. You always say when you're having a fight with someone, "I saw him or her in a new perspective."

But there was no new perspective to see from in a nine-by-eleven room. There was only one, and that one always close up.

But we did have a fight, I have to confess, we did have one fight, often, and it was about food. My theory about marriages and fighting is that—well, everyone knows Tolstoy's thing about how all happy families are alike and how unhappy families are unhappy in their own way. *My* theory is that all unhappy marriages have many different quarrels in them, while all happy marriages have the same quarrel, over and over again.

And that is how you know that it's a happy marriage—that there's one quarrel that two people have from the day they're married to the day they die. It's not that they don't have a quarrel, it's not that that quarrel is not, on its own terms, often quite violent. It's just always the same—so that the couple come to know all the steps and the dance of that particular quarrel. It becomes their ritualized steam valve, their anger dance, their shake-a-spear moment.

And the standard repeated quarrel of every happy marriage is more often than not some kind of quarrel about food. As I've written elsewhere, at doubtless exhausting length, it's human nature to turn a mouth taste into a moral taste—to make a question of how something feels in your mouth into a question of what it says about your world. That's the basis of every dietary law known to man. When we imagine God, we don't imagine him indifferent to appetite. No, we imagine him enraged and enraptured by what we're eating—he tastes bacon and declares it bad and tastes matzoh and can hear a whole heroic history when he breaks it. Every mouth taste instantly becomes a moral taste. And so when we need to fight— and no marriage can survive without some useful friction—we fight about food.

My uncle Ron and my aunt Rose, for instance. They spent most of their life, through about sixty years of marriage, having the same argument about food. My uncle Ron insisted that the reason they give you large portions at restaurants is in order to charge you more. And my aunt Rose insisted that the reason that they charged you more at restaurants was that they had given you such large portions.

And they carried this argument along like a Beckett play, from Philadelphia to Florida and then into the hospital where my uncle Ron had his vocal cords removed, and would say, forced into a high falsetto, "The reason they charge you more is because they want to. And they trick you with the large portions." She said, "No, Ron. That's not the reason at all. They have their costs. They have to charge for them."

My grandparents had a single quarrel. I should add at once that there's a weird thing about my grandparents, which I have to explain in order to explain their argument. And that is that I introduced my grandparents when I was about two years old. Not literally, but essentially: I only have, or had, one pair of grandparents, because when I was about two my father's father—now, follow this—met my mother's mother. And they divorced the other spouses and they married each other. That's a true story. So I only had one set of grandparents.

And what was touching about it is that my grandparents strongly resembled my parents—my mother's mother like my mother, strong-willed and intelligent; my father's father like my father, peaceable and humorous—and so I had a kind of 'toon version of my parents who lived in Florida. My grandparents' food fight was about the *language* of food. My grandfather came late to this country and my grandmother earlier, and so, he complained, secure in her knowledge, she would never explain to him what important food expressions actually *meant*. When he was eighty-eight and I was visiting him in Florida, he took me aside and said, "There's something no one will explain to me, even though I've been waiting for someone to explain it to me for seventy years."

"What is it, Grandpop?" I asked, as solicitously as I could.

"What do people mean when they say, 'You can't have your cake and eat it, too'? *What else are you supposed to do with your cake?*" he demanded. It's a good question. It haunts me still. (Of course, the intended meaning is clear enough: you eat the cake and it's gone. But the form of the imperative undermines it, that "have." It implies a kind of Schrödinger's cake, at once tangible and still in front of you, and, simultaneously, in your stomach. I got his confusion.)

So it shouldn't be a surprise that Martha's and my fight in the Blue Room was about food, too. For reasons that were both generational and peculiar, food already had an undue importance for us then. Or at least it did for me. The restaurants of New York enraptured me—we didn't go to any, but I loved the idea of them. I would lie in bed below the hair-trigger glass shelving, after we unrolled and enwrapped the "triple fold" sofa every night, and read what was then the premier guide to New York dining out, Seymour Britchky's *The Restaurants of New York*.

No one remembers Britchky now, but at the time he was the terror of the New York restaurant scene, the last credible entry in the once-long Manhattan roster of monster/master critics—his tone "scathing," like that of the characters whom one saw celebrated in forties film noirs, the ones whom George Sanders or Clifton Webb would play, always in a silk dressing gown and cravat with a writing desk in the bathtub. It's a vanished tone now, in the age of mass amateur reviews on Open Spoon or Table Talk or whatever the current forum is called. ("I took my honey here for birthday dinner, and—wow!—what a blowout. Five stars for sure.")

At the time, though, his criticism, first issued in a newsletter and then collected yearly in a book, seemed thrilling in the power of its sneering, the certitude of its exclusions. The power critic of this kind depends on the lightning turns of his contempt and his favor: no one should ever be sure where he will land, or on whom. Clement Greenberg, the equivalent in the art world, would excommunicate a generation for splashing paint incorrectly, then embrace another for making giant wan watercolors. I turned Britchky's pages over and over in bed, relishing the authority of his judgment, reading about restaurants where we could never possibly go. It was a time, the last time, when the reign of three-star French luxury restaurants was still taken for granted in New York. All of the ones he graced with three and four stars were of that kind, all the beautiful "La"s and "Le"s, now gone: La Caravelle, La Côte Basque, Le Lavandou. (That last was particularly fine, offering a delicate plate-painting style no longer chic. Once, Martha's father did come to town and take us there. I still can recall each *plat*, and still think it the best meal I've ever had.)

Britchky, my mentor, knew no limits. He concentrated more on the manners and mores of the restaurant as it worked its way through the meals than he did strictly on the food on the plate. "The lesser of these captains," he wrote about those at the Four Seasons in the Seagram Building, "will lie as easily as he will blink, and he informs you, unblinkingly, that there are no desserts on the menu that are not on the cart. He does not want the trouble that crêpes entail, or to spend the time waiting for soufflés, or to take the walk to wherever the cheeses are kept." I shared his mocking indignation at the poor captain, whom we had seen right through, together. At other moments, he could be scathingly satirical of the false hopes that diners brought to tables: "Pairs of lonely ladies, whose office salaries are supplemented by alimony, share their troubles here," he wrote of a long-forgotten Italian place called Claudio's, "trying to make a special evening of an ordinary Tuesday, spending too much money in a restaurant they figure must be fancy because they never heard of most of the dishes." I loved that sentence. It was like Maupassant with ratings.

But all of that world of menus and prices and sneaky captains and pathetic aspiration, fascinating though it was—and I actually developed the habit, shameful as it sounds, of jumping up, actually leaping in my sneakered feet, when I walked past La Côte Basque or La Caravelle to claim just a microsecond's glimpse of the gleaming interior, briefly but beautifully visible as you rose above the curtained windows that sealed the restaurant off from the street— all of that was beyond our reach. The only restaurant we could (very occasionally) afford was a hamburger joint on Second Avenue, or else pork schnitzel and potatoes at the old Ideal Restaurant on Eighty-sixth Street, where, in accordance with the New York principle that everything attracts its own, those pale, pasty-faced Central European families would gather at five-thirty in the evening for cheap and pallid dinners. (The way in which any restaurant instantly compels the clientele appropriate to it astounded me; if someone opened a restaurant serving human parts one morning at 8:00 a.m., the city's cannibals would have filled it, happily, by suppertime.)

So if great food were to be had—fine food, French food, *leap-worthy* food—I would have to cook it. I used to try every night; my mother was a wonderful cook, and she taught her sons how to cook. For our wedding she had given me a series of haute French cookbooks: Simca Beck's *Simca's Cuisine* and a book of Roger Vergé's and something of Michel Guérard's. Inappropriately haute—inappropriate for the space and my skills, I mean—their recipes demanded poaching and roasting and marinating and above all sautéing, even flambéing, along with all the other high-heat and smoke-making procedures of a French country kitchen.

I had a tiny three-burner gas stove, with a matching Easy-Bake–style oven beneath, to produce all this. (We had had to haul crisply baked cockroach bodies out of the oven when we first cleaned it.) But I have never cooked so ambitiously, before or since. I would stand there in that corner, creating pillars of smoke and flame, which would then go pouring out of the single window and out onto the street. Everyone was convinced that we were running a crack den. But that was the only way I knew how to cook. Sometimes, hard as it is to believe, we had people "over" and I made them *côtes de veau Foyot* and Grand Marnier soufflés. (I wonder what they thought? Well, I know what they thought. I can still see their faces, even through the burning haze.)

And so I would sauté the little bit of filet of beef, with its nicely reduced sauce, and put it out there on the dining table, and Martha would come along and, bravely waving her way through the veils of smoke, she would sit down and cut into it and make that face—you know that face—and say, "Oh, can I have this a little better done?" because, yes, that was her nature.

She was a well-done person. And she had married a rare husband.

This was a huge abyss, much larger than any religious abyss that could divide the two of us. She *actually liked well-done meat!* When you're courting someone, you don't actually believe that when they say "well done" they mean it—you think it's a kind of affectation that they've developed and that they will obviously give it up the moment you start living together. (She had, I found out later, felt the same way about my Sinatra records.) I had, in our college years, believed that was true for Martha's taste for "well done," that it was just a kind of flirtatious gesture—who could actually like things that are well done?

Until I went to her parents' place for an outdoor barbecue, and I saw her father put a hamburger down on the grill and leave it there for the appropriate five minutes, and then another five, and then another five, and then another five. . . . Fifty minutes had gone by; the thing had become as dense as a hockey puck, just sitting there, sizzling miserably, on the grill.

Of course, there was a reason Martha came from a well-done family. Two generations back, her ancestors were Icelandic peasants. And, basically, *everything* for them was rare—they had no fire, they had no trees, they had nothing to do but hack off a small piece of raw lamb or pry open a rock mussel and eat it and then wait a day and hack off another bit of the lamb or pry open another mussel. So moving toward well done was, in her family, a sign of escaping from your peasant past.

Now, my parents were rare people. But it was exactly the same kind of generational mechanism that had made them so. They had grown up in Jewish families where there was nothing but pot roast and meat loaf—that was still, in Florida, my grandmother's cooking. Things that were cooked past blood, things cooked not just past rare but beyond recognition. My parents' way of claiming their identity as European-minded and Francophile people, as intellectuals, was to have everything as rare as humanly possible. Blood was old Europe, steak tartare far from Florida, pink inside was Paris.

And I believed in rare, as a moral principle, because . . . well, because my parents had brought me up to believe in it, just as passionately as Martha believed in well done as a moral principle that she had been brought up with. But it was not (I thought) just a clash of family values. There was obviously an element of sexual rejection in her constantly turning down pink and bloody meat that I would offer her night after night. The symbolism was a little too self-evident to be put down to mouth taste. When I offered my young wife something that was beautifully pink and bloody and she made a face that said, "Can you take this back and change it?" its meaning was all too evident and echoed through this little space all too clearly.

So, one night in that first bleak-cozy winter, I went off to a fishmonger's on Eighty-sixth Street and I bought some tuna. Now, the early eighties were a kind of pivotal moment in the history of American cooking, because it was the moment when we passed from tuna fish to tuna. Tuna fish was, of course, the thing that comes in cans: you mix it with mayonnaise and you have it in sandwiches. Tuna, on the other hand, is the beautiful pink thing that is the fish eaters' substitute for filet mignon, the thing you cook very rare and you serve in the French style.

So I went back to the Blue Room and I sautéed this beautiful piece of tuna and I gave it an *au poivre* sauce made with brandy, filling the place with black fumes—it would often have been wise, at dinnertime, to have an oxygen tank strapped to your back. Martha pushed her way through the dense thicket of smoke to the table, gracefully breast-stroking aside the dark cloud, and cut into the tuna. It was properly rare.

"I can't eat this," she said.

It was, again, a crystal-goblet moment, a fish-out-of-water moment—that moment when something precious is about to fall off the table and break and you know it even before the fall is finished, the break actually made. You know you're going toward disaster. You feel the real risk. You know that, while in most of the petty squabbles of early marriage resolution is coming right after the quarrel, this quarrel is something more.

I succumbed to the moment's potential, because the rejection of the rare tuna seemed to me so fundamentally hostile. I did what I've never done before or since: I got up from the table then and there and I grabbed my raincoat and I headed for the door like a bad husband in a sixties sitcom.

Headed for the door . . . There really wasn't very far to go, what with there only being three steps between the table and the entrance. Still, I went there, and I opened it.

Then Martha, with a show of force and conviction and inner authority that I would not see again even during childbirth, summoning up a spirit all the more impressive for rising from such a gracious and fundamentally noncontentious person, went to the door and stopped me.

"You are going back and you are going to *finish cooking that fish*!" she said.

We looked each other in the eye and we knew that this was a fateful moment in the history of our marriage, and I went back and I finished cooking the fish.

About a week later, the super, Mr. Fernandez, came to our door—there was something mildly thrilling about having a super named Mr. Fernandez—and explained that everyone was complaining about the amount of smoke that was coming from our little basement apartment. Apparently, it was rising right up through the six stories of the building, setting off smoke alarms. I realized at that moment that, in order both to keep our lease and to save our marriage, I was going to have to change my approach to cooking.

One way we could help ourselves, I had already realized, was through a magic word of common invention but of our special use. And that magic word is "medium." The beautiful thing about "medium" as a word is that it slides over insensibly toward its near companion—to "medium well" or "medium-rare." Your partner hears the "medium," and the waiter alone hears the "rare" or "well done," and you get to belong to two categories of moral taste simultaneously. It is a wonderful word, "medium," and it can save any marriage if you use it properly. Even if the only place you ever go is out, once a week, for a hamburger on Second Avenue.

And since I wasn't going to be allowed to sauté and flambé in that nine-by-eleven room any longer, I had to do the only thing I could do instead—and that was to slowly braise, to stew everything that came to me. And the beautiful thing about braising and stewing, as I discovered in the Blue Room, is that it only has two moral components to it, two degrees of feeling—tough and tender. You are no longer implicated in rare or well done, or even mediating with medium. Things are either properly tough and have to be cooked down, or they are appropriately tender and ready to be eaten. And they more often became tender than remained tough, because I took the time to will them so.

The truth, in retrospect, is that what Rose and Ron did not know, or quite see, is that if you make a good marriage, the prices may stay the same. But the portions mysteriously grow larger.

4

My First Job

After our first year in the Blue Room, Martha said to me, "Why don't you go look for a job?" She had already begun working for the documentary filmmaker D. A. Pennebaker, whose "archive," consisting of thirty-some years of loose film reels, needed . . . something. What the something was had been left to her to discover. It had to be organized. And she was originally it.

"Working" had never quite occurred to me, really, as a pathway in life. I mean work for pay, of course—I was working hard at Renaissance iconography and Byzantine icons in graduate school. And I was working in another, more far-fetched, way as well. Once a week, I would write a piece for *The New Yorker*'s "Talk of the Town" section—a larksome high-hearted thing, bending toward wistfulness in the end, and all this emotion neatly compressed within fifteen hundred words—about something or other I'd seen or experienced in the city over the previous week. A man reading *Le Monde* on the subway; something happening on the bus; the first snowfall. Then Martha and I would walk the fifty-plus blocks from the Blue Room to the old offices of *The New Yorker* on West Forty-third Street, and slip the short essay under the door, or hand it to the baffled and impatient receptionist. (I didn't know—a meaningless-seeming distinction that would years later nonetheless prove significant in my working life—that these small letters "from a friend" were actually called "Comment," not "Talk." Or that, still later, I would become friends with that receptionist, and an auditor of tales about her fascinating love life with the writers on the other side of the door.) At the time, the pieces would then come bouncing back from the magazine with a celerity that suggested the entire transaction were being conducted on a particle accelerator, with messages written and returned at something approaching the speed of light. And of course I would patiently work on my songs, one after another, picking them out on the guitar and committing them to hissy cassettes. "God Bless the IRT," I told Martha, was the best but not the only of the crop of the "new work." She listened attentively, as she always did, and offered "notes" on my notes.

But the only thing I'd ever done in college that you could call "work" was work in the library of the business school three nights a week during the summer. So I took that out into the world, and I got a job at a place called the Frick Art Reference Library, which was, and still is, I suppose, a library above the Frick Collection in New York. I knew that collection well. There were beautiful Rembrandts and Bellinis in it, and Martha and I loved most of all Fragonard's feather-light but heart-deep series, *The Progress of Love*. I had even made a mental note to adapt it for the ballet, after I was done with my careers as a Broadway composer, popular essayist, and seemingly effortless restaurant-frequenting man about town.

The Frick Art Reference Library sat up above the picture galleries, and it was like a little piece of the nineteenth century on East Seventieth Street. I don't mean the good nineteenth century, the nineteenth century of wonderful Christmas teas and gaslit streets, the nineteenth century we envy. I mean the bad nineteenth century, the nineteenth century where miners were shot en masse, and everyone died of communicable diseases. There was only one phone booth at the Frick Art Reference Library, and on it was a sign, "Please disinfect phone after using." There was a blue bottle of disinfectant alongside the sign, and napkins. You really did have to disinfect it every time you used it, though I never knew what illness you were disinfecting it against. I always imagined that it was something like consumption or neuralgia or lumbago or catarrh or some other complaint of the Civil War period. I went there, and to their eventual great chagrin, they gave me a job, and the job I got—my first job, my first experience of grown-up toil—was running what's called "the authority file."

An authority file is a filing cabinet filled with cards—little three-by-five cards were used in those days, before anything was digitized. It gave, and I suppose still gives, the name of an artist and his or her birthdate. If that's all you have, if you don't have a death date, in an authority file the card sits above the rod, hasn't been "dropped below the rod." And when you can find a death date to pin to the artist, you drop the card below the rod.

My job consisted of trying to kill off as many artists every day as I could. Newspapers would arrive from around the world each morning, from Spain and Russia and England and elsewhere. Sometimes, they would be several weeks old. Another sub-librarian would clip out the obituary sections. Then I would have to pore over them, searching the obituary pages for the names of artists and news of their passing. When, delighted, I found an artist's obituary, I would take out the artist's card, type the death date on it, and go see the head librarian and ask her whether we could put the artist's card below the rod.

We would do it together. First, I would remove the long rod from the cards it held in line through the uniform punch-holes in their lower thirds. Then, while I held the cards together, she would drop the one with the new death date into its place, and then skillfully push the rod back through the entire tunnel of punch holes, putting the small fatal hole in line with all the others, with the rod running through them. It was pretty skilled labor, and a sort of funeral for art, held on the sixth floor. At first I liked rooting for the elderly artists to outlast the head librarian, although there was something fateful in their daily fall. It was like living with the Fates, and watching them at work.

Of course, if you do a job like that for a while, you begin to get this strange, *Twilight Zone* feeling that you are responsible for the life and death of artists. *You* are cutting the thread of fate for some poor aging Abstract Expressionist counting out his days in Mexico, some surviving Fauvist hanging on there in Provence. Their cards linger precariously above the rod, day after day and year after year, and then, one morning, you find yourself making history in the way it is really made, by adding a death date to a single card.

The problem was, I was about as badly cut out for that job as any human being could possibly be. I'm none of the things a librarian should be now, and I was none of those things then. I'm terribly disorganized and I don't keep good records, and I don't remember where I put anything. On my first day at work, they gave me the scepter, the orb, the symbol of being a member of the closed court of the Frick Art Reference Library—and that was a key to the stacks, because all the stacks were closed and you had to come and beg entry to them. If you were a woman, you had to wear a skirt. If you were a man, you had to wear a jacket and tie, and then you might be allowed to consult a book, but only if allowed by us librarians, who held the key.

And they gave me this key, and they explained how important it was, and within two hours, I had lost it. I still don't remember where I lost it or how I lost it, but I know that I lost it. And for the rest of the year, for want of the missing key, what I had to do whenever I needed to go into the stacks to look for a book was to linger, kind of clandestinely, by the edge of the door, until some other librarian, with her key about her, went in, and then I would slip in beside her, making pleasantries all the while.

This is a terrible way to be a librarian, to have to wait for chance encounters, a bit like one of those white slavers who wait at Charles de Gaulle Airport for American women in Liam Neeson movies. That was my life, and that's how it was spent, trying to kill off aging artists and waiting for somebody else to go into the stacks to retrieve a book. On my lunch hour, I would slip downstairs into the collection. I would look at the Rembrandts and the Bellinis. They seemed different. Even the Fragonards had lost some of their featheriness. They seemed stodgier than before.

I was learning a necessary lesson in the duller side of life. I was getting a glimpse at how much glummer and grimmer New York could be than I had imagined. Upstairs at the Frick looked quite different from downstairs at the Frick. What you saw when you sneaked behind the collection wasn't the obverse, secret side of the paintings, encoding some occult signature. It was just a grim little nineteenth-century space, with all the charm of a blacking factory.

At the Institute of Fine Arts, the lectures and seminars I was taking weren't, as I had hoped, a sort of seminar in being Kenneth Clark, a key to the mysterious glamour of museums. Instead, they were something between courses in stamp collecting and puzzle solving. Most of them were mindlessly devoted to "iconography," solving essentially meaningless little symbolic riddles that stood on the margin of the pictures' meaning. (Old pictures did have little puzzles in them, but no one at the time had cared about them much: Renaissance people cared about the picture's style, magnificence, original contributions, about the tremor of the thing.) Or else the classes were devoted to connoisseurship, learning the sequences of one artist or another without caring much about what the pictures meant.

The one exception was a seminar on Picasso I took with William Rubin, the great chief curator of painting and sculpture at MoMA. But even that ended, if not badly, then at least ambiguously. God knows he was filled with vitality—he looked as if he lived on a diet of organ meat, and the very name of Picasso was sacred to him. I went without food for four days as I readied my seminar report on Picasso's portraiture. When, finally, I delivered it and Rubin was, if not rapturous, then at least not disapproving, I slipped over to the Bemelmans Bar in the Carlyle hotel, which I still associated with the kind of glamour I had come to New York intending to experience, and I ordered the only drink with whose name I was vaguely familiar: a Black Russian, a vile combination of Kahlúa and vodka. I drank it down, and, sitting there on the banquette in my jeans (since I had no suit pants) and sneakers (since I had no dress shoes), I promptly passed out, slipping to the terrazzo flooring, and had to be helped out of the bar by a crew of pointedly efficient Italian waiters.

While I worked, and waited, I also wrote a play and a poem. The play was to be called *The Anatomy of Art* and it was a satire, though of what I don't know—the art world, I suppose, though I scarcely knew enough of that world to satirize it. I recall that it had a long opening section of verbal misunderstandings, of which I was peculiarly proud, though I can't remember the exchanges now— irritatingly, I can only recall the punch lines, which seem like Dada non sequiturs without the setups. The funniest line in the play, I recall, was an exchange between a museum guard and a winsome young woman curator that ended with the riposte "No. Mostly they lived on oats." I can no longer remember what the setup was that made that funny, but I remember that I thought it was, unusually so.

Then, at my desk, I wrote an epic poem in heroic couplets about the art world. I found a few scraps of it the other day. It was called, I think, *Cathedrals of Art*—I was impressed by Florine Stettheimer's charming heraldic paintings of New York life in the twenties, just then coming back into fashion. In the titles of all of them she used *Cathedrals* to indicate peculiar New York establishments: *Cathedrals of Commerce* referencing department stores, and *Cathedrals of Art*, museums. Mine was a wry, satiric poem, again about the follies of the art world, about which then, as I say, I had something less than the vaguest idea. (When Robert Hughes actually had his mock-heroic couplets on the art world published, a few years later, I felt mildly resentful, even though by then he was a friend. His were more skilled than mine, and much more vitriolic, but, though published more widely, they didn't live any longer.)

Finally, one day, after a year of dodging, I noticed that there was a key in the door to the stacks, someone else's key left in the key-hole. And I thought, "Oh, this is my chance. I'll act now." I slipped the key out of the door, out of the lock, and I put it in my pocket, and I went back to reading obituaries.

And then, about an hour later, someone came up in a state of agitation and misery, and I said, "What's wrong?" He said, "All of the librarians are locked into the stacks and we can't get them out, because the master key is missing!"

There are certain moments that arrive in life as a true test of character. You know the kind of person you are after that moment. You are the kind of person who goes and says, "I took this key. I'm sorry. Let me release all the librarians from being locked in a black, inky well, surrounded by books." Or you are the kind of person who turns around, slips down the stairs, goes back to his nine-by-eleven basement room with the key still in his pocket and, thirty years later, still has the key locked in the top drawer of his desk. What did I do? I chose a middle way. I could have left and walked away with the librarians locked in the stacks. But I didn't. Instead, I left the key on the floor, for someone else to find.

I did learn something there at the Frick Art Reference Library. I learned that there's somebody eyeing your card at every moment of your life. None of those artists knew that I was down there, peering over fate's shoulder. Over the progress of every love lurks the authority file, with its fatalities.

And a more important thing had happened. I wrote a sentence. It was my first true sentence. I used it to start a story. It went, "I am a student at the Institute of Fine Arts, and I work part time at the Frick Art Reference Library." It couldn't have been simpler, could not have been flatter or more naïvely declarative. And yet I knew at once that, writing it, I had broken through, that in the simple accumulation of obviousness lay a path toward writing more potent than all the puns and poems I had written. Wherever you were going, the power of sentences lay in their simple additive observations. It was a truth that I glimpsed, and that then escaped me. It escapes me still, as I pursue it, still.

I had also learned that, no matter who you were or what you did, you were only going one way, straight below the rod. Even if no death notice turns up for you today, your card stays above the rod until one does. The claw of the head librarian gets us all in the end.

=====

Oh! I remember! It was a joke about the National Endowment for the Arts. That's what it was. The museum guard explains that his father had been a dealer—that his father had had a stable that he kept fed. The pretty young curator, thinking that the stable was one of artists, not horses, replied, "NEA?" meaning that she supposed that's how the father (and there was a father/fodder pun somewhere in there, too) kept them fed. And he replies, "No, mostly they lived on oats." No wonder I was proud of it. Puns like that are only produced under the pressure of waiting for old men to die in Europe, and your first sentence to appear in earnest.

5

Seeing Theo

After I lost the sort-of job I had at the Frick Library, killing off old artists who had once been young, I got a job, sort of, at the Museum of Modern Art, talking about old pictures that had once been new.

Those were, and probably still are, the two kinds of jobs you can get as a newcomer to the city: the sort-of job, and the job, sort of. A sort-of job is one that's really a job but that you don't really want to do—a job that no one would really take if he had a choice. People worked for years at the Frick Library, but no one was really *lifted* by the experience. A job, sort of, is a job that *could* be good if you actually had it, but really you don't, not in the way normal people have real jobs. These days those kinds of jobs are called internships, but thirty-five years ago, though they might ask you to do something for almost nothing, they didn't quite yet have the nerve to ask you to work at something for nothing at all.

The job I got at the Museum of Modern Art was like that. Not really a job—you couldn't live on what you made doing it—it was still fun to do, within limits. Three times a week, I was to give museum visitors a lunchtime lecture on famous pictures in the collection. They would pay me fifty dollars for every talk.

Given Martha's and my capacity, undiminished to this day, for accelerating from nothing to Parnassus in a nanosecond, or at least to the basements of the Upper East Side, which was, after all, what had got us to New York, we saw this job, sort of, as a good omen. In fact, when we stood in the museum garden, we noticed that there was a good-looking modernist building directly across the street, on the north side of Fifty-fourth, with casement windows and curved Bauhaus segments. Like all Bauhaus buildings, it had, obviously, an institutional look, and we were pretty confident that it served to house young curators with bright futures. (This, we later learned, was not actually the case, certainly not on $150 a week.)

The job, sort of though it was, certainly suited my verbose nature and family pedigree. Various lost uncles on my father's side, I knew, had once worked as boardwalk pitchmen in Atlantic City, where they would demonstrate, say, spray starch for housewives. *Tumlers*, amusing men, they had the habit—observed by me as a small boy, once—of starting each spiel in a low-key, friendly manner, attracting a crowd not with carnival barker intensities but with high-hearted confidence: they couldn't *wait* to tell about the spray starch.

I adapted that approach to the pictures at MoMA. I would park myself in front of a picture—*The Starry Night* was a popular choice, as was *Les Demoiselles d'Avignon*, anything with a *story*, even if what you were about to repeat was the orthodoxy that the art annihilated the tale it began by telling—and just start talking, free-associating shamelessly.

"Don't read the labels!" I would call out, loudly, to the puzzled and docile crowd. "No, don't read them! If you read the labels, you won't be looking. Come here and let's talk about what we really see!" There was enough authority in that cry—and in the promise of deliverance from having to read those tedious blurbs, or at least from this guy's continued shouting—to draw a small crowd around.

Like every teacher, cheap or skilled, who promises to "talk over" or "have a discussion about" something or other, I meant: Now you'll have your chance to listen to me. What was Vincent looking at when he painted this picture—why a starry night? What did he see?

Off I would go on a careening roller-coaster ride—the seat belts unfastened and the old wooden tracks rattling for dear life—of mixed metaphors, rhetorical turns, labored analogies, the whole riff made remotely decent by the passion with which it was offered, which was real enough. "Vincent had a way of looking outside that crucially enabled him to look inside. Where others saw pinpricks of light punched in the fabric of a uniform black sky, Van Gogh saw ecstatic spirals and tumbling whorls, a night sky pregnant with possibility that revealed itself in the very act of creation—as though he were some prescient prophet of what our own age would see in the birth of galaxies and the making of stars . . . that seemed to populate the cosmos, as though it were pregnant and laboring to bring forth not just a new art but an entirely new universe, rooted inside the painter's mind. It is a picture of the ecstatic whorls and spirals that he felt spinning within himself. . . ."

If I was in good form, there wasn't a pause for breath. Then I would work my way round to the lovely patch in one of his letters, which I had committed to memory, where Vincent writes so beautifully about how illness and suffering and madness might merely be the star-tunnels that take us on train rides to another world. Just as magicians learn that the most obvious tricks impress people the most, talkers learn that anything committed to memory and recited with emotion will, in an age when nothing is committed to memory, impress people even more than something intelligent, freshly said. (The great art critic Robert Hughes, I would learn much later, whose Jesuit education in Australia had beaten into him long pages of verse and classical prose, could stop a dinner party dead just by reciting some epistle of Pope's to an audience that couldn't remember the headlines in the *Times* from that morning. That he got more satisfaction, and perhaps more credit, than he deserved, or actually wanted, from the rich ladies at those parties, was part of his vulnerability.)

I was good at it, the first thing in New York I *was* good at. Shooting tendrils of words to grow around frames and pictures, interpenetrating stories of artists' lives—training anecdote and adjective through a trellis built around the artwork, to make its light a play of shade and dapple, as a trellis overgrown does the Italian sun. Those trellises of anecdotes and adjectives would eventually become my daily work, and, after I started learning to put the words on a page, my very comfortable prison. But for now, the one thing I did do well, or at least confidently, was speak in public. This is, as public speakers know, an easy thing to do. Most people are terrified of speaking in public. I was terrified of most things people are good at—skateboarding, or driving cars—but I wasn't scared of public speaking. Not being scared in the first place is usually just a sign of lack of imagination. The people who aren't frightened of climbing vertical rock faces haven't added up the risks and decided to defy them. They just don't feel the risk adequately in the first place, as they note ruefully to themselves while they plunge, as eventually they will, back down toward the ground. The person who isn't afraid of public speaking hasn't overcome his fear of being ridiculed. He just likes being heard so much that he doesn't notice how ridiculous he is.

The people coming in at lunchtime were hungry for a little bit of humanity. They were coming to the Museum of Modern Art, but they didn't really care about the Museum or the Modern. They cared about the Art. If it had been the Museum of Modern Artists they would have liked it more. They had made the alteration in their own heads anyway. They didn't care to know anything about the complicated scheme of influence and ideas that the cadet art historians had learned so laboriously: how this simplification led to that stylization, which led to this abstraction. No, they wanted to know what had moved the mover—they wanted to know who had broken the poet's heart, and what he or she had broken her heart against. To tell them that this broken heart was one in a long chain of broken hearts leading to Andy Warhol or all-black flat pictures was unsatisfying. They were more interested in the hearts than the chain. The more you told them about the drama of the life of the person who painted it—Mondrian fleeing Europe, Vincent being fled by Paul Gauguin—the happier they were. It was a simple lesson and, for someone who had been taught academic art history, audacious, inasmuch as the last thing we were being trained to talk about is whom the person who made the picture made it for, and who else he wished would look at it and love it. Even though, in truth, that is the most revealing question that you can ever ask about anyone's art—whom did the artist mean it for, and why was he hoping someone else would love him more for having seen it or read it? A Malevich black square becomes a Joni Mitchell lyric, once you know about Mrs. Malevich.

People listened. John Cleese came once, and, in a mad improv, I suggested that there was some connection between Basil Fawlty and Van Gogh; he beamed, warily, from the back. No one recognized him, at a time when his American fame was still blended into the, to an American, one-of-a-kind Pythons. (Years later, I met Cleese at a New York theatrical occasion; not only did he remember the moment, but saw it less as the kind of lovable thing that happens when you are admired by bright, voluble strangers than as the sort of first reckoning with the chaotic principle of celebrity that throws even a noonday visit to a museum out of whack.)

I felt unreasonably pleased with my approach, but there was soon a damper. "You're doing *docent* work?" was what William Rubin, chief curator of the museum, said as he was passing by. (He had seen me give that seminar report, though not, of course, seen me collapse from hunger and mixed drinks afterward.) There was in his amused tone—unforgivably and unmistakably—a sense that this was women's work. It's true that in those days in art history most of the students were women and most of the professors men. But a lot of the men who were studying were rich young men who took it arrogantly for granted that they would get further by studying than the women would get.

This information—that talking well about pictures was a fine thing, but a feminine thing—was useful. "Art appreciation" was considered weak, unscholarly—"feminine"—while an appetite for art was acceptable and "masculine." There were, I was beginning to learn, actually two sensibilities at large in the New York art world.

The first was that stamp collector's sensibility, with each artwork slipped, so to speak, into its neat little plastic jacket in a chronological album. The other, more promising approach was the epicurean, each thing relished as a sensual delight, almost as a sexual fetish.

Bill Rubin *ate* the pictures in his gallery. When he talked of the "jammed little biomorphs" in a mint De Kooning, the little biomorphs became as edible as ortolans. If you had handed him a knife and fork and a big white napkin, he might have dined late at night, experimentally, on a Cubist collage or two. In the seminar during my first month at school, his caressing passion for the Picassos he was showing us and for the African art he collected put me in mind less of a professor explaining art than of Sydney Greenstreet in *The Maltese Falcon*, greedy for the missing bird. When he showed the profile of a Bawang mask, it wasn't a semiotic triumph; it was a visitation from another planet. "This," he said of the Picasso guitar, "looks like an unprepossessing object, but it's as potent as $E = mc^2$." The objects were not suspended, like the beautiful things Martha and I had wanted, on invisible wires through space. They were presented raw and whole on the plate of history.

Perhaps ours had been a wan, provincial way of seeing beautiful things. Aestheticism, I was learning, is as various as any other kind of desire. One might think this would be the first thing anyone would learn about it, but in fact it is the last thing anyone teaches—the aestheticism of the moment is always being presented not as aestheticism at all but as a self-evident morality exposed when the previous aestheticism got torn down.

Rubin was the director of MoMA in those days but he was not—not remotely—like the kind of museum director one finds now, who could easily slide over and run Sotheby's or Apple or the Veterans Affairs Department. He was simply passionate, with a brutal head, a Roman head, like one of the lesser Caesars, with close-cropped hair and a sharp jaw and a surprisingly slow, conspiratorial, crinkling grin; he walked with a silver-tipped cane, a crooked walk that also left him the cane to gesture with. He always wore a suit, and in the lapel the red ribbon of the Légion d'Honneur, or its rosette.

He was one of a generation of New York Jews who had become not the popes or tsars or dictators, but something more like the doges of modernism—like the old Venetian doges, they had a permanent respect for the other members of the assembly, and understood that power passed to them institutionally: power kept was power shared. With the art critics Clement Greenberg and Harold Rosenberg and Meyer Schapiro and Leo Steinberg, Rubin had in common an oracular authority and severity, as well as a maturity I recognized as possible only in one from the other side of the great cultural divide of the sixties. On our side, the post-sixties side, boyishness was a common trait, if not always an appealing one. Boyishness was part of the inheritance of the "cult of youth." Having grown up in a decade, the sixties, when the people who made all the good art were our own age, changing year by year almost in perfect unison with our own changing sensibility—deepening from 1964 to 1965, and then brightening psychedelically from 1966 to 1967—we felt that our extended youthfulness was not an affectation. It was the logical extension of our experience.

The Rubins of the world had an authority that derived from an earlier time, when military service was part of the general experience even of aesthetes. To have been part of the Second World War was hugely helpful to an art historian. It taught you a healthy cynicism about motives, and an even healthier belief in big accomplishments. Bill assumed that everything that Picasso did was for a carnal or money motive—to impress a girl he wanted to fuck, or to fleece a few extra bucks off the Americans—and he loved to mock his students when they suggested a higher, or more grad-student-approved motive, earnestly insisting that a picture had been made under the "influence" of one highbrow book or another of the kind that Rubin knew Picasso never read. But he also believed that consciousness had been altered permanently by these carnal and self-interested acts; he knew this, because he had seen idealism mixed with blood from the beginning.

Bill *loved* Picasso—he didn't appreciate him, or recognize the range of his influence. He loved him, with a carnal infatuation for his objects and his aura that moved me by its innocence, its being so plainly a crush. He had been close to Picasso—and had found the right, wry, man-of-the-world tone to speak with him about art. For, though artists are serious about art in the final instance—serious about nothing except art—they refuse to be serious about it in the first instance. No artist worth her salt wants to talk about her influences, her visions, her breakthroughs, and above all she despises being asked what she "meant by" whatever. What she means by the work is the work, which contains all the meanings going. She found out what it meant by making it, and you find out what it means by looking at it. Training in art history is still mostly training in what *x* "means" and "stands for"—regarding *Les Demoiselles d'Avignon,* we ask what Picasso meant the brothel to stand for and the masks of the women with syphilis, or the like. Artists want instead to talk about their art as a chef talks about dishes: an assemblage of good things, brought together to solve a problem. Cooking is not an art in the sense that art is art only because, though it seeks balances among opposites—vinegar and oil, sweet and spicy—it does not stand on its contradictions, as art does.

A dish that does not contain two different flavors is unlikely to be any good; a work of art, I was learning, that does not include two forces or drives pulling in starkly opposed directions is never going to live. And this truth is expressed in personalities as much as in paintings. So that in later years, when I came to know Chuck Close or Richard Serra a little, it was the neat split of their personalities that marked them as artists: Serra's near brutality of manner combined with the obsessive delicacy of his taste; Chuck's obsessively, almost autistically impersonal and systematic realizations of faces as landscapes combined with the good-humored collegiality that moved him in realizing them. Faces became landscapes, and landscapes, surveyed in objective detail, turned out to be the faces of friends.

The sensual appetite for art—that was the mark of the real vocation. That, and the slightly more disconcerting ability to tell prettiness from beauty. It was the gift that would have enabled someone to distinguish Matisse from Raoul Dufy in 1905. "Dufy was the most talented painter visible in 1905 among the Fauves," Rubin once said, as dogmatically as only he could. "But anyone with an eye would have seen that he would amount to nothing." I was terrified. For I knew that I would have placed my bets on Dufy. The inability to tell pretty from beautiful was my weakness, for which, in truth, I wasn't entirely sorry.

But the engine of that difference between pretty and beautiful was already starting to be visible to me. It lay in the same openness to contradiction. Nothing is truer than that art is what starts off ugly and then gets beautiful, whereas fashion starts off pretty and then gets ugly. It's another form of the rule of incompatible forces, newly reconciled. Beauty is the woman in a Picasso portrait of the forties, perfection and imperfection pulled together, with the features out of order but the face intact. Prettiness is beauty without an opposing principle present in the same picture or paragraph. What made Rubin original was that he saw the contradictions of beauty not as intellectual knots tied by deep thinkers but as dishes made by cooks who had freed themselves from the limitations of our ordinary foods and hungers.

It was dawning on me—slowly, because, though I have a quick tongue, I have a slow-to-dawn-on mind, a paradox that has made me miss many obvious things while talking my way past many apparent difficulties—it was dawning on me that the museum *was* like a church, but not at all in the way that the Tom Wolfes of the world meant: not in inculcating a set of rules but precisely in *not* teaching rules, proposing instead a way of being, of putting on an unconscious and inherited daily routine of belief, of wedding hunger with practice. The appetite in the art world was not really for ideals like "beauty" but for objects, objects that would be as dense with significance as a black hole is with matter. The real art appetite was for consuming history with your eyes. "You're not looking" was Rubin's ultimate dismissal. Far from being an ideologue, he was a romantic obsessive. All these things meant more than they seemed, as glasses of wine and biscuits and scraps of parchment

mean more than they seem to adherents of other faiths. Really looking required not earnest sentences—pronouncements and cunning
comparisons and by-the-book reversals of expectations—but a sort
of suave, secretive complicity. When my parents came to New York,
I ostentatiously admired Bawang masks, standing alongside them
in profile to look. They seemed impressed by the impersonation.
Understanding would come from looking, as enlightenment somehow came to adepts of meditation just from sitting. But it was hard.
There seemed an awful lot of eyestrain involved.

———

Looking was hard, but talking remained easy. Sometimes, the same
people would come day after day to hear me speak. Amid the generally docile crowds of tourists and day-trippers, grateful for someone
to listen to amid all the visual confusion, there was a hard core, now
vanished, of MoMA regulars. The museum in those days was not
yet fashionable but it was popular, genuinely so. Rubin knew this:
"We hang the pictures for our audience," he said. He meant not rich
folks, or art folks, but just folks, of an odd kind, who came to the
museum on weekends and at lunchtime, a few of them to hear me
talk.

There were "wholesalers" from the garment district not far from
there; grandmothers who made it their habit to come twice a week,
as they had been doing since they were young. Almost invariably,
Matisse's *Tabletop* was those gentle ladies' favorite picture, and I
worked up a sweet, short eulogy to it, which got me fine cred with
the over-seventy crowd—what might now be called my base, since
it has remained enthusiastic. (My son, Luke, twenty-odd years later,
insists to this day that he never feels comfortable coming to a reading of mine without a defibrillator.)

There were more aggressive attendees, though. There was, for
instance, the man with the needlepoint *Guernica*. Not long before,
the real *Guernica*, Picasso's legendary protest picture, had been
repatriated, as the painter had wanted, to a newly democratic Spain.

He came up to me after my talk on *Ma Jolie,* that strange, dark, rooftops-of-Paris painting, with its stenciled title meaning "my pretty one," and that I had managed to make sound as if it had been painted by Jerome Kern and P. G. Wodehouse.

"It's hard for me to keep coming back here," he said provocatively, and then waited for me to take the bait.

"Oh, I'm sorry to hear that. Why?" I said, being constitutionally unable not to take bait when it's offered, even if the hook looks bright and shiny and sharp, just beyond the wriggling worm.

"They betrayed us when they handed over the *Guernica*," he said.

"I think they sort of had to hand it over. The deal was that when Spain became a democracy . . ." I said, trying to spout what I imagined was the company line without starting a fight.

"Spain's a democracy?" he said. The question didn't take considering.

"They didn't have to move it," he continued to insist before he paused. "But I'm doing something about it. I'm reproducing it, and my *Guernica*'s in *full* color."

He went on to explain that his "passion in life" was making needlepoint reproductions of Picasso paintings from the museum, working from his own photographs. He was a burly little guy with a spade beard and a thinning hairline. He came back, again and again—once or twice, he actually brought his little needlepoint frame, on which he worked as I spoke. It wasn't rude, just diligent.

He kept inviting me over to see his needlepoints. This sounded to me a little suspicious, so, failing that, he actually brought photographs of them to show me one lunch hour. Like some old-fashioned pornographer exhibiting his choicest postcards, he took me into a corner to reveal his "album" of needlepoints—photographs slipped under plastic—with a mix of guardedness and pride, making it plain to would-be gawking passersby that they weren't invited to *this* party.

He had colorized all the pictures as he turned them into embroidery. The Cubist *Ma Jolie* was done in a sort of ecru, "to show the forms better"; the *Girl Before a Mirror*, originally in the reds and yellows of a Spanish medieval apocalypse, had been given a tasteful turn in blue and mauve pastels. She seemed . . . homier than she had before. The *Guernica*, which occupied a two-page spread, was remade in a sort of ocher-and-lime harmony. It stood out from the rest. It actually looked pretty good in ocher and lime, about as good as it did in black and white. (It was both an homage to Picasso and a critique of Picasso's failures as a colorist.)

What was odd and interesting was that, whether purposefully or not, it was, in its way, a "camp" enterprise—an ocher-and-lime *Guernica*—that made you laugh because it undermined the pretensions of a certain kind of high modernism. But it wasn't presented as a parody—and God knows its creator didn't think of it that way. It had the *form* of a joke, but you weren't meant to laugh at it, not even with the ironic smirk that might have greeted a Lichtenstein pop art cartoon painting. It was a completely sincere form of unintentionally parodic self-expression.

If I had been more prescient than I am, I might have seen the needlepoint *Guernica* as the first small domino to fall—or the first blade of crabgrass to invade the lawn—signaling the appearance of a new kind of art in the 1980s, in which all the older kinds of camp and parody got played as straight as *Hamlet* or as, well, the *Guernica*. Though I didn't know him yet, a young man of a similar spirit was working not far from me, at the MoMA membership desk; within five years, Jeff Koons would be presenting life-size Italian ceramic figurines of cartoon characters with the same mix of desperate sincerity and bizarre bad taste as the needlepoint *Guernica*. But I didn't know that then. (Neither did my *Guernica* guy, of course. He possessed the sensibility by, so to speak, anticipatory accident, rather than guile. But, then, you might have said the same about Koons. In fact, later on I did.)

There were others like him, lots of them, more of them than you might have imagined: people whose connection to the pictures in the museum was visceral, eccentric, and all-encompassing, religious in that other, deeper sense—part of a search for self-definition rather than for admission to any kind of club of in-the-knows. The folk culture of modernism in New York, I was learning, was stronger and more original than the professional culture of modernism, which seemed merely expert and religious. The high culture was filled with icons and priests and competing theologies. The folk culture was filled with amulets and shamans and superstitions.

They came to the Museum of Modern Art, every day, or almost every day, at lunchtime, and what they wanted was not a sense of history unfolding in synoptic fashion, with Cézanne nudging the Cubists, who in turn nudged the Futurists, who nudged the next movement, one long row of dominoes falling in curatorial order. No, they came because they were convinced that these strange pictures, these distorted faces and abstract planes and unreal landscapes, were not windows into a form of experience stranger than any they were normally allowed access to, but were windows onto experience that looked like their own in its very strangeness. They *lived* the pictures as parts of their lives, just as intently and fully as the burghers in Siena and the merchants in Florence had once lived their altarpieces. They didn't understand that they were supposed to feel alienated from the work. Why should they? They had been looking at it their whole lives. It didn't *feel* alien. It felt familiar. The only history it belonged to was their own. They had made a kind of imaginative leap past the apparent difficulty of the pictures, which had seemed so formidable to a popular audience when they were first exhibited, to see the pictures' difficulty as no more difficult than life already was—they were at home with strangeness, because, after all, the strangeness outside the museum was likely to be stranger and more alienating than any a painter could conjure up. The oddity inside was downright comforting.

They did not grasp, as I would try to do tumidly in lectures, that the girls dancing in Matisse's *La Danse* were cartoonlike forms subversively designed to flatten the robust Rubensian bodies of illusionistic art, that these were not women but ciphers merely *standing* for women. They saw only girls dancing, and if they were girls in outline, well, what else would you expect in a picture? Stylization they took for granted. Everything they saw was stylized. What was new and inspiring was Matisse's personal struggle to make his stylizations ring in the world. Their idea of Matisse's *The Red Studio* was our Blue Room to the nth. It was a place dreamt up to compensate for what life was like outside it. They saw modern art romantically, instead of academically, and I was beginning to suspect that this was the way the people who made it had seen it, too.

Martha came a few times to listen to me. She remained busy with her own version of the same kind of job, sort of, organizing D. A. Pennebaker's vast trove of outtakes, thirty years' worth, for which the great documentary filmmaker had vague Utopian plans. It had fallen on Martha, ten months into her filmmaking career, to achieve them all. She both loved the sudden, unexpected proximity to the heart of the documentary film world in New York—and was slightly alarmed that, though she had just arrived at the heart, anyone would expect her to, so to speak, crack open the chest and perform surgery.

This, though, is the truth of New York life. The intern becomes the authority with staggering suddenness, if things fall out that way. The master or mistress hires an assistant almost absentmindedly, desperately, and the assistant accrues power with amazing speed, since the one thing she can do is limit the overflow that led to her hiring. She liked to run away from her other internship, at the Museum of Broadcasting, and come to the modern museum at lunchtime to hear me speak, though she would often start crying—not racking sobs exactly, but tears all the same—just as I started speaking. Afterward, she assured me that this was only because she was emotionally so invested in my performances, so concerned that I do well. I wondered if there wasn't some sort of oblique censure registered in the act. (Even now, when I am speaking in public, if I look into the first row I see her lovely slanted eyes dissolved in tears. She still makes the same assurance, and I still have the same doubts.)

But two of these passionate listeners stood out from all the rest, and they were Larry and Maxie.

Larry came first. He was a tall string bean of a guy, in his late twenties, in a bad stiff suit. I noticed him standing at the back of the group once, and then again, and then the following Tuesday again. The next time, he gathered up his courage and came up to talk.

"I really enjoy hearing you," he said. "Tell me, where could I go learn to talk about pictures the way you do?"

Knowing my younger self, I'm sure I was a little miffed at first. "You could take art courses at the Met or somewhere," I said vaguely.

"No, I mean, where could I go to become an art historian. That's what you are, right?"

"Studying to become one," I said, in the tone of a rustic: "Right hopin' to be so, sir."

"I have a whole lyrical, aesthetic side that I can't express," he said bluntly, with an impressive amount of honestly delivered pain. "I'm an accountant. It's hard to be lyrical when you're an accountant."

I saw that this was probably true, and I immediately felt protective of him. Or maybe I felt competitive? Larry wanted to be an art historian. It seemed to me the last thing in the world any sane person should want to be. But reluctantly, I became his mentor—his Bill Rubin. I brought him a catalogue of night-school courses at Hunter College, and instructed him on how to discriminate among them. I wondered if the chain went on this way, bluster educating the half-baked and mesmerizing the innocent—was this in fact the germ line of education? Was it possible that each of us was imitating the next most visible guy, with no actual person at the center, no real authority, just the long chain of mimicry?

I did the best I could:

"Look," I said, "you enjoy coming here to listen to me and to look at the pictures, and that's the last thing you'll find yourself doing if you become an art historian. Keep this feeling pure—let it be the pure thing you have."

"You have no idea how terrible it is to be a certified public accountant," he said. He was trying to be amusing, but he was also entirely serious—almost angry with my complacent, patronizing counsel. "I did it to please my mother, but I want to do something better."

He caught himself slightly, not wanting, I realized, to lose my good opinion, or mentorship, through an undue display of rebellion.

So I helped him enroll in a class at Hunter—the kind that we called "Pyramids to Pollock," an overview of man and art from first to last act. He seemed happy.

Maxie Schacknow was a more ornery kind. He came to hear me speak about Vincent van Gogh. He stood scowling in the back.

"You didn't mention the picture he didn't paint," he heckled.

"Well, he painted all kinds of pictures," I said.

"Fuck that. There was one picture he never painted." He waited for me to name it and then, despairing of penetrating the kind of thick skull that was by now familiar to him, went on. "He never painted a portrait of Theo! He painted his mother. He painted the goddamn *berceuse*"—he meant the woman on a rocker, imagining, I guess, that a *berceuse* was a job, not a song. "He painted the god-damn *post*man, for Chrissake!" He was enraged about that, in par-ticular: he meant Joseph Roulin, whom Van Gogh did indeed paint, and in his uniform, too, several times. "But Theo, his brother, lives for him and supports him and cares for him when he's sick—and no portrait."

"I think they were never together long enough once he arrived—"

"Bullshit," Maxie blurted. "I mean, excuse my French, but that's bullshit. He just never saw that he should. Van Gogh was a great artist—but a *terrible* brother."

"Well, many great artists are poor family men—" I began.

"Family man? That's how you treat your wife and your children? How you treat your brother? That's not a man. Terrible brother." His eyes gleamed. "That's why I'm doing it."

"Doing what?"

"*I'm* painting a portrait of Theo. It's the picture he should have painted, and I'm painting it for him. In his style, of course. I wouldn't do it in any other style. I mean, a Monet? No. A Degas of Theo? Of course not. A Vincent of Theo. A Van Gogh of Van Gogh. I'm working on it now."

I suppose I edged away, just a little. There were a fair proportion—not many, but some—of outright crazies who came on weekdays at lunchtime. It cost too much to just come in out of the rain, so to speak, but not that much if you had a few dollars (nowadays it's twenty, or some Disneyland-worthy admission, but then it was much less). Still, he didn't look crazy. He looked like a guy in the garment business who painted Van Goghs on Sundays.

Maxie asked me to come and see him exhibit at a street fair, down on Washington Square. It was a crowded show, with acres of the kind of painting that I had been raised to have contempt for.

What was odd was that, removed from the halls of MoMA, he was clearly something of a star among the Sunday painters. The others—I will never forget an adorable landscape painter with the dream painter's name, Honey Ruskin—deferred to him every bit as much as we deferred to Rubin. I sensed that the truth of the "marginal" was that the margins were so broad that once you were in them you no longer recognized them as the margins. The "margins" for the marginalized looked like the mainland, with the mainstream merely a horizon in the distance.

════

A sign above his paintings announced that none of the paintings were for sale. People went back and forth, admiring the pictures. One woman asked him the price of a *Road with Cypresses*.

"That's a Van Gogh, lady!" Maxie said, rising from his director's chair. "Offer me ten million and we'll talk. What's the price of a Van Gogh! The nerve."

She withered away. By the end of the decade, even ten million for a Van Gogh would seem absurdly cheap. By the end of the decade, ten million for a Maxie might not have seemed absurd. But we were only on the verge of the explosion, and not quite there. When I interviewed him five years later, all his imaginary prices had gone up accordingly.

"You look like an educated group. You remind me of my son.

He won a twenty-thousand-dollar scholarship to college. From his father. Come look at the pictures." We were alike in spirit, I thought, *tumlers* of art.

———

At last I saw his portrait of Theo—though I can no longer recall whether I saw it then or at a subsequent street fair in Washington Square. His Theo was a black-and-white sketch for the painting. It was, of course, a pastiche of many elements in other Van Gogh portraits, less "skillful" than audacious. There were irises behind his head, as I recall, but made to look like iris-patterned wallpaper. Vincent's patina of heavy brushstrokes became a sort of toothpaste-tube application of raw paint. Theo's face had been carefully traced from a photograph, and, though daubed with flesh-colored pigment, it looked oddly photographic—a Chuck Close face peering out from a wrinkled, surging expressionist background. Its sincerity was absolute. The background came from one of Vincent's self-portraits in Arles. But Theo's forehead was higher and his brow was smooth.

"That's deliberate," Maxie said, following my eye. "I didn't wanna potchke up the paint there. I didn't potchke up the paint because I wanted to show what a mensch Theo was. What a brother. If you potchke up the paint, the way Vincent did with the postman's beard, it makes it look watery, you know what I mean, like the beard's on fire or going somewhere. You don't potchke, you got a *rock*."

The other painters came round to admire Maxie's pictures and accept his strictures. One of the things I was learning in New York was the insuperable rule of the rabbit hole. If you go into an academic art studio, filled with plaster casts, you expect to find the classically minded artists embattled and bitter. But they aren't. There are too many of them to be embattled. What they are mostly is amused, the absurdity of the avant-garde establishment being too obvious to them to need much criticism. In return, the avant-garde establishment can't be angered by the Beaux Arts–minded artists. "The realists, like the poor, are always with us," one of the wittiest of the avant-garde magi said to me once. Numbers insulate, and in

a city of eight million enterprising artists, there are always so many
of every kind that no kind seems marginal to itself. I met a man
who taught students to paint frescoes in the classic Tuscan manner.
He was preoccupied with rumors that another émigré Tuscan might
be opening his own fresco studio. A Don Quixote in New York is
chiefly annoyed at some other, overread knight who might be mus-
cling in on his windmills.

Meanwhile, Larry the CPA was pursuing the class at Hunter. "If
it's Tuesday, this must be the Rococo." It was that kind of class, the
kind of thing that graduate students were expected to teach, having been taught by people who also taught them contempt for it.
But Larry wasn't contemptuous of it. He didn't find it shallow, or
reductive.

He would arrive every week with a set of questions, queries.
I would see him waiting to ask them, at the edge of the crowd—
perhaps no longer really listening, I thought, feeling mildly hurt,
eager to show that he had been promoted into a different relationship with the speaker.

His questions were polite and sharp, sometimes disconcertingly
so: If the cave artists were so great, why do we like primitive art
that isn't lifelike at all? . . . How can you tell the difference between
Baroque and Rococo? Wasn't one sort of all spirals and the other
all . . . If they were so religious, why did they make everything look
so sexy? How could you talk about the naturalism of Greek nudes
when they didn't look like anyone you ever saw if you saw them
naked? Why did Malevich choose a square—aren't there squares
everywhere? What was the big deal about Picasso's guitar being an
"object in space"? There are lots of objects with space around them.
And why did we admire Van Gogh's self-portraits so much? Wasn't
one more or less like the next? Why weren't they just, well, an ego
trip?

They were, I realized after a time, a CPA's questions—exactly
what you would get if you merged an accountant with an art historian, in some odd X-Men hybrid. He was probing the fine print,
looking for the exemptions, double-checking the ledger. He hated

the sloppiness of the sums by which art history was usually rendered. And, I had to admit, an accountant's questions were good questions to be asking, probably better than an aesthete's, at least likelier to lead to some significant discovery. If we quantified our assertions, what would be left of their extravagance? All the aesthete could do was aestheticize; the accountant could add.

And yet being exposed to the sloppy accounting of aestheticism didn't alienate him from it. "I want to do this. I feel that this is what I ought to do." It was an impressive display of stubbornness on the part of someone who had rarely shown it in his life. "I think I've figured out something," he told me one day. "What you do is, you read the footnotes. Then you see what books they refer to. Then you get the books. Then you see what books the footnotes in the books refer to. Those are the important books." Volumes, as they say, could not have told more.

Maxie's sentiments led me to feel protective of Larry's. "Look at Theo," I said to him, "Theo van Gogh. He was a sort of accountant, really—not an artist or an art critic. But he took care of his brother, and that made him indispensable to art."

Larry looked at me dubiously. "My brother's not a painter in Arles," he said glumly. "He's an accountant, too. In Syosset."

I saw the issue—one Theo supporting another, one accountant supporting another no less: no unsung heroism there. I still pressed the point.

"But I don't mean literally supporting your brother as a painter. I don't mean it literally; I mean, you know, being part of the whole kind of family of people who help make art happen. Sort of in the support structure." I smelled the lie even as I spoke it. The "support structure" for art was made up of the hugely wealthy who bought it, and of dealers who wore Armani suits and looked as streamlined as Bauhaus façades, not well-meaning accountants, however fraternal in spirit.

"I heard about Theo," he said to me, more tired than triumphant. "He didn't even get a portrait." The invisible people were banding together. They might no longer be content to haunt the house. They might decide to storm the castle.

=====

After I saw the portrait of Theo, Maxie and I went for coffee. (He had tea, I think, with many sugars.) He explained to me that he had been born in Williamsburg but grew up mostly in Brownsville. "I worked as a shoeshine boy, and at a slaughterhouse. But I always wanted to be an artist. I don't know why. My father made mannequins for Finkelstein's, on the Lower East Side. My mother designed quilts.

"Then I got married. If you want to be an artist, you can't be a family man. Van Gogh, he knew that. So I tried other hobbies. I did ham radio for a while—monitoring the ships." He snorted his snort, at the pretension of "monitoring" from your basement. "In 1958, I opened a textile brokerage business with my brother. But always at the back of my mind there's this picture of Van Gogh's called *The Langlois Bridge*. I saw it when I was young, you know? So Evelyn, my wife, tells me, Get off the damn radio! Find another hobby! So I took painting classes, and I painted one picture and then another, and now I paint seven days a week, every minute I can take from the business. I've painted one thousand two hundred and forty-five pictures. I know the amount for certain, because I number every one."

"That's great, to have a passion like that," I said, trying to avoid a critical assessment while congratulating him on the intensity of his commitment—a verbal trick that would come in handy over the next decade with painters a lot more famous than Maxie.

"Why didn't Vincent paint Theo?" he asked me. I noticed six or seven empty sugar packets.

That question I thought I should have at least *some* answer to.

"I don't know," I said at last. "Maybe because he was the invisible man in his life. We all have invisible men somewhere in our lives—people who believe in us but who become so familiar that we just can't see them. I think that Theo was his invisible man."

Maxie paused to consider this for a moment. "Fuck that," he said finally. Then he coughed slightly and leaned forward.

"What do you think my painting's worth?" he asked.

"Sorry," I said. Of course I had heard him, but needed a moment to think of what to say.

"What's it worth? My portrait of Theo van Gogh? To a museum like yours."

Like mine! I realized that he thought that my lunchtime presence was a sign of my authority at the museum. If you talked up the goods, you must buy and sell the goods. It was a natural conclusion for a garment factor to make. I was being courted, I realized, not for my wit but for my access.

"What's it worth?"

I realized that his was the same mistake I had made thinking that somebody who knew Art Garfunkel could sell Art Garfunkel a song. The space between the top rung and the bottom rung in New York is smaller than you might think—cats look at kings all the time, interns talk for auteurs—but the separations' being small doesn't make them any less separate. Rungs remain rungs. Cats are cats and kings are kings, and kings buy what's on the castle walls and cats don't even get a vote. A cat may look at a king—may even talk to the king more freely than you might imagine. But the king won't let the cat decide what to spend on pictures. That's the king's business.

The best answer would have been, of course, "Try to be realistic. It really isn't the sort of thing any museum would ever buy." But we are all too cowardly to say such things, or too courteous. Or maybe courtesy and cowardice are one in the end. (The people in Paris who didn't fight duels with D'Artagnan were courteous because they were afraid of his edge.)

"It's priceless," I said at last.

I thought that the sententious baldness of the response might be seen through instantly, as Vincent had seen through Theo.

But Maxie seemed to find it satisfactory.

"Yeah. I know," he said, "I'll never sell it. Someday I'll have my own museum—not outside, but with walls and all that crap—and I'll put it there."

I smiled. The portrait of Theo was still there four or five years later, when I visited him again, at the same street fair.

———

When the museum acquired Vincent's *Portrait of Joseph Roulin*, I went with Maxie to look at it. He wasn't crazy about it.

"The eyes don't follow you," he said, taking it in one lunchtime. "That's bad. That beard is good. It's the color in the curlicues that makes the beard stand out. Van Gogh is a colorist. Me, I'm an accentuist. I accentuate the lines." He walked around. "Look at it from over here! From over here he's got a sneer! Why should a mailman be sneering at anybody?" He looked some more. Finally, he said, "You know what, this picture is a big disappointment. Those two big yellow buttons on his coat—your eye goes right for them, so you don't see his face. Also, the way those three flowers in the background [on the wallpaper pattern, he meant] crowd the beard. And—that *smirk*! Give me the *Langlois Bridge* anytime! Give me the *Road with Cypresses*! Actually, my portrait of Theo is a better portrait than this portrait. You know, looking at this picture and thinking about Theo reminds me of a time when my brother Harry was in his shorts, delivering some goods, and a postman got right in his way. Harry said to the mailman, 'Get out of my way!' The postman just stands there. So Harry slugs the postman! It's funny how this picture reminds me of that story."

It seemed like a fair interpretation, or at least as fair as any other. It struck me that the thing that made the picture sublime to many of its highbrow viewers—the dignity that Vincent gives to a "simple" postman—was exactly what bugged him about it. He hated mailmen. They were timeservers. They got in the way of hard-charging factors making their deliveries.

Years went by, and eventually I wrote something about Maxie, and then lost touch with him. Not long ago, when he came to mind again, I did what no one could have done thirty years ago—I

Googled him. I was stunned—no, I was astonished, I *plotzed*—to find out that Maxie Schacknow's museum, makeshift arrangement of the art fairs, had, in the end, actually come to exist. A now defunct but still live page showed that there had been a Maxie museum in Florida, the Schacknow Museum of Fine Arts on 7080 Northwest Fourth Street in Fort Lauderdale—the same sad town where my grandparents had gone to "retire" and die.

There was still a "mission statement" with a photograph of the museum: "The purpose of SMOFA is to provide a venue for artists, some well known and some obscure, to share their work with the community. The Museum was founded by Max Schacknow, a self-taught, Brooklyn, New York born artist, who realized how difficult it was for unknown artists to showcase their talent."

He had done it after all. He had made a museum with walls to show his pictures in. The portrait of Theo must have emigrated there.

There was even a review that sounded as though a younger version of me might have written it. "And how credible is a similarly photocopied brochure soliciting membership in the museum when it can't even get the names of some of the best-known artists in history right? Of the six membership categories named for those artists, only two—Picasso and Renoir—are spelled correctly. Would you want to shell out $75 for a 'Reubens' membership (does it include a sandwich?), $500 for a 'Rembrant,' or $1000 for a 'MichaelAngelo'? The Schacknow Museum of Fine Arts is a fine idea, but unless Max Schacknow starts paying attention to the details or hires someone to do it for him, he'll never have a first-class museum." That was Maxie's museum, for certain.

So he had been a millionaire! Small potatoes by New York art-world standards, but a big enough benefactor to bully and entice art professionals in art-starved retiree Florida. He had become an anecdote I told, but I had missed the range and power of his vision. He had not only painted this picture, he had built a museum to hang it in, and had then died with his work intact. He had done what Vincent dreamed of doing

Then, about six years ago, in 2011, a Dutch art historian discovered that a self-portrait of Vincent that had been in the Amsterdam museum for years was, in fact, a portrait of Theo! He had painted a portrait of his brother after all. It had existed all along! I felt a small, regressive, smug triumph: they *had* been looking at the labels, and it *had* been a mistake. It was hidden in plain sight, and the reason it had been accepted for a century as a self-portrait was that, though distinguishable from Vincent by a set of infinitesimal clues that took a century and more to put together—the slightly blonder color of Theo's beard; the turn of Theo's ears—Theo had been made otherwise indistinguishable from Vincent. The actual portrait, unidentified for so long, was of a man who bled into his brother's image—or was, perhaps, trapped in his brother's shadow. An invisible man, even in his own portrait.

As always, what was really there to look at was what was always there to be seen. The mysteries of art are on the surface, open to the eye—because that's where the mysteries of life are, too. Sibling love and sibling rivalry, the needlepoint *Guernica* and the portrait of Theo—any attempt to mystify the pictures with occult symbols or buried allegories missed the source of their actual emotional power, which is right there to be seen if we are willing to look past the labels. I had not been wrong about that, even if my saying it had been shamelessly designed to draw a crowd.

There was, I think, some strange moral equation of ambition and absurdity and self-obsession, of self-assertion and self-denial, in the intersection of Maxie's and Vincent's and Theo's ambition with my own. They provoked in me an act of moral and aesthetic accounting that I still seem unable to conclude. (Larry might have done it.) There was some tangle of truths about ambition and art that I could just detect within this comedy of unfulfilled aspirations on Fifty-third Street. My own ambitions were quickly gratified by the instant sugar high of attention in the gallery, no matter whose it was. But attention was what everyone wanted, whether a genius like Vincent painting or Maxie copying him or merely me, talking, or Larry copying *me*. However small or sad the act, the ambition was always the same, and it was nothing so grand as to be "understood" much less advance the history of art—it was simply to have people listen and look. Reading Vincent's letters, we're stunned by his simplicity and his devotion—but, God, he wishes people would *pay attention.*

Maxie was absurd, certainly, to think that he could be Van Gogh—but, then, to everyone but Theo, Vincent had been absurd to think that *he* could be Van Gogh. The pieties of humanism often cover up the brutalities of ego. Maxie's portrait of Theo looked like a picture painted by Maxie because it was dutifully selfless, a catalogue of Theo's traits and treasures. Vincent's actual portrait of Theo looked like . . . Vincent, because Vincent, being an artist above all, was, above all, occupied with the mystery of himself. His brother was entirely hidden within his own face, under his own hat. Beneath the pieties of art lie the brutalities of talent. It really *is* all in how good you potchke up the paint. Paintings are a series of egotistical assertions, rooms in Maxie's museum. Some of them turn out, by a strange architectural alchemy of the self we call art, to be places where we all can live.

Art begins in paying close attention to the one thing outside ourselves that we believe most resembles ourselves—to a face, or a flower, or even someone else's portraits. But ambition is simpler: all we really want is not to have passed this way without notice. The same impulse that got me talking at lunchtime without an audience listening made that other art-lover work with a needlepoint over his *Guernica* and had Maxie building a little museum with his name on it, and all the artists' names misspelled.

At least I was learning something real. The history of art looked more human than the art history books allowed, and ambition had more pathos in it than they allowed, either. *Don't let me leave here trackless and alone,* is all we plead for with fate, and ambition is a reflection of that panic. Ambition became art when we learned to be willing to defer the immediacy of the attention in order to make it count for more later. That's what Vincent had believed, anyway. But it was a challenge to this lunchtime *tumler,* and would always remain so.

Talking at MoMA at least made me realize that the only thing I would ever be good at was spinning tales, telling stories. I would never be a real critic, much less an "iconographer," a scholar of Renaissance pictures. My allegiance was to the excitement of the moment, the interchange between speaker and picture and audience, not the interchange between the picture and history. I was going to have to get out of art history one way or another and, somehow, find a place in the world of writing, some place where what was wanted was words, even silly words, in the one right order, even if it meant becoming in the end that terrible thing, a writer of labels.

Oh, and Larry? Years later, rummaging through art magazines, I was startled to see what I took to be his name on a paper, duly foot-noted, about—Tatlin, was it? There is always something frighten-ing about seeing one's own name in print unexpectedly—it always has the look of an indictment. My heart stopped when I saw that I was referenced, at the end and dismissively, for something I'd writ-ten: "Gopnik here makes the error" or "Gopnik sneers at . . ." It was the eternal exchange between writers and scholars, between people who are here to tell tales and the ones who are out to find facts. He had become my story. But I had become his footnote.

6

The Simple Logic of Summer Shirts

After I was fired from the Frick, and then discovered that the pleasures of talking about art at MoMA, though real, were not very lucrative, I decided to look for a real, a paying, job. (We were officially still in love with the Blue Room, but, unofficially, both ready for a better, or at least a bigger, home.) I found a job quickly, through a school friend. It was at *Gentlemen's Quarterly*, at that time not yet exclusively called *GQ*, and still exclusively a men's clothing-and-grooming magazine. They needed someone to edit the fashion pages, and, my qualifications for this job being exactly zero, I got it.

In those days, the back and forth between real jobs and sort-of jobs was freer-flowing than it is now. People advanced. They started as fiction editors at *Mademoiselle*, as the beverage editor at *Esquire*, and next time you turned around they were running a publishing house. To be in print was an astounding thing in itself; to *control* print, to be an editor, even of trivia, was to have power—as if in today's terms there were only fifty or so computers with Internet access in the whole city, and the ability to post was limited to those who owned them and would let you use the keyboard for an hour or two. The fiction editor of *Playboy* was a significant person; the movie reviewer of the *Soho News* was, too. The copyeditor of *GQ* was not exactly on their level. But he was a citizen of the inner city.

On her series, *Girls*, I was, as I've said, startled to see Lena Dunham's Hannah—having landed a job, of *exactly* the same station, at *exactly* the same men's fashion magazine—indignant at its limitations, and for a half-second I felt generationally censorious: didn't these kids today know how lucky they were? The entitlement! But, then, Hannah, I realized, was terrified of getting stuck there—once a regular paycheck arrived, she thought, they had put a flowerpot over your head, and it was pointless to struggle. (There were several other would-be poets and essayists placed in that office, trapped alongside her.) In the eighties, fluidity of opportunity made up for absurdity of occupation. You did a silly job, but having jobs was not in itself silly—one led to a better one. Now twenty-somethings feel *impaled* upon their first jobs. We felt . . . impelled—impelled upward, however illusory that feeling may have been. One day you were serving hors d'oeuvres at a cocktail party; a few months later you had a contract with Gordon Lish for a collection of your short stories at Knopf. Things like that happened. After you had the contract it might dawn on you that there was more money to be made per hour handing out tuna tartare on crispy crackers than publishing short stories. But the path from the crackers to fame seemed short. Nowadays the path from obscurity to ubiquity is instantaneous—you just write something nasty or nice on social media. But the ubiquity turns out—and here's the joke they didn't tell you, the punch line they forgot to share—to be not very different at all from complete obscurity. Everybody's speaking at once.

So I was excited, not depressed, to have the possibility of a job. My friend explained it casually: they needed someone who would edit the fashion copy. I nodded wisely, as one who had done this often. It called for meticulous attention to detail, he went on, and a tedious concern for the fine points of presentation. Since no task could have suited my abilities less than one calling for meticulous attention to detail and a tediously exacting concern for the fine points of presentation, I leapt on it at once.

And found myself soon in the office of an elegant Englishman whom I'll call Peter Taylor. "This could be *delicious*," he said. ("Delicious" was, I soon discovered, his all-purpose adjective of praise.) He, too, didn't seem to view my obvious incapacity to do the job as any kind of barrier to getting it. By a twist that I would learn was nearly universal, the glamour in those precincts of being a graduate student in art history—a thing actually so lacking in glamour as to be almost the definition of tarnish—seemed to elevate my candidacy. You would *want* an unprepared copyeditor who came from graduate school—just as, I discovered, having landed a job editing fashion copy at a fashion magazine added a note of real-world glamour to my life among my fellow clerks at graduate school. The great satirist Stephen Potter, inventor of Lifemanship, wrote once that the core of metropolitan living was what he called the "Two Club Gambit": one had to belong, in London, to two clubs, the Artillery and the Arts, and be the odd man out at both—arty among the military men, combed and contained among the artists. Potter was right in his social observation: authority in one place derives from an occupation in another. On a more Lilliputian scale, I was instinctively doing the same. Fashion magazine people imagine art historians to be interesting; art historians imagine fashion magazine editors to be glamorous. The complete absence of either glamour *or* interest in either place is compensated for by the shared illusion among both about what it is that the other place possesses.

———

Having been shown the top of the ladder at the magazine, I was quickly passed right down it, to the senior copyeditor, and had the actual job explained to me. I would learn soon enough that this was the pattern of all more-than-sort-of New York jobs—a few congenial seconds with the ultimate boss, and then a quick plunge to the effective supervisor, for whom the ultimate boss was not the congenial character you had just met but a Sphinx of arbitrary decisions and random, crazy choices, of which you were obviously the latest. Job hierarchies in American life tend to look remarkably clear from the top—the boss is the boss and gets an office like one—but the middle and the bottom tend to get all compressed together. (Already existing in that time, this segregation would only increase over the next thirty years, until the boss now usually has the splendor and isolation of a Byzantine emperor, while the underlings share the sweaty, unwindowed squalor—not to mention the morale, and often the longevity—of Byzantine wrestlers.)

The job, it turned out, was very complicated without being particularly interesting. It required some math and an X-Acto knife. In those days, before computer typesetting made "leading" the spaces between characters easy, all the words, or copy, on a fashion "spread"—photographs of clothes with type describing them—had to be "flush right": lined up exactly even against a right-hand margin. Nowadays you can do this with the press of a key on a keyboard, but in those days you could only do it by giving someone a "character count"—the exact number of characters, including letters, spaces, and punctuation, that filled each line. The someone was called a "fashion copyeditor."

I was to be him. The fashion copyeditor had to take the descriptive text written by the fashion copywriter—a higher creature, though confusingly, by the rule of perpetual unease essential to any capitalist hierarchy, subject to the lower-ranking fashion copyeditor's constant improvements and changes—and alter it in order to make sure that it broke down into the precise number of characters that the art director had prescribed for each line, without any hyphens at the column's edge, or "widows" on the line below. (Widows were left-over lines that only came partway across the designated space. They were called widows because they seemed useless and unfulfilled, I suppose, an insensitivity encoded in copyediting.) You did this with an actual X-Acto knife, applied to the lettering.

The form that the fashion copy took was as neatly stereotyped as a haiku or sestina. Each little block of type had to begin with a two-word "cap"—a little starter, preferably with a pun of some kind, that set the tone for what came immediately below: "The White Stuff," "Loose Change," and "Collar These," over simple spreads of shirts, were some I recall from my first summer. Then there had to be a description, exact enough to identify the clothes being described ("Double-breasted nail-head wool suit," not just "suit with nubbly surface"), the name of the designer, and then, in parentheses, an approximate price—("about tk"), an actual price being disliked by the advertisers—"tk" meaning "to come," an abbreviation having apparently been invented by an earlier copyeditor who could not spell. The choice of clothes, and the prices, too, were arrived at by a complicated negotiation between the tastes of the fashion editor, the art director, and the advertisers, though how intense, or craven, that negotiation could be I was not to learn till much later.

I seemed at last to be in the middle of the real world. Even my schoolwork seemed to be improving from my exposure to Madison Avenue style. At the same time that I had begun my adventures in fashion copyediting, I had found in Cesare Ripa's seventeenth-century Italian *Iconologia* ("Dictionary of Images") an image of Ambiguity, personified as a young man with a lantern. I was going to deliver my next seminar report on him, on the way that the half-light illumination in Baroque painting was always—I had a hard time writing "sometimes" in those days—to be understood as a sign of ambiguity, of moral confusion and youthful striving. An iconographic "catch" of this kind was still regarded as an art-historical prize.

I was excited—I identified with the ambiguous youth, in his mismatched suit—though the professor of the course was oddly, disturbingly larksome. Once, a hopeful student had pointed out that the mismatched socks in a Carpaccio seemed like those in a print of a traveling *commedia dell'arte* troupe—so shouldn't we take the painting, whatever it was, as a representation of a performance of a Nativity rather than a representation of a Nativity? "No," the professor said, with a long Lewis Carroll sigh. "No. It wasn't just actors. *Everyone* wore mismatched stockings then. It made life so . . . so *easy* when you reached into your sock drawer in the morning."

I wish I could say that I walked through the job at *GQ* with a dry, mordant awareness of its absurdity, or at least its triviality,

and the larger absurdity or triviality of fashion magazines generally. Not a bit of it. For one thing, it didn't *feel* trivial. With its rules
and orders and precise numbers, its conventions and insistent con-
junctions, the this-with-this and not-with-this—not to mention the
irresistible note of commercial imperiousness that drove it all, the
entangled injunctions by which only an approximate price could
ever be mentioned for fear that the garment might be found somewhere at discount or at a markup, enraging the trusting reader or
disappointing the faithful advertiser—no, it felt as though all the
forces of the world, commercial and aesthetic, had converged on
this photograph of clothing on handsome tall people and that *you*
had been placed there as their judicious umpire. These seemingly
neutral pages, which one flipped idly in a barbershop or at a newsstand, turned out to be as intensely felt, as organized and rich with
inner referents—as filled with what would later be called hyperlinks
to other worlds and needs—as densely and obscurely referential, as
any page of Cesare Ripa. And they weren't necessarily less reward-
ing when you got to the end of the page's meanings, even if the
page's purposes were purely commercial and designed to sell men's
clothes, not offer an encyclopedia of icons.

And, then, there is no greater pleasure in a working life than
being inducted into a new kind of shoptalk, with the ooze of expertise cheaply earned in a few afternoons of listening. Nowadays my
family mocks me for the Broadway-ese I have lapped up hanging around actors and directors: we "track" a narrative thread to
make sure it "lands"; we wonder if we should "put a button" on
something—i.e., create a sharp crescendo to provoke applause. In
that period, I felt the same way about the tawdry shoptalk of fashion
magazine copyediting. I was high on it, intoxicated with gutters and
widows—with "spreads" that bled (i.e., went right over the spine of
the magazine) and spreads that didn't; and drop caps that might or
might not be italicized. I knew that only an outsider called a magazine anything except "the book." Despite what now seems to me an
almost insane narrowness, at the time it seemed far more thrilling
than anything I was learning in art history.

For the truth is that academia, though long on technical-sounding jargon, has no actual shoptalk, aside from the desultory gossip of sabbaticals and tenure-track positions and the like, which I had grown up overhearing. But shoptalk isn't gossip. Shoptalk is secret technical language. It is the argot of shared practice. It is inviting, inasmuch as it inducts the new speaker into a charmed circle of initiates; off-putting, inasmuch as it prevents the new speaker from wondering just how charmed the circle really is.

At graduate school, new names for old things were constantly being generated—"deconstructed" for "explained," or "praxis" for "what he did." Intellectuals believe that making up new names for things is the same as having new thoughts; professionals are taught the professional names for things in the belief that this will make having new thoughts unnecessary. Louis XIV discovered that having competitions for meaningless medals and geegaws among aristocrats kept them from starting rebellions. It took capitalism to discover that teaching people a specialized professionalized vocabulary helps keep them from asking what the profession is for. The point of the talk is to keep you from thinking too much about the shop. It worked, for me.

———

Having become the fashion copyeditor, I had, after memorizing that technical vocabulary, to learn a rhetoric. The rhetoric of fashion—even men's fashion—in those days, as probably in these days, too, depended on a simple, puzzlingly repeated tale of previous confusion from which we had now blessedly—just this month!—recovered. This myth of eternal return went this way: Until recently, the whimsical, the arbitrary, and the showy had reigned. *This* season, though, simple logic, classic lines, and common sense had mercifully dethroned them. Put away your show-off shirts! Come home to the elegant drape and flow of natural fabrics. "Return to Classics," "The New Informality," "Simple Pleasures," and "The Six Classics a Man Must Have"—invariably those were the headlines that would arrive on the fashion stories I was expected to edit. The previous styles, now condemned as repellently self-conscious and artificial, had of course been heralded, a season or so before, in the same terms: we were getting rid of everything starchy and fixed, and play and fun and ease had become the watchwords of the new dispensation.

The rhetoric of fashion, I was learning, is *always* a rhetoric of the triumph of the natural over the artificial, even when what is being pushed or presented is so obviously mannered that it might as well have been an imposition from a dictator on Mars. Even the self-evidently strange is always announced as the serenely self-evident. Among what we called "our sister magazines" the rule was even more extravagantly enforced. In those years, Japanese designers were just coming into prominence with their mismatched buttonings and irregular hems—but they were not presented as pleasingly strange. Instead, they were shown as logically in tune with their time: They were thoughtful, not capricious, specially made for thinking women. They made you aware of how unduly dated your Chanel suit really was. Now, in *Comme des Garçons,* you could be free from the encumbrances of cute, and a woman could dress as wise as she really was. The new clothes corresponded to another *kind* of nature, that of women's inner lives. In this way, the art world and the world of fashion, the two rabbit holes I had fallen into, were rhetorically out of tune while being in deeper harmony. Everything in the art world had to be announced as new even if, as with Expressionist figure painting, just then coming back into style, it really wasn't; everything in the fashion world had to be announced as classic, even if it was entirely new.

No one told me this, of course. That's not how the languages of life are learned. It was just implicit in the system of rewards. About six weeks into the job, I was given a spread of cotton shirts to "edit." I brooded, fixed the widows, and then, boldly crossing out whatever the proposed headline was—"Shirtings for Summer," or something like that—I wrote over it: "The Simple Logic of Summer Shirts." I soon saw, by the approving smiles around me—or, rather, by the absence of changes made by those still higher up—that I had landed on the right formula, like the lucky Renaissance man reaching into his drawer and finding the ideal pair of mismatched socks.

I worked at home, on the floor of our basement room, while Martha was away cutting or archiving film. But two or three times a week I would come into the office, on the eighteenth floor of the headquarters on Madison Avenue in the Forties. I loved being there. In those days, the magazine was largely read, and entirely edited and composed, by gay men—and yet kept up a pretense, in its pages, of its being written by and for straight men. Not weird, prematurely married straight men, like me, but ones who were shown, month after month, off on Australian beach holidays with perfect abdominal muscles and an accompanying, rather indifferent-looking, six-foot-tall blond girl in aviators. The men had six-packs and big, toothy smiles, and tousled sun-bleached hair. Their "girlfriends," in swimsuits or nightgowns—never lingerie—stood beside them, bored, in almost every spread. The girl models were like the Christian Bibles ostentatiously placed on the entrance table of secretly Jewish Marrano households in Spain: there to declare an allegiance no one really credited. The staff photographer, a kind of genius, would place both boys and girls in processional friezes of beauty that announced, in their absence of heat or evident interaction among the models, the actual condition of desire, while leaving it to the fashion writer, and the fashion copyeditor, to pretend otherwise.

It would be too simple to call the actual appetites of the editors and the readers "closeted." I did not have the sense, talking to my universally genial and fashionable colleagues, that they were discontent with the deception. They were *aware* of it, certainly—but they knew that the attempts to make ours seem less gay a magazine only made it seem more so. The excess of the encoding was so *obvious*, the falsity in its pages so marked and theatrical, that the real tastes of its makers and readers shone all the more brightly through the transparent masquerade. The attempt to make the magazine seem less gay than it was only made it even gayer than it might have looked.

Indeed, the simple presence of semi-dressed boys and girls

together made its covert orientation plain. Straight men, God for-give us, prisoners of our simple compulsions, like our semi-naked ladies straight, all by themselves, somewhere we can gawk at them without competition or distraction. For the secret of the "male gaze," already gaining currency then as a term in art history, is that it *isn't* a gaze, slowly glancing over its objects. It is a *gawk,* always coming back to the same two or three oversubscribed features. Straight men can't get enough of breasts spilling over and bottoms in thongs. And though there are obviously gay equivalents in raw-appetite images, when gay appetites leave the house—exit sex magazines for style magazines—they do tend to be, so to speak, better dressed. (When *GQ* became radically straight, in subsequent years, its sexual politics consisted of getting a well-known model to take off her top. I will not pretend to have been displeased by this, but I knew that it was, as pictorial orchestration, oddly *flatter* than the old dispensation.)

My colleagues were all gay men, of a kind essential to New York life, but whom I was meeting for the first time only now. For the most part my sense was that they were of two generations. There were older gay men—the senior copyeditor, who oversaw my stuff, was one, and so was the British-born art director—who, having come up through the ranks, so to speak, in the closeted fifties and sixties, kept the traits of that kind of gayness (the dandyish turn, the lisping speech, the campy humor and "effeminate" turn of wrist), and then a younger generation, for whom "pride" involved something like uncontroversial acceptance of their own nature, unmarked by tribal traits. Though the older staffers were willing to be much more obviously, caricaturally, "queens," they were, oddly, much less willing to be "out." They still held on to the older caution and reserve—the vocabulary of "confirmed bachelors" and "part-ners" and even "roommates" that homosexuals had been caged in for so long. Though they were far more unmistakably gay, address-ing their homosexuality openly was bad manners. In their minds, I sensed, being aggressively "out" was vulgar. It was, indeed, part of the essential vulgarity of heterosexuality that straight people *were* "out" all the time. Normalized sex was less interesting than marginalized sex for the same reason that drip-dry shirts were less stylish than linen ones. Being "in the closet" was not so bad. What was kept in the closet, after all, were all the elements of style.

The younger editors, on the other hand—one, the managing editor of the magazine while he waited for his career as a Neo-Expressionist painter to ripen, and whom I'll call Stephen Jones, became a good friend—had few of the self-conscious traits of gayness. Stephen, if anything, cultivated a quiet power and reserve that came from a kind of calm judiciousness about appearances. He was far more naturally "masculine" than I was—able to negotiate restaurant lines and recalcitrant waiters and the little annoyances of New York life. Where the heterosexual man is always, Sinatra-like, the victim of his own perpetual fear of humiliation, of being made a social second, Stephen's kind of homosexual had learned a more detached attitude toward the small social rivalries of the city—distance from the normal hierarchy of humiliations was essential to those creating their own new hierarchy of normalcy. When we left the building, I would, in those days, go nuts if someone stepped in front of me to hail a cab, in that perpetual bizarre New York game whereby the area controlled by a taxi hailer is so ill defined that no law, or social rule, exists to stop someone from doing so without apology. Stephen would not—some part of him knew that there would always be another taxi, and another part of him knew that making a scene was the sign of someone who was not significantly whole, integrated, and showing yourself whole against a background where you had long been made to feel partial was the real end of good behavior. Being dignified wasn't just a good thing. It was the whole thing. Control was the essential emotion the times called for. "Control freak" was a new (it first appears around 1975) and far from wholly pejorative phrase of the time. To be controlled without being crazy seemed the wholly enviable goal. Making sense of being gay meant accepting all the ways in which normal masculinity failed to make sense.

And then, suddenly, it was the beginning of the plague years. I recall in 1982 and 1983 the first stirrings of gay plague, as it was called then. As always at the beginning of bad times, rumors of how easily the affliction might be dispelled were the signs of its seriousness. "If you drink plenty of vitamin C, you'll be fine," I recall the art director announcing over lunch. When the vandals surround the city, the first tone of the citizens within its walls is of reassurance, not panic. ("They can't get in here. I have a cousin at the gates who says they're starving and ready to go home.") The rumor of an easy cure is the surest sign of an approaching pestilence.

The strange truth, taboo to say even now, is that the appearance of this terrible scourge—an often fatal infectious disease largely concentrated within a minority group—would result not in more persecution but in an open acceptance of the minority unprecedented in human history. The mechanics by which this happened are still astonishing to contemplate: basically, not that the sufferers became "victims" but that they became more than appetites. Images of suffering are humanizing to all but the hardened fanatic. Watch men die struggling for dignity and you cannot deny their humanity. If this is the "politics of victimization," then all our impulses of empathy with strangers are the politics of victimization. We learn to care about those who are not like us not when we learn they want the same things we do but when we learn that they feel pain in the same way we do. They weren't ennobled by victimization. They were humanized by suffering. That's what suffering is meant to do. The trouble is what it does to those who suffer.

═══

My incapacities for the job were many, but one of the worst was simple: I didn't know the language of clothes. Shirts were shirts, pants pants, suits—even suits—were suits, and though I could tell a two-button from a three- and a double-breasted from a single-, I could not then have told a pinstripe from a chalk stripe, a gabardine from a herringbone. Though I now knew the names of the forms that you used to write about clothes, I had nothing to fit inside the forms. Since telling a pinstripe from a chalk stripe was all the telling there was to do in this case, I was stymied. "The Simple Logic of

Summer Shirts" had been a serendipitous leap, where I could use a smartly abstract term to disguise my ignorance of the actual subject. I could have tried going on in this way—"The Impeccable Dialectic of Winter Scarves" and the like—but even I couldn't have worked that stunt indefinitely.

It was made harder because the fashion "spreads" were laid out on "boards"—big heavy paper stand-alone "two sheets"—and they gave me Xeroxes of these to take home. But you could only make out the shape and general silhouette of the things from the black-and-white Xeroxes. All the subtleties that I had promised Peter to use my "well-trained" eye to note were lost on the copies, though they were clear enough on the "boards" themselves, color prints with a lovely veil of tissue paper stretched over them for protection. (These were the final versions from which the magazine would be shot in those days, the "camera-ready" art. The impeccable and untouchable Ur-text. Were these to be lost, all would be, the loser included.)

Fortunately, I did know someone who did know all those subtleties, by nature and by nurture both. Bringing Martha up to the eighteenth floor to tell me what I was looking at seemed plausible but difficult. It seemed simpler to contemplate taking the boards home to her. Even now, thinking through the enormity of this action, I blanch a little. If I didn't then, it was mostly because I was moved by desperation. I had to show her the clothes to find out what they were. So I waited until the end of the day, and slipped into the art director's emptied office and put the boards under my overcoat—an awkward fit—and took them down in the elevator, and then took them on the subway to the Blue Room.

That night, after I had made our "French" dinner and cleared the cockroaches away from the stove—they came scurrying out when you lit the burners, an odd little Dr. Seuss–style action that I had become accustomed to in a frighteningly short time—I sat down with her. (I made elaborate French dinners, most often from Pierre Franey's *60-Minute Gourmet* collections, night after night—*poulet Eugénie*—or things from Simca Beck.) She was *freezing*, she said.

She was always freezing, and how fetching she looked in her flannel nightgown and bikini panties, her usual at-home garb. Looking thirteenishly lovely, she pored over the boards, the thrill of illicit congress complementing the pleasure of expertise—as though the "boards" were diagrams of a Nazi blockhouse that I, a Polish patriot (played by Matthew Broderick), had smuggled out of the headquarters and that she, a Dutch woman physicist (played by Geneviève Bujold), would now have to study, so I could sneak them back (to music tense and percussive, by Elmer Bernstein) into the German headquarters before they were missed.

"Now, this shirt is linen, so it has a lovely weight and a glow. It glows against the dark background—don't you see?" she said. "A glow like chiaroscuro." I wrote it down.

"It's the chiaroscuro that makes them special," she said firmly. An inspiration dawned on me, and I passed a line through the existing two-word blurb, authored by the poor, mere fashion writer, and . . . edited it. I gave it a new two-word tag. I looked at it several times. I read it out loud to Martha. It seemed like a breakthrough.

———

"That's de*lic*ious!" It was later that week, and I was in the office, and Peter, the editor, had come round himself to praise my little alliterative invention.

"Chiaroscuro Chic!" he repeated, for that was the "tip-in" I had invented. "You know, that could actually be the spread title. 'Chiaroscuro Chic!' "

I kind of hoped he would declare this, but he didn't. "This is delicious," he merely repeated.

I cannot, over the long abyss of time, describe, or for that matter defend, my pleasure in the praise. Partly because I always take undue pleasure in praise, and partly because it was the first time anyone had ever praised my writing as writing not for the artful deployment of argument, but for the potent combinations of words. I felt like Charlotte the spider, having landed on "Some Pig."

Eight weeks later—there was a two-month lag time between the last changes to the copy and the appearance of the magazine—we happened to go to Barneys.

"Look!" Martha called out.

I did what I think our fathers would have called a spit take, or I would have if there had been coffee in my mouth. There, across the room, was a five-foot blowup of the spread with linen shirts—my two-word benediction now almost the size of our blue room: "Chiaroscuro Chic."

It was my first time putting words into the center of anyone's consciousness, and I felt unreasonably pleased—no, I felt *reasonably* pleased. All writers ever do is take pre-existing units, words, arrange them, and insert them into other people's consciousness. Words are always arranged, never invented. That these words were cloyingly arranged and inserted not so much into anyone's higher consciousness as into the maw of commerce did not alter the poet's satisfaction. The bard singing *Beowulf* for a bad king gets as much pleasure from his alliterations as the one who sings for the good one. What he's after is not the virtue in the listeners' hearts but the look on their faces. Getting the thrill of the look on their faces is why he invented Grendel. Getting more of it is why he went on to invent Grendel's mom. The essential magic of writing is elemental—and unlike any other art form. You're not really making something so much as assembling something—once the assembly is completed, you hope it gives the illusion of originality. Like my professor's Renaissance man dressing in the morning, you reach into the sock drawer of words hoping to find an interestingly mated pair: among many choices of mismatched socks, some mismatched socks match surprisingly well. The socks, or words, exist already; the eloquence of their mismatch is your own to make.

I have since published five-hundred-page books, have official pages that argued for classical liberalism, been whimsical with children and passionate about gun control. I've even seen some of the results translated into Italian and Korean—but the secret guilty pleasure of the writer, as opposed to the citizen the writer may also be, is simply the sneaky delight of seeing the words strike home. For the first time in my life, they had. And what home was more home to us than Barneys on Seventh Avenue—how much closer to home could it get than to see your words mounted so big among the actual shining shirts and glowing sweaters they superintended? I was, professionally, happier than I had ever been, and as happy as I have ever since become.

———

"Chiaroscuro Chic"—the two words shot me to the top of the ladder, although in this case, of course, the top and the bottom were so close together that you could hardly tell them apart. Really, on the strength of eight words and two phrases—"Chiaroscuro Chic" and, before that, "The Simple Logic of Summer Shirts"—a career in fashion editing opened up before me. "Delicious!" he had said. Greatly encouraged, I began to meditate, and then deliver, ukases and interdictions about fashion and grooming from our basement room on East Eighty-seventh Street. Shave only in the shower! Apply moisturizer no fewer than eight times a day! White socks with jeans were now acceptable! (They were to me, but I had to dress that way.)

I realized that writing with certainty was all the certainty writing offered. If you said it, then it was so. I wandered the five steps from the "living room" to "the kitchen" and the bathroom and, on Martha's parents' old jumpy Olivetti, I pounded out, with ever-increasing confidence, rules and diktats and nonnegotiable dogmas on grooming. It was slightly frightening to realize how easily fashion and grooming rules and tips could be conjured out of nothing—that out of nothing was in truth the only place whence they *could* be conjured, since the truth of it was that the obvious rules (soap, toothbrush) were the only rules that counted, while the rest were not rules but mere tics and half-truths and why-nots. I busied myself rewriting advice that the staff writers the magazine employed had offered on how to style your hair and how many times a week to shampoo it, given all the styling.

The truth is that there *is* no right way to, say, apply moisturizer, because there is no wrong way to apply it. The verb and the noun are the same, the action and the item identical. You . . . moisturize. You don't moisturize well or ill. You're dry, then you're . . . moist. Yet, having invented a rule about, say, shaving in the shower, I followed it religiously. I became a true believer of a faith I'd fabricated. Indeed, to this day, when I read something in a fashion magazine on a plane—a nutrition tip, a recipe—in *Men's Journal* or *Men's Health*, I take it instantly to heart, and attempt to apply it, despite knowing, in some recess of my consciousness, that it must have been invented by a freelancer just as young, ignorant, and pressed as I was. I have drunk eight glasses of water, started the day with coconut oil, fasted for eighteen hours to improve my digestion. . . . Perhaps the truth is that fashion can *only* be diktats, and our respect for fashion is our secret respect for the necessity of an arbitrary principle in life. If there *were* a logic to summer shirts, after all, everyone would have learned it by now.

Not long after, the English editor called me in—I was at first in a Frick-like panic about having somehow lost the key—and offered me a promotion. I was offered the full-time, in-the-office job of grooming editor. I pointed out that I would still have to be at graduate school, but, somewhat to my shock, they agreed to let me come into the office three days a week, while devoting Mondays and Fridays to school. Eight words had done all that, lifted me from the ranks of the indigent freelancer to the truly employed, a man with a job. (I devoted Mondays and Fridays instead to my own writing, but they didn't have to know that. Meanwhile, studying for the Ph.D. orals would somehow take care of itself, though how I wasn't sure. The habit of dividing myself, amoeba-like, into new entities, each part assigned an ambitious piece of work, so that there could end up being five or six simultaneous versions of me, all working on different projects, was something I picked up then, and never entirely lost. It means a lot of work gets done, but a lot of details get dropped. The inter-amoebic communication, so to speak, can get disjointed.)

I got a real full-time salary—less than it would now take to put a

New York child through one month of private school, not counting lunch, but at the time it was all we needed to stay in New York. We could even think of finding a new apartment. On the day I got the promotion, it began snowing on my way home, and I found Martha and we went out to dinner at one of the German places—we called this one, Kleine Konditorei, "Austrian," out of some bizarre geographical instinct. The snow fell harder, and we were all alone. I had goulash, and she had goose. Martha had a marzipan cake and I had Black Forest cake. The snow kept falling. We leapt home, one block, through the snowdrifts, even though my sneakers got soaked. Martha's La Squadra sweater set, with its woven top and big zigzag pattern, made her look like a sexy Charlie Brown—or like the little red-haired girl wearing Charlie Brown's sweater. The snow kept falling outside our window. Once again, I was happier than I had ever been. I haven't been happier since. I would never be so happy again.

They put me in charge of *all* the grooming copy in the magazine— lotions, conditioners, cover-ups, and shampoos. Not a line about moisturizers could go into the magazine without my scrutinizing it first. The one thing I was not allowed to touch was the thing I liked best, the fragrances. I had loved men's colognes since I was in college, and would have loved to try my hand at editing their copy. But the fragrances belonged to an editor of their own—being a thing of such delicacy and refinement, I assumed, that they demanded a separate set of skills. In reality (as I later learned), it was because they were such an important advertising category that they needed to be treated with more diplomatic expertise—knowing who got how much copy, line for line, Calvin Klein or Ralph Lauren, depending on how many ad pages they'd bought—than I was thought to possess.

I was given, at last, my own cubicle, commensurate with my stature—in a room that I shared, three days a week, with two other people, a fact-checker, the only woman at the magazine; and an accountant, who had been called in to bring some order to what was, apparently, the magazine's confused balance sheet. He was a subject of secret fun among the staff, who mocked the stiff, Styrofoam (polyester, really) jackets he always wore. He had an accountant's dogged sense of the real amid the rich fantasy life of the editors.

This fact of the extreme simplicity of grooming products, especially compared with fashion spreads, was reinforced for me by the most acidic of the older generation of gay editors. "Let's *face* it," he said. "There are two kinds of lotions: one tightens the skin, and the other moistens it." He shrugged, and then developed a mildly devilish little grin. "Skin is like sex, you know. You can either make it tighter or make it wetter. That's all. And either one only lasts for minutes—hours, at most." I blanched a little, but he wasn't trying to tease me. He was right: everything in life is either tighter or wetter. Astringents and lubricants were all we had to sell, and both were, in every sense, temporary solutions.

The attitude of the editors toward their readers, I learned in more detail in my three days a week at the office, was not hostile exactly. But it was condescending, taking the form of absolute refusal to actually use any of the "products" we turgidly analyzed and eagerly pushed upon our readers. "Fashion victims" was their not always unkind phrase for the people who took our counsel seriously. This didn't make them less eager to impart it pompously. "All I know of fashion is how many white shirts you have for summer," the editor-in-chief confessed, and he was wise enough to know that Gatsby's famous abundance of colored shirts in Fitzgerald's novel was a sign of a touching vulgarity, not high style. There were certain words—I suppose like the words of a sermon, "faith" and "transcendent" and "sacrament"—that they never said, but that still had to be used in print: "sartorial" was one; "stylish" still one more. We might produce a magazine devoted to sartorial stylishness, but we weren't dumb enough to believe in it ourselves; that's what gave us style. It was a confounding formula, and, in its way, a disillusioning one: Martha and I *had* believed in all those pieties, at least a little, had thought that having the one right dress and suit would matter. In the temple, they disdained the holy things. Getting educated,

I was finding out, was always a business of discarding pieties for practices. The pieties might be art historical ones at MoMA or "sartorial" ones at *GQ*. They were still pieties, and needed to be replaced by the daily fullness, the lived experience, of the practice they encoded, no matter how absurd the practice might be. (That the pieties might be replaced with actual principles was a revelation that would arrive—or that I would postpone—until much later.)

Still, making awful puns and creating candied alliterations was a thing I was actually good at. It was what I had been trying to do at the Frick Library when I should have been monitoring the pulse rate of artists, and now I could make a sort of living at it. It was better than talking about pictures, because it punctured the world; it was like drilling a toggle bolt hole right into the side of the big store of New York life. Now I could hang up my own shelf. I wrote it; a million print copies showed it. The space between word and reality was *slightly* disappointing. In my fantasy New York, well-dressed men had quiet assignations at piano bars in the mid-Fifties; in the real one, the "well-dressed" men were actually the anxiously dressed ones, and no one would be caught dead in the mid-Fifties. And there were no pianos.

I became a fixture in the office. Eventually, I even got to go to the "Clements meetings," named, I believe, after the weary-looking market researcher who presented them. These were high-nervosity, closed-door events, in which Mr. Clements would come in and supply information about how highly "scored" each page and feature in the magazine was. Invariably, the fashion pages scored high, the feature pages just behind them, and whatever little actual journalism or writing there was scored least.

But the highest-scoring page, month after month, was always the same. It was the very last page in the issue: "Next Month in *GQ*," simply listing, in bullet points, some of the features we would be running in the next issue. There were no pictures, no "tags," no prices. That these features were always essentially indistinguishable from the present month's features did not alter the excitement the page seemed to create among our readers. Next month's issue is coming! Next month's issue would be the one to read! At last! Here comes next month.

I sensed then an essential truth—or at least as essential as truths can be in the magazine game. Magazines are—or were then, when they mattered more—essentially vehicles of fantasy, far more than even the most hardheaded ones can be of fact, or information of any kind. *Every* magazine in a sense only exists next month. They sell fables of aspiration, and get their power from being quietly attuned to a social class just beneath the social class they seem to represent. Playboys do not read *Playboy,* and voguish women do not obsess over *Vogue,* and twelve-year-old, not seventeen-year-old, girls read *Seventeen.* Our magazine, ostensibly directed to an audience of upwardly mobile young executives, was read by high-school students. But had we addressed them directly we would have failed, as the *Playboy* of those days would have if it had taken off its smoking jacket and put on the baseball cap its readers actually wore. An elaborate artifice of shared fantasy had to be sustained in order to sell advertising pages, which was, of course, the aim of the enterprise. The final artifice was . . . next month. Everything we did, we did in order to sustain the illusion of next month's issue.

And yet, even learning all this, I was happy, because at least it seemed a real thing learned. In the museum, the lessons had all been about the fixative power of fantasy: about how people could attach themselves obsessively to art in ways that really only illuminated their own desires. In the fashion world, the lessons were all about how fantasies got made and used and exploited and sold. I was a fish out of water, certainly (I always seemed to be a fish out of water, even when in a backwater pond, as at the Frick). One thing you learn about fish out of water, though, is that they are never really out of water. If they were really out of water they would die. No, what we call a fish out of water is really just a fish in another *kind* of water, trying to pass as another kind of fish. Since all fish are fish-shaped and live in water, they do better than you might think. A fish in a new kind of water is still . . . a fish in water. The real problem is that the water is almost always moving faster than the fish knows, and is part of a river or a stream or a current heading toward a bigger body of water with bigger, meaner fish living in it. A fish's problems are not water. A fish's problems are always other fish. It's the neighborhood, not the water, that's the worry for the fish.

=====

I had earned a reputation at the magazine as a dab hand with a sentence, and so, swallowing his pride of place, Evelyn, the cologne-and-aftershave editor, came to me one day with his copy. He was a gentle, mustachioed man, who had once been a small figure around the Warhol Factory and had now subsided into good smells.

"I can't solve this," he said fretfully. "Would you look at it?"

Eager to mend fences with the fragrant side of things, I took his copy and looked at it.

"I can't solve this," he repeated, as though it were a quadratic equation rather than twenty-seven characters on eau de toilette.

I looked it over. It read: *"When she smells the residue of you she will—"*

"I just can't finish it," he wailed.

"I like the internal rhyme," I said, professionally.

He looked at me blankly.

" 'Residue' and 'you,' " I explained. He tried to look at once lucky and expert.

"What if you just insert an ellipsis?" I said. "You know, three dots. When she smells it she will . . . You know. Leave it open-ended and mysterious. What will she do? We don't know. Leave it to the readers' imagination," I said.

His look of dumbstruck gratitude touches me still—it touches me almost as much as the ellipsis idea shames me. It made it all the way into the issue, too.

=====

I finally gave the seminar report on ambiguity and Cesare Ripa. As I have done too often in lectures—I still do it in keynote lectures at the obscure colleges where I tread to make my family's living—I went a bridge, several bridges, too far, overloading or overlarding the talk, not content with the merit of the reasonable core insight that the play of light was symbolic of uncertainty. I pushed it past the point of reason so that chiaroscuro became the key to the whole period. I always did that. I do it still. At the end of the seminar report the professor said, "Thank you for a vivacious report." It was far from an unambiguous success, even though the light in the seminar room was low. Chic suddenly seemed a more interesting path for those who cared for chiaroscuro than scholarship did. So *that* was the path I would now follow, wherever it snaked in the half-light of the fashionable.

A few months later, everything changed. I was away from the office on Fridays and Mondays, and, having left on a Thursday night, I came back on a Tuesday to find that the entire staff had altered. Entirely! A new editor-in-chief was in place, with a new assistant editor, and a new fashion editor. In those days, mass firings were part of the glamour of magazines. (Now they just shut the whole thing down, and no one notices.) Usually in the days after Christmas, long-standing editors-in-chief would learn that they had lost their jobs in a morning column.

The coming of the new editors, who had been instructed to turn the magazine into a "general interest" men's magazine, modeled on the old *Esquire,* was an accident of great good fortune in my own life. On that Friday morning, the publisher had come in and fired the entire staff. Off at school, I was in the position of the mob guy who had, luckily but unknowingly, fallen asleep under the Stutz Bearcat while the St. Valentine's Day Massacre was going on. On Tuesday the new editor, Art Cooper, called me into his office. Bearded and besuited, in Ralph Lauren worsted, he had none of the gentle nimbleness of the old editors, but he had far more literary heft and purpose. His ideas for the magazine's future were in an odd way antiquated, or seemed so: he wanted to restore it to the manner of *Esquire* magazine in the sixties, when that magazine was sort of the distilled genius of Madison Avenue, wise-guy covers and pinpoint prose. Still, it seemed like a good ambition. I explained that I had just published my first short story, which I had, though very obscurely.

To this day, I don't know if he thought I had been planted on him by Personnel or if he acted on a hunch, of exactly the kind the new mob boss might have had in Chicago, that a guy this lucky had been saved by the Fates for a reason, and might bring us all luck, could be the clubhouse rabbit's foot. In any case, he told me to go out and hunt for "quality fiction" for the new magazine, and I did. It was a wonderful break, a kind of ascension, from grooming editor to a literary one in a year and a half. I doubt that I was sufficiently grateful.

Yet, oddly, considering I was far more at home and better employed in the new regime, when I think back, it is the older one that educated me. Style, as I had assured my readers, seeps inside your skin more than you know, and the gallantry of gay style, that equanimity that saw the absurdity of dressing up and still thought it worth doing, illuminates my life still. After the end of the decade, in the early nineties, I looked at the masthead of the magazine I was first hired by. So many of them, the men I had known and worked with, were dead. The ambiguities of ambition might be half lit, but life and death are binary. "Does God ever judge / us by appearances? I / suspect that He does," Auden wrote once. It might have been their epitaph, and their entry to heaven.

Anyway, I learned a lot then, and from them. I still like ellipses and alliterations. I still try, every morning, to leave the house taut, moist, and scented. I will always wait for next month's issue to arrive.

7

Men Making Pictures of Women Wearing Clothes

When I think of those years, and of the moment we left the Blue Room for a wider world, I think first of all of the light writer. "Light writing" is the root meaning of photography, and it was Richard Avedon, the photographer, who became our surrogate father, a best friend, a mentor of a kind—he was our introduction to the world of power and glamour in New York, and, in another way, the source of our first disillusion with those things.

The experiences I've related in these chapters are mostly the ones everyone has: a small apartment, a silly job, another silly job that gets more sensible over time. But the experience of being adopted by a charismatic mentor, though in one way it's what we come to New York for, is not the experience that everyone who comes to New York gets. When we get it, we know it. Everything after seems imprinted by its good fortune. Those first shaping experiences move us from being strangers to citizens; the experience of a charismatic mentor changes us still more, from citizens to subjects, people who, for a little while, have the illusion of themselves as privileged, members of the court.

It is the norm of city life for the dukes to sweep away the D'Artagnans in their carriage. (Auden says somewhere that as an old man he still expected exactly that, an aristocrat to swoop down, saying, "You please me, child. Jump in.") The duke's motive may be partly careerist—dukes need spry young aides—or even carnal, but it is most often an older version of the same ambitious urge that strikes the young. That primal motive of ambition, which I had first sensed giving talks at the museum, is not to be "major" but just to be *there*, seen and heard, and our pursuit of being present, right in the center of things, the room where it happens, often takes its first form in our adoption by some charismatic pseudo-parent. (Among my closest friends, one had William Maxwell as an editor-writer father, another had been adopted by Nora Ephron, still one more by a great movie critic.)

The duke's reasoning is not that different from the recruit's. I have passed through there and made myself "here," the duke thinks, but it will mean nothing unless I impress my hereness on one who has not yet quite got there. In the end, though, time defeats experience, as it always will, and the protégé almost always outlives the mentor—the one who is not yet there will still be here at the end, and D'Artagnan writes the book about the duke.

Which the duke both wants, and doesn't quite. All intimate relationships are complicated, and the ones we have with adoptive charismatic fathers and mothers perhaps the most complicated of all. Not that ours was ever unhappy. From the day we met, in 1985, until his death in 2004, every morning, across twenty years and two continents, would begin with a phone message, and every evening ended with another from Dick, and we were always glad when the phone rang. Sometimes, often, we spent hours together between the messages. The joy lay partly in the specificity of who he was. Irving Penn, the other great photographer and rival in the same fifty-year marathon of art and fashion, once called him a seismograph, an instrument for measuring tremors. Dick hated the implicit condescension of Penn's remark, its suggestion of instinct and journalistic brio rather than intention and art. (You knew it infuriated him, because he mentioned it, often.) But it was not entirely inapt. There *was* something tectonic about him, something of eruptions and shocks, radiating out through the seams into other lives—fault lines within a single personality that, sheared together, made inordinate waves. He always shook a little, with emotion, and he shook others with his own. When I think of him, in any case, I see a needle leaping on graph paper, oscillating highs and lows, more than a scroll unrolling with stately sentences. Love can never explain itself, but it can bear witness to its movement: the paper rolls, the needle leaps, and if nothing is really understood, still, the tremors get set down.

No, never unhappy, but always complicated, and relating it in a way seems too *final*, too valedictory. I have never felt ready to write about Dick, or us, because to do so, I now suspect, would seem to surrender the boyishness in which we both participated—and which, in an odd way, we both believed in, as a role to play—for a note of mature retrospection, of appraisal and reflection and even, I suppose, regret. To remember is to keep alive, they say piously. But to remember is actually to entomb, to inter emotion, at least a little. At least, I have never committed a vital memory, a moment of bliss or confusion, to paper or pixels without seeing it dim a little in my own recall, even evaporate entirely. The living emotion seeps into the page, where it fossilizes. What we care about most needs to be spoken of in a present, or anticipatory, tense—*Someday I'll have to write that story down.* Written down, it's over and done. Epitaphs are chiseled, and they speak less of the permanence the epitaph aspires to than of the full stop, the ending, it superintends.

With all that sticky stuff said, let me now recall in large, handmade letters—less like the epitaph engraved than like a quick, improvised series of postcards—how we three met and lived together for so long, and hope a touch of incoherence will be the stuff of life.

We met for the first time in July 1985, when I was working at *GQ*. He had finished his great work *In the American West*, portraits of working people and drifters, and each of the fashion magazines, *noblesse oblige*, was required to send a writer up for half an hour's interview and a photograph. Art Cooper sent up a staff writer, and he ordered me to go with him, knowing my background in art history. Of course I was curious, and so I went. Avedon was a hero in my arty and intellectual family—but, by an irony that he could never quite understand, it was the fashion photography that a family raised on irony loved most. My little brother, Blake, had spent his teen years trying to launch a career as an Avedonian fashion photographer, complete with whatever white no-seam backgrounds he could find in our austere house—in a house painted exclusively white, it wasn't hard—and whatever models (chiefly Martha) he could find to arrestingly estrange from their white surroundings. Then he had succumbed, as we all did sooner or later, to the family curse of academia, and went dutifully off to Oxford to study art history.

The wryly wrought surface of fashion photos, that was what we were taught to love—and the passionate, earnest, and finally sincere portrait photography that Avedon made, the work of a boy who had come of age in existentialist Paris—was, we thought, a bit jejune, a little naïve. (Over the years to come, I would spend an undue amount of time trying to convince him that the sincere existential portraits were *really* fashion portraits, and that the fashion pictures were existential. There was enough truth in this idea to float an argument, though not really enough to land it safely on the ground without a horrible, *Hindenburg*-style explosion.)

The writer Art assigned—his name comes back to me, as two oddly matched monosyllables, like a title: Pope Brock—and I went up together to the studio, a red-brick townhouse off First Avenue on Seventy-fifth Street. I would go there again so many times that the layout became as familiar to me as a lyric from a pop song. Downstairs was the studio, where Bill Bachman, his PA, sat behind a desk, composing a simple white card with Dick's appointments for the day, from dawn till night, typed out. The famous photograph of Dovima and the elephants flew overhead like a flag—the only fashion photograph on display. Nearby, Norma Stevens, his personal manager, kept busy, always warm, always alarmed. A small kitchen to the right was filled with granola and muffins and, often, with impossibly beautiful women, waiting their turn. They looked, somehow, younger and thinner and, though certainly not *plainer,* simpler than one had imagined, canvases to be painted. Only up close did one recognize the perfection of each feature. They were usually unstimulating—underdressed, without makeup, tall, more thin than slender, in overalls or black leggings—less like beauties waiting to be immortalized than like oddly attenuated stevedores, waiting in a union hall in Hoboken for a job call. A small army of assistants paced seriously back and forth, ears almost visibly twitching, waiting for a command. They were, exclusively, men so small as to be practically dwarflike, since, as one of his art directors pointed out to me, they all had to be smaller than he was. This was a choice he must have made unconsciously, since when it was pointed out to him he was genuinely astonished. If a model stood next to an assistant, they looked like Boris and Natasha in a *Bullwinkle* cartoon.

Then down the hall, toward the place where the garden would have been in a normal Upper East Side townhouse—I didn't see the sanctum sanctorum on that first morning, but would be inside it many times after—was the studio itself, filled, somehow, with foggy gray light and a one-page "seamless" hung from the ceiling behind: the wide page of paper, neutral or pure white, that produced his signature pure white backgrounds. His usual camera was an old-fashioned twelve-by-eight—the camera that Mathew Brady had used to photograph Lincoln and the Civil War. Much had already been written, as much would be written later, about this choice—about the fine grain, and the antique referents, and the rest. But when I asked him about it, he said, with a look of wonder that smart people can be so stupid: "It's so I'm not behind the camera. I can hold the release in my hand while I talk to whomever I'm photographing." It was one more clue that the processes of art were less mediated metaphysically by formal tricks, and rested more obviously on human urgencies, than I had been taught at school. "To me Art's subject is the human clay / And landscape but a background to a torso; / All Cézanne's apples I would give away / For one small Goya or a Daumier," I knew Auden had written, and I had memorized it. But what I hadn't known, yet, was that even for Cézanne the apple would only matter if it called up a breast in the painter's mind. Art's subject was *always* the human clay; if it looked like anything else, it was always because you were missing the most obvious thing about it.

He was a tiny man—but he didn't seem tiny to me, because, being a short man myself, I was half a head shorter than he was, with the extra half-head being supplied by his thick and silvered and black hair, swept back, as Saul Steinberg would say, "like a circus pony." He was a tiny man, though, where I was merely a small one. Tininess radiated through him, like a condition, instead of being compressed as an inadequacy. He had delicate features, delicate hands, thin legs, and quick-hitting feet, always ready to dance. I am peasant-built, short-legged and barrel-chested. Yet, at the time I met him, when I was twenty-five and he forty years older, we were somehow exactly the same size, so that, in years to come, when I had an interview to give or dinner to attend, I would borrow one of his beautiful linen suits—double-breasted but cut narrow, so that it had a nonvoluminous effect, cross-buttoned but still slim—and wear it. ("How do you keep it from becoming creased?" I asked once, a natural accumulator of grease stains and folds and lines. "You sit very, *very* still in the taxi," he said sternly.)

His voice had an authority and a depth that his delicate form belied. I found it thrilling, because it was the same educated Jewish voice that I recognized from Leonard Bernstein's *Young People's Concerts*—the voice I had come to New York to hear. It was the sound of wise and educated but entirely cosmopolitan New Yorkers. Bernstein, of course, was only latterly a New Yorker, Bostonian really, but it was the accent of a coast and of a buoyant time, the forties, and you heard it still in the most unusual places, in interviews with Alan Jay Lerner or Arthur Laurents. It was, in plain English, the sound of educated Jewry born in the twenties, raised through the hard thirties—Dick, I would learn, as a boy still sneaked down every night to the basement to look at the stationery of his father's bankrupt department store, Avedon's Fifth Avenue—and flourishing in unimagined possibility and accomplishment in the forties and fifties.

Then, striking the rocks in the sixties, some of its speakers foundered for good, and were left with bitterness and nostalgia, while a very few had made a new style and a new way in the midst of change. He had found that new style, but his voice hadn't changed as he had. His was an "r"-less dialect—my wife's name came out forever as "Maaahtha"—but it wasn't the dropped "r" of "New Yawk" cab drivers and Ralph Kramden. For the absence of consonants in his voice was met by an overcharge of humming vowels, short vowels made long—it was not merely "Mahtha" but "Maaahtha"! It was a big voice, not "ringing," as in a bad novel, but hoarse and resonant—it had all of the 1940s in it, a moment when artistic-minded American Jews suddenly found themselves not only unembarrassed but empowered. It was, in his mind, the Gershwin sound. (Dick grew up on East Eighty-sixth Street, around the corner from where we live now, and that name, "the Gershwins," contained the whole of his aspiration. Not music alone but a whole way of life was entangled, in ways I still don't entirely understand, in the name "Gershwin," for him a sound as thrilling as the sound of "the Guermantes" and "Parma" were for Proust.)

He was effortlessly elegant—and even as I write those words down, I see him grimace at them. Though a hero and an "icon" of fashion, he hated that kind of talk and called it, lovingly but lucidly, "Fash-wan." He disliked both the camp world of fashion and the French emphasis on "chic." His beloved French collaborator of many years, the editor Nicole Wisniak, he loved in part for her want of ordinary French chic and its replacement by French hyperbole. (A bad meal for her was a massacre, a bad play a catastrophe, a bad hour a nightmare. The hyperbole wasn't hysterical. It made the ordinary seem amazing.) He loved fashion as a simple form of manners, a way of being courteous to others by being pleasing oneself, or else, as a form of adult dress-up, a way of aspiring to a more romantic way of living. He liked beautiful and strange objects because they expressed the strangeness of the human condition. All the usual "amusing" and "charming" and "elegant" crap he disliked.

On that first afternoon, he showed Pope and me his new book, as he always showed everyone everything—not grand and distant, but intimate and peering, *leering*, right over your shoulder. As he turned the pages, he twitched nervously, waited for you to say the right thing. He smelled faintly, richly of limes.

The pressure of his superintending presence was too much for poor Pope, who couldn't think of a single thing to say. Trained in such performances, I pressed my MoMA lunchtime improvisational button.

"It's so much about . . . August Sander," I tried, allusively.

"Yes!" he said. It was, if not the secret woid of Groucho Marx, at least not the wrong thing said. "I *love* Sander—that Germanic, secretive, creepy thing. Sander is all over it." This was encouraging, like playing a game of hot and cold and being told that you were getting warmer.

The pages turned, stigmata of anxiety etched between the eyes of every one of his subjects—these drifters and slaughterhouse workers. The effect was ravishing, though I had my doubts—I have them still—whether the actual American West of the mid-eighties was not more truly composed of fast-food workers and Latina domestics and insurance brokers and assistant managers at rental-car dealers outside Phoenix than by these tragic Sam Shepard characters. But, beyond the unsmiling poise, the graphic authority and emotional vibration were overwhelming. It would be years before I fully understood that all of them were citizens of Avedonia, his own made-up land, created, like all artistic universes, from a handful of memories extended outward until they became the archetypes of his creation. It was a world as distinct as Francis Bacon's, or Beatrix Potter's, or William Faulkner's, and as essentially mythological: the journalistic basis was barely nodded to, and then he was making up his characters.

Encouraged by the Sander hit, I think I mentioned Shepard, and Mailer's *The Executioner's Song*, and I may have thrown in a reference to Goya, just for good measure. He started like a man with electrodes attached and activated at hidden spots of his torso—he twitched and reacted more actively than anyone I have ever seen. He seemed to risk a heart attack with every incoming allusion.

His degree of awkwardness and elegance combined—the boyish and lopsided walk, the shy grin, the oscillation between severity and sweetness, his comically large glasses shrewdly recognized to be more becoming than more conventionally becoming ones—gave me some new idea of what real elegance was, not arid and classical, but a series of spontaneities. I felt all that within fifteen minutes.

We chatted for a few minutes more, and I mentioned, in passing, the avant-garde director André Gregory, whom I had worked with as a boy actor.

"Oh, you know André," he said, with careless, mischievous complicity. "He'll call in the middle of a sitting, and you're sure it's about Chekhov, but it's where had we gotten the William Greenberg's coconut cake." I didn't know that, but I liked the note of familiarity, Chekhov sliding into coconut cake. (Greenberg's, I would learn, was a not terribly good Upper East Side bakery around which Dick's generation had an almost erotic fixation. Sinatra had sent a coconut cake from there once to Ava Gardner in Europe, and she had torn it apart, looking for the ring. Sinatra, Dick explained, intended only, good Hoboken boy that he was, for it to be eaten.)

I went back to my office and worked. The phone rang.

"Adam!" the voice rasped at the other end. "It's Dick. Can you come for dinner tonight?"

I was startled, shocked now, too—and, God forgive me, a little suspicious. Gay pickups happened occasionally in my life—I was cute without being beautiful—and I had learned to deflect them, mostly by being doltishly unaware of their content. (I wasn't feigning doltish unawareness; it had begun as genuine doltishness, and then itself became a manner and, I suppose, a mask. Curiously, the invitations never happened at the magazine, where I was respected as the house heterosexual. Or maybe it's just that no one tries to convert the *Shabbos goy*.) Martha was out of town, up in Canada with her mother, working on a documentary. So I went up to Seventy-fifth Street for the second time that day. This time I rang the bell at the smaller door. It buzzed open, and I faced a high, steep staircase.

I would climb those stairs, with wife and friends and, eventually, babies and then children, so many times in the next twenty years, that to try to recapture my first sense of it now is difficult. It beckoned you to ascend. There were beautiful white cards—his day and night schedule for the next day—placed on several steps, and at the top, barely visible, a pair of small feet in small boots (boots from John Lobb in London, I learned later, bought decades before, and kept in perfect polished shape).

He embraced me, not awkwardly at all, and then he led me into the most beautiful room I had ever seen. Some rooms, like the Blue Room, we think of as beautiful, or I had been taught to think of as beautiful, because of their being well put together, a form of austerity perfectly arranged. This was a room devoted to overcharge and extravagance and personal iconography, private symbolism.

Can I describe it adequately, or at all? Let me try. It became my favorite room, and the pattern of my own later organization of existence, my template of the best way to live. The walls were lined with soft white fabric, onto which you could pin up any image, a changing small circus of images that had snagged on his mind, and that he had torn or raggedly cut from magazines and newspapers and postcards. They were neither conventionally lovely nor tabloid-odd but informed by a distinct sensibility that knew exactly where the beautiful intersected the strange. There were his heroes. There was a torn-off cover of the *Post*, with Salinger bearing down on a photographer; Chaplin out of character, as romantic young poet, curly hair and open smile; an eerily vindictive and determined Van Gogh baby; Brodovitch, his mentor, elegantly sorting photographic prints on a tilted easel. Movement everywhere: a Minoan diver falling through air; a Remington chief pointing a bow and arrow; a Fra Angelico angel, as chromatically plumed as a peacock, rushing the news of the Annunciation to a still-startled Virgin, and then, among them, anonymous athletes caught sliding into second, or suspended over a balance beam and pinwheeling through space—or perhaps a dancer leaping from a found stage into unseen wings, or a fullback caught in full-frontal horizontality flying toward a first down, or a postcard of Astaire in air, knowing body and naïve smile. There was even a tabloid photograph of a bank robber, caught in a security camera's gaze, striding balletically toward the exit, holding gun and hostage. A world turning and alight and alive. I peered discreetly and tried to find the line that connected them all—and the even more extravagant line that must connect these found images to the stoic and severe black-and-white portraiture of his own that lined the other side of the long room. It was as dense as a Victorian living room and its density seemed a reproach to modernist austerity. What did it mean? . . .

Then, on the far wall, a long table, white Formica, with a forest of blooming foliage at one end, and steel shelves on the other, and these filled with bright ceramic plates from Siena. A sink and stove stood behind them, unashamedly busy. Silver candlesticks, Baroque and polished, clustered on the table. We lit them for dinner to beautiful and almost comically religious effect. I suppose I was still in the spell of my strange family, who imagined modernist severity to be the proper accompaniment to modernist accomplishment. In truth, I learned later, it was a design for living that he had absorbed from the studio arrangements of the great artists who had still lived in France in the 1940s. The neatly framed pictures and gray flokati rugs and Breuer and Mies chairs—that whole Bauhaus order—they regarded as hopelessly vulgar and bourgeois. Instead, there were books piled horizontally on books, pictures left in their frames on the floor leaning up against the wall, tiny bijoux placed on side tables, pictures hung asymmetrically up, one skiing above the other. The aristocratic and the absentminded, it seemed, went hand in hand in these rooms: if you showed too much pride in the beautiful things you owned, you must not have owned many for long.

His motive for asking me up for dinner, I soon realized, couldn't have been simpler—on the surface at least, where motives actually first move us—or more touching. He wanted a friend to talk with about books and pictures. The people who made books and pictures, whom he knew too well, wanted to talk about everything else except books and pictures—preferred to talk about real estate and advances and gallery owners' and publishers' perfidies. Twenty years later, I would have been in the same condition, but at that point I didn't know enough not to know enough, hadn't gotten enough experience to talk about my own experience in preference to other people's versions of their experience that we call art. "Intellectuals don't like to talk about ideas. And art historians never talk about art," he said plaintively and openly. He had made his life among them, and it was true: the intellectuals gossiped, with a malicious voracity that Irish washerwomen would have regarded as unduly small-minded, while the art historians, who liked his company for the glamour of it, engaged in broad, airy generalities when they talked over dinner—his whiteness, they would tell him, was like the minimalist background in Robert Ryman's paintings, which it wasn't—as they patronized him genially over his own grilled swordfish.

Instead, we talked about Cartier-Bresson ("He's the Tolstoy of photography," he said with the authority of one who can say things like that). Diane Arbus, he said, was sort of "spooky," rather belying the notion that they had been particularly close. We talked about Velázquez's popes looking like CEOs. "Aren't masterpieces wonderful?" he burst out happily after a while. "Why don't we go to the Frick this weekend. It's been *years* since I've looked at those Whistlers. They changed my life when I was twelve. Whistler and Fred Astaire were the two greatest influences on my life." It made instant sense: the dandified, nocturnal, high-minded elegance, mixed with an American nervosity and restlessness and lightning grace. A small boy seeing Whistler while trying to tap-dance. Perhaps his work was no more—or less—complicated than that. Judgments that were always original and occasionally profound—like the one about Cartier-Bresson, a perfect aphorism—mixed with boyish enthusiasm for the simple existence of art. This mix of awkward and elegant was, I suppose, the essence of his charm, for charm is always simply courtesy offered spontaneously, the gracious thing offered as though it were the obvious one. (Cary Grant is the most charming of actors because his wit is always offered as aplomb, simple and self-evident, imperturbable in the face of every incident.)

So I witnessed that night a love of art, and a hatred of pretense, and I sensed another quality I could not yet quite name but was intuiting, and that I would later think of as "aristocratic," although he was a Jewish kid whose father was a failed haberdasher. Its essence was an adaptation of manners to the moment for the emotional ease of those involved—a readiness to let oneself look silly in pursuit of a social occasion, a knowledge that the spontaneous adjustment of self to circumstances was what the good life meant. Middle-class people knew rules, but aristocratic ones grasped the spirit of generosity the rules had been meant to codify—they broke them in order to restore their true purpose.

So, once, at a meaningless social occasion, I saw Dick, meeting an old hairdresser who had been with him on many shoots and who was clearly badly ill. "Ara," he said. "How are you?" And then, after only a moment, "You look *terrible*!" The wrong thing to say was the right thing to express, and the friend broke down with a weak grateful smile for the awkward empathetic gesture. His favorite story—he told me that first night, and I would help him write it down for many staged purposes eventually—was about how horribly out of place he had felt as a young photographer at the table of Jean Renoir, the great French filmmaker, who had a long table where old friends gathered. Renoir took him aside and said, "It is not what is said that matters; it's the feelings that cross the table." The simple dictum seemed to Dick the essence of humanity. Brodovitch, he also told me that night, had given one last class and had said . . . nothing. I anticipated that this was to be taken as a great Zen gesture, and was already nodding in appreciation—but he made a disappointed face: it was rude, and showed a lack of feeling for the students. Aristocratic disdain for the fixed decorum of life was always essential; coldhearted contempt for other people's feelings was always wrong. It was a complex formula, a practice that you had to practice.

A few key words landed in my head, and I locked them away to emulate and imitate and, perhaps, someday understand. There was "correct," meaning the right thing rightly done ("She was always so *correct* in hallways . . ."); "disgusting," meaning the wrong thing done wrongly; "all wrong," meaning the right thing done badly ("So he had us over for fish and it was . . . all wrong"); and "wacky," an affectionate version of "all wrong" ("Mike always chooses the *wackiest* restaurants to share confidences in"). He loved bizarre behavior designed to exhibit an unconstrained temperament, hated it if it was a display of pure egotism. Since pure egotism and an unconstrained temperament were near neighbors, it seemed like a minefield to walk through between right and wrong. You needed a sapper or two to go into the minefield before you, I thought. If they were missing a few fingers, all the better—it was a sign that they hadn't lost more. I learned later that many of these terms he had picked up in Paris and London in the forties and fifties, where he had had his moral, as opposed to artistic, education. (The artistic education had been more purely American.)

Above all, I was struck by his favorite murmured response to something that pleased his eye, whether a Cartier-Bresson of men walking at odd angles in the Palais Royal, or Julia Margaret Cameron's portrait of Tennyson, all pious beard and mad eyes: "Isn't that beautiful and strange!" or "It's so beautiful and so strange." There was a strange beauty in the seesaw balance of the "and." Not strange—which would have gone a long way in my family. Not beautiful—which went almost all the way with Martha. Not "strangely beautiful," which implied romantic mystery, or "beautifully strange," which implied romantic excess. But beautiful *and* strange, as independent categories but seen at once with both eyes, the ever-exciting discovery of a new marriage of kinds. *That* was what drew together all the imagery on the wall—beauty undercut by an unexpected informality, or by madness, or by rage. The second baseman, tipped over by the approaching runner, became beautiful by desperation. Sweet infancy became lovely when alloyed with anger. And everything not in motion so much as in action, as though the assertion of frantic energy was in itself redemptive, as though you could dance away any damnation.

He spoke with an intimacy mixed with a strange tensile steel core of ambition, of push: he avoided the neat formulas of graciousness.

"None of them are any good at all," he said brutally of the current generation of fashion editors. "Just PR people. There aren't any fashion editors left." Around ten, his face drained and he said, "I'm having such a drop. Forgive me." I went back down the steep stairs, and home.

I went home, and phoned Martha in Montreal, and told her, in tones like Wally Shawn's in the Andre movie, about my dinner with Dick. Whatever he had invited me for, I had obviously failed to deliver. The next morning the phone rang at eight-thirty, early for us then. "Adam? It's Dick. That was such fun last night! I was so sorry to have had *such* a drop. Can we have lunch on Saturday and see the Whistlers?" I was startled and pleased. And from then on, truly, for almost twenty years, he became our alarm clock: Dick calling with some news, thought, thing read, scheme or plot to advance his career or mine, usually, well, wacky, or all wrong, but never disgusting. And then, before midnight—slightly drunk, to use his own words, on the sleeping pills he relied on, unscandalously, his generational tipple—he would call again with the day's score. Matins and vespers, rung as reliably as a medieval bell ringer would. New York prayers, which are the same as plans, and not unrelated to plots. Though the plots, invariably, involved complicated carom shots in which the editors of one fashion magazine were to be played against the impresarios of some fragrance maker—Calvin Klein's eagerness for an ad would be parlayed into a tripled fee for a cover shoot, or the "branding" of a camera in his name—and almost always turned out to be too elaborate or fantastical to be executed. He was, I said to Martha, playing chess while the world played checkers. Diligence, dutiful forwardness, was the rule for advancement, a truth that he applied to his own daily work, but which fled him in those early-morning megalomanias. He was right, at least inasmuch as the basic lever of "power" in that world was always the same—simply being desired elsewhere—and it vanished when you weren't. But being desired elsewhere was a function of being good here and now; midnight machinations had nothing to do with it. He knew this without being able quite to *learn* it, and screwed up a few promising prospects because of it, pushing too hard or corkscrewing his ambitions too elaborately. I think he enjoyed the morning megalomania, the midnight machinations, for their own sake, like a kind of Manhattan Tom Sawyer, plotting to free an already liberated prisoner or, in this case, to advance a career already advanced, to score a coup by craft already earned by art.

═══

A week later, after we had walked and talked, I confessed that Martha and I had always tried to live with nothing but beautiful things. He invited us to dinner. (Martha wore the white Kenzo dress she had bought in Paris on our first, teenage visit there; years later he would photograph her in that same dress, hugely pregnant, on the verge of giving birth to our son, his godchild.) "I'm so relieved," he said. "I was thinking all week: What if she's a lemon? Well, we could have lunch. But that throat and that hair . . . Now we can have dinner every night."

In an era of cocaine and punk, we were champagne and Gershwin. But it was where we had always intended to be. They were always my tastes, and finally someone shared them—though he shared them with a sure grace that I envied. (I mean by that that he always chose the one right record to put on—mid-fifties Sinatra, whereas I was still a little lured by "Summer Wind" and the tacky sixties organ; Mel Tormé with George Shearing and only with George Shearing—not as a series of ukases and snob values, as I had grown up with them, but in the same spirit of emotional overcharge in which Martha chose her clothes.)

═══

On winter weekends, for ten years, we would go out to Montauk, where he had a house. In those days, Montauk was still a decently underinhabited part of Long Island, well clear of the Hamptons and their desperate social masquerades, where a handful of similar figures—Warhol, the designer Halston—had bought properties. (In *My Dinner with André*, Dick's place is referred to as "the Avedon estate," which infuriated Dick. It made him sound too landed.) Our weekends out had a beautiful regularity. Usually, Dick and I would drive out together on Friday afternoons, while Martha finished her day in the editing room. Then she would take the jitney or the train, and we would go out to pick her up and start dinner.

The weekends were pure joy, bookended by absolute terror. Dick was the most hair-raising driver I have ever driven with. The problem was that he lived for human faces—was addicted to them— and he could not, just could not, have a conversation with someone without looking at them, usually searchingly, to see what they were really saying, or how they were responding to the story he was telling. This meant that he negotiated the Long Island Expressway with his eyes and head turned right toward you in the passenger seat, not the front-facing direction generally recommended at fifty-five miles an hour—speaking and laughing, and, more disconcertingly, *listening*, intently, while the traffic roared and honked in disbelief at the station wagon veering and lurching from one lane to another. It seemed scary then. Now that I can drive, I know how really scary it was.

I'm aware that, in reading this, the reader must think: Oh, he was looking for a father! Perhaps I was, but only in the more special sense that, having a strong father already, I was always comfortable in the presence of another. Indeed, in those days, I was subject to an illusion that I later came to recognize as semi-universal: boys with good fathers, like me, tend to trust the entire world, perhaps unduly. I saw it in another friend, Wilfrid Sheed, the wonderful critic and novelist, whom I would usually try to visit when we were in Montauk: he went through the miseries of Job in that decade, from pill addiction to cancer of the tongue to a recurrence of adolescent polio, and yet was always oddly resilient, optimistic, even blithely unaware of his own close shaves. (Having become, like so many writers of his generation, over decades of ever-rising ingestion, a stone alcoholic, he saw his own drinking sweetly, as mere sociability. It might have been, once.) He put this down, grumpily rather than evangelically, to his faith—but his Catholicism, I realized when I read his beautiful memoir of his parents, was really a faith in his Catholic father, Frank, who had instilled in him a sense of trust in the universe, the greatest gift we can give our kids, even if it is always at least partly an illusion projected on a universe that in fact wishes no one well, or ill. Dick's father, I was to learn, had not so blessed him, and the bouts of paranoia and pushiness were both designed to impress an untrusting father, absent the blithe confidence that the universe, like the good father, would always embrace you in the end. This is a roundabout way of saying that I was never properly scared when he was in the driver's seat, since, trusting my own father, I trusted anyone who drove. (Martha, a good driver with an absent father of her own, was, over the years, with gentle, mostly invisible diligence, able to nudge Dick out of the driver's seat and take it over, leaving him in the passenger seat and me in the back, where we belonged.)

There was a complicated sexual triangle among us, not less potent for being unconsummated, no less real for being marginally incestuous. His sense of sex roles—what came to be called gender roles—was touchingly rooted in the 1950s. Though I did all of the cooking in our couple, and in Montauk, too, Dick, who admired Martha's mix of femininity and career seriousness, assumed that she, being "one of those great women," cooked as all the great women did. Alice Trillin and Nora Ephron had participated in what Calvin Trillin once called "the domestic deviation," meaning that being expert in the kitchen was part of their feminism, rather than a rejection of it. Dick took it for granted that Martha was a master cook, and for twenty years would direct every culinary question to her, often leaving messages asking for instructions: "Maaatha—when do we turn the temperature up on the lamb to get it crusted?" "Maaatha—it's me. When you're doing the risotto with wild mushrooms, do you heat the stock to boiling first, or just to a simmer?" Martha would turn to me for instructions and then call or respond with the answers. Even if, as I sometimes did, I gave the answers myself, he always remembered them as hers. "She's a filmmaker and a beauty—and what a cook," he would announce to someone, selling her (none too subtly) to a newcomer. They were all parts of a single description of what a woman was, and one could never convince him that I was the chef. Even all the visual and palate evidence over countless meals and Thanksgiving dinners that this was so did not alter his admiration for Martha's cooking.

On bitter winter nights in Montauk, we would build fires and make plans. Sometimes Dick would call me in to look at Martha, curled up in a chair, her top lopsidedly buttoned and stretched around her, her yellow legal pad on her lap, her splashy smile. "Look at her!" It was a compliment to me, of course, and to us—but there was always feeling in his craft, sincerity backlighting his strategy, whether personal and improvisational or photographic, and so I knew that he delighted in the beauty of girls and women in a way that made my own lust-marked appetites feel vaguely second-rate. It was heterosexual and erotic without being lecherous. "Most men want something from women," Martha said. "They want to fuck you, or gauge the chances at least, or they don't. But a heterosexual man who loves women without lechery—it's so rare that you give everything." He put it more simply, but with a sense of bedazzlement more moving for having been professionalized for so long. "Men making pictures of women wearing clothes," he mused once by the fire. "It's such a little thing. But it's so big in art."

He made us feel possible, and brought us outward. A tiny elegant man with a gravelly authoritative voice; a man of the forties remade by sixties politics; a master of the decorative arts who relished only the anti-decorative ones; an optimistic romantic who dreamed only of being a grim existentialist—he was the sum of his contradictions. Indeed, I learned from him that character *is* contradiction, a lesson he imprinted in every one of his portraits, so that, talking about one of his masterpieces—Oscar Levant, or a Wyoming drifter—he would draw attention only to the incongruity of a hideous mouth with an elegant brow, of a tightly clenched fist with an easy turn of the leg. What seemed at first like Roman portraits of grim similarity, a march of unsmiling ugly orneriness, were, once one had become sensitive to the micro-phonetics of their language, always revealed as studies in the paradox of personality—the enigmatic sense of human character that Rembrandt had achieved with half-light, Dick sought in harsh light, trying to make of the opposed inner life that scarred a human face something whole.

So it was no surprise—indeed, in the best sense, no contradiction—that he himself embodied as many opposing passions as his portraits. Or, in a better sense, it *was* a contradiction, between the sigh of mischief and a search for the monumental, and the one that gave his work life. I had been trained away from accepting that art, all art, is a scene of contradiction. Rather than being resolved through war, the myriad interpretations were likely to be all correct, and this was not a sign of tepid middle-of-the-road-ness but of real intelligence; the sign of real intelligence in interpretation was the ability to say how the tensions became articulate, rather than the habit of arguing for one or another trait as the foremost one. "Both at once" was almost always the right answer in life. But "both at once" always arrives one at a time—you'd have to go back to look again and again, at a Braque or a new friend, and simple duration of experience made up more often than not for a lack of instant understanding.

As with all strong personalities, his attraction and charm could sometimes turn treacherous. The straightforward and puritanical tend to leave little room for ambiguity, and though they make few friends, they leave fewer feuds—whereas the charming are necessarily evasive and two-faced and create mixed emotions wherever they go. He had many embittered ex-friends. Strong personalities who try both to delight and to control do delight, and do control—but the underside of delight is disenchantment, and the underside of control is rage, and many disenchanted always trail in the wake of the enchanting. Their promises cannot be kept, at least not completely, and though their promises were (they thought) meant to be understood as enchantments, fantasies, and fables—the charmer charms the snake, he doesn't converse with it—a fable no longer enlivened by faith is simply a lie, and earns the anger of those who feel themselves deceived.

And, then, the gift of charm is the gift of instant intimacy. He's my best friend, sees through me, my truest confidant. But of course instant intimacy, though not a scam, is an instrument: Dick used it to make what he needed, if not merely to get what he wanted, though the two are hard to separate. As with any great theatrical director, once the work was done, the intimacy was not so much withdrawn as suspended. For those caught short by the suspension, the sudden withdrawal of messages and conversations and dinners felt like (as in one way it was) rejection. (At first, we felt this at times ourselves.) Of course, the cynic would say, with as much truth as cynics possess, that the project, the getting what he needed, was just a longer one with us: a scribe and a pseudo son and daughter. But the cynic's account of motive, though not entirely false, is not remotely true: all motives are always mixed, lust becomes married love every morning, and what we can do for each other is inseparable from what we need from each other.

And so the most charming people one meets often tend to have the worst track record in making inexplicable enmities. Blunt Dr. Johnson had many non-admirers but few ex-friends. But blithe and ingratiating Boswell spent his life caught in a labyrinth of other people's exasperations. The disappointed become enraged, and feel swindled, instead of just disappointed. Nora Ephron had many protégés, who loved her, but all felt that the great bright horizon that she held out never quite materialized—because the horizon was herself, which one could seek but never quite become. "So quick bright things come to confusion," and big, still brighter ones are often what bring the smaller ones to confusion. The moon tugs on the waters, and the little boats struggle with the tides even as they admire the shining silver object above their heads. If they knew that the moon made the tides, the boats would be angry at the moon. But they blame the water, or each other, and the moon shines on.

⸻

Our meeting was, in retrospect, the great turning point of my life "in town." A mentor can seem to resolve our problems—but even more to make our problems seem to vanish, becoming not problems at all. The mentor magician, and Dick was mine, is the kind who fills with you with confidence that all the things that looked terrifying don't really exist. The mentor teacher—I had one in my teacher Kirk Varnedoe—shows us his subject and then ourselves. The mentor magician shows us his world, and then our possibilities. He makes the world's contradictions look like connections, hidden to lesser eyes. Of course, mentors can teach us only what we want to believe, for as long as we want to believe in it. Falstaff showed that it was possible to be both witty and woozy, a drunk and a man of language with a sharp tongue, because Prince Hal wanted to be both. Then we sober up. Look before you leap, the mentor teacher teaches. The mentor magician says, Leap, and look after, and— what d'ya know!—you're on the other side. This works out because most of the terrors are in your mind, and most of life's leaps are easy. Until the day comes when they aren't, and you have to jump by yourself.

Eventually, of course, that day came for Dick and me. It had to. The last trip he ever took—to San Francisco, to shoot people engaged in the 2004 presidential campaign, we shared. Although he was in first class and I was in coach—he still came back, as the flight attendants fluttered worriedly around like pigeons in a pigeon coop, to sit on the edge of my seat and show me the boards of his new spread, white-haired now but leaning over with the same avid eagerness as he had shown twenty years before. Never for one moment was I disillusioned by him—but over time I gained a sharper sense of the sources of the illusion. When we are befriended by magicians, they are not the less impressive when we know the way the tricks work. That gaffed deck that Sky Masterson's father feared is all the more interesting when you know *how* it squirts cider.

So I came to understand that Dick's capacity to charm was insep- arable from his need to dominate and control—as, of course, my capacity to *be* charmed was inseparable from my need to have sto- ries to tell, people to inhabit my life who could become characters within my writing. Even at the height of our friendship, when he asked me to write an essay for the catalogue of his museum exhibition, "characterize" him is what I did: I portrayed him as he was, an amazing original presence, walking the length of Fifth Avenue with an unnamed friend, me, full of schemes and strategies and plans. But by showing him so, I owned him a little, as, by choosing us, he owned a part of me.

He took it, I see now, in good spirit, but he was wounded by it, too. Wounded that it was his presence as much as his portraits that I chose to write about, and though I would have sworn on stacks of Bibles—or, in our case, on stacks of paperback Kafka and Billecart-Salmon champagne cartons, our equivalent—that it was meant as pure admiration, unalloyed love, I also see now that, as in any moment when we write about another, there was a power contest in it, too. I was asserting myself as a writer who could control *his* portrait, as he asserted himself as an aristocrat who could make mine. The moon keeps the boats swamped, but also creates the tides that let them voyage. You're grateful to the tide for pushing you a little farther from the safe, familiar shore, even when you know, in the end, that the voyage out is one you'll have to make under your own sail.

For the time being, back then, many things that had been building up and seemed unresolvable seemed to have been resolved by his company that summer: the need for a Blue Room, an inner space, with the wish for entry into the world; the possibility that the glamour of fashion lay in seeing past its frauds and making that discovery exuberant; the desire for worldliness and absolute commitment to work. Through his example, it began to seem possible to have a bigger room that kept the blueness. Contradictions were life, and life was leaping over them. Things were strange and beautiful. Their being strange didn't make them less beautiful. The "poetry" of love we'd made so far wasn't adequate to the plurality of life yet to be found. It seemed like enough wisdom to leave the Blue Room with.

Part Two

THE BIG STORE

8

SoHo, 1983

I t remains the strangest and luckiest thing that has ever happened to us. Over the Fourth of July weekend, Martha spotted an ad in the real-estate pages of the *Times:* "Snny lft. lndmrk bldg. Reasonbl, No fxtr fee, No agnt." On Tuesday, she went to take a look, mostly out of mordant curiosity about exactly where and what the catch was.

She called me later that morning at my little cubicle at *GQ.* It was *lovely*, she said, and for some reason the owner was inclined to rent it to Martha if she could meet her husband. Could I race downtown to be, well, seen? Mrs. Franz—as I'll call her—who owned the building and lived there, was a landlady out of *My Sister Eileen*, a charming middle-aged woman with a heavy Middle European accent. What she showed us was just as described: a spacious, sunny loft in a landmark cast-iron building. The rent was very reasonable, and was "stabilized." There was no fixture fee and no broker. Mrs. Franz invited us into her apartment for coffee and sweet rolls, and after asking us some weirdly unpointed questions (not "How long have you worked for your present employer?" but "Who is your favorite composer?"), she brought out a lease. We signed it, and then she double-kissed us and we kissed her back.

The staggeringly reasonable monthly rent I recall to this day. It was $832 for fifteen hundred square feet. Facing a red-brick wall, the loft didn't have a view, but a well of light between buildings filled the place every day. There were three cast-iron Corinthian columns holding up a tin ceiling above a honey-colored hardwood floor.

To say that this was an unusual event in the history of Manhattan apartment hunting is not to begin to capture its improbability. No one found an apartment in the *Times,* and if you did, you didn't get it, somebody's friend or broker having raced in ahead of you. For a couple of months after we moved in, we walked around jumpy, waiting for the other shoe to drop—would Martha be impregnated by the Devil? If the deal had been offered, I think we would have thought it over, and then raised little Beelzebub happily enough, in exchange for the space—but it never was. One of our friends said that we must have won some kind of contest that the landlords of New York cynically allow one couple to win every few years, just so that people will stay in the game.

Overnight, really, we went from the condition of clerkship, crowded like Cratchits into our basement room, out into a real world with space and huge windows, and not just any real world—the world of art making and selling that until then we had been remotely witnessing and longing to inhabit. Nobody could figure it out, least of all us. We would have been just as likely, and, in a way, as lucky, to have ended up on the Upper West Side, or in Chelsea, neighborhoods we would have taken in a second for even a bit more space and light. It wasn't fate that brought us to SoHo at its height as an art world village. It was just chance. But it had the look of purpose, and I suppose chance that has the look of purpose is exactly what we *mean* by fate.

The SoHo we moved to in 1983 *was* still a village, a village of art. The cobblestone streets and cast-iron buildings and loading docks were all lined with galleries. There were art supply dealers there, too, some witting, some not—there was still a working lumberyard on Spring Street, Pearl Paint on Canal, bulk sellers of plastic, metal, and discontinued hardware on Canal Street as well. The sense of art in process, being made—canvases arriving, and sculpture being anchored—was still evident. There were also old-fashioned, nineteenth-century-style businesses in SoHo. The ground floor of our building was occupied by a ship chandler's, a supply depot for ships. The sides of most cast-iron buildings were palimpsests of advertising for the original function, which was still legible. The side of ours read CHOCOLATE COVERED CANDY.

═══

For the people who had settled SoHo a decade earlier, in the early seventies, the real SoHo was already deep into its decline—even unrecognizable. The very first SoHo, where a few brave art dealers, in flight from the impossible rents on Fifty-seventh Street and Madison Avenue, had set up shop was for them gone—and the artists that had followed there, who had lived without hot water or kitchens, pirating electricity, had either left or else acquired all those comforts. Clothing boutiques, a newsstand, two bookstores, and a few restaurants and other appurtenances of a normal New York neighborhood were beginning to settle in place, with more arriving every month. The people who had settled SoHo in 1969 claimed not to be able to recognize it in 1980. They were already writing stories about its ruin, even as they sublet their lofts to the new arrivals, making money while they mourned.

But to less discerning—or more spoiled, or perhaps simply less snobbish—eyes it was still intact. There was only one convenience grocery store, De Roma's on West Broadway. Dean & DeLuca, the prototype of all chic and specially sourced modern "gourmet" grocers—had opened up in 1977 in its first dark premises on Prince Street. I say "opened," but it kept gallery hours, with a gallery's sobriety, trafficking in beauty and expensiveness that couldn't be thought of as in any way convenient. Still, there were many more art galleries than there were shops. You could buy a Stella sheet-metal piece more easily than a six-pack of beer. And it was still largely artists who inhabited the beautiful lofts with their cast-iron columns.

At night, one could see the original settlers, the art-making giants of the previous generation, striding the streets—Donald Judd and Carl Andre and Frank Stella and Chuck Close. They still made objects, but the art world had been dominated by what was called conceptual art the whole decade before—poetic-philosophical ideas, in theory unsellable, enacted by the artist and then memorialized in photographs or in little diagrammatic papers pinned to the gallery wall. And a few odd conceptual projects still went on: a man and a woman chained together for a year walked the streets, suggesting how eccentric and luxuriant a culture must be that could support such things.

In the early 1980s, SoHo the village remained even more isolated than any other in the city, neatly bound by geographic limits. Whereas most New York neighborhoods are nebulous hypotheses, leaking out and over their borders, lapping the shores of the next neighborhood one decade and then receding the next, SoHo had boundaries as fixed as a walled medieval city. It was bordered on the north and south by two double-wide streets. The northern border was Houston Street—pronounced "How," not "Hew," a thing that I had learned, to my pain—creating an effective moat between SoHo and the Washington Square Village a little farther north. On the south, SoHo ended neatly at Canal Street, helping to retain some of the significance of its name. Originally an actual canal, it still sealed off the southern end of the district as confidently as any waterway. And then Broadway to the east, and Sixth Avenue to the west, closed the frame. Nowadays, the crosstown boundaries have become leakier—by the end of the eighties, they were already changing—so that a loft east of Broadway can be sold as SoHo prime. But in our day, the four lines of Canal, Houston, Broadway, and Sixth still enclosed the village—which remained, however absurdly, the beating heart of the Western art world, and the current inheritor of the entire Western art-making tradition. Of course, great art was made and sold elsewhere—but the life of new art was concentrated here, its buying and selling, reviewing and arguing, fêting and eating and drinking. Europeans came to test themselves against the locals, as American artists had once gone to Paris or Rome to go ten rounds with the big guys over there.

I see now that, whereas the Blue Room times were private above all, with their public meanings borrowed from Bloomingdale's or Mr. Frick, the time that we experienced afterward in SoHo was not, and so must be written from three points of view at once. There is an eagle's, or, rather, pigeon's, eye view of the village and its inhabitants and their practices; a philosophical-theological view of what they believed about art and why they believed it and whether, or how much, they really did; and then a micro-view of how one shared consciousness—one couple—actually got settled and painted walls and paid rent and bought unexpected cheeses and fought off mice and rats and mosquitoes in one of the warrens between Houston and Canal. All three, entangled, are my tale.

===

It is a curiosity of the history of art since the Renaissance that it has proceeded distinctly from capital to capital—from Florence to Bologna to Rome to Paris and then at last to New York—with an art district in each city, so that its history can be told village by village as much as epoch by epoch. There has always been one big art town and one hot art district within it. The muse of painting—if there had been one, the Greeks leaving her name out of the lists as superintending a form too artisanal for divine intervention—needing only a man or woman with a marker and a flat surface to make marks on, is the one whose devotees are most in need of sociability. Painters clump in groups. For visual artists, talking nights succeed making days—perhaps because, the competitive, I-can-do-anything-better-than-you-can aspect of visual art making is basic to its existence: images only make sense in sequence, with each gesture an answer to a previous one, the cool irony of Warhol articulate only after the unmediated angst of Pollock. These effects bloom best in close quarters. Poets can write in isolation; painters rarely can, because their art depends on outdoing or outpacing other painters. (They can *find* themselves in isolation, like Cézanne and Van Gogh after Paris, but they first have to lose themselves in company.)

Artists talk openly, excitedly, about their art, with each other and sometimes even with critics, because talking doesn't compete with their real work. This makes the history of art since the Renaissance an antipodal history of lonesome studios and bustling clubs, empty garrets and cafés at night, making and arguing in close-order drill. The talking shops of SoHo were its little restaurants. Bob and Kenn's Broome Street Bar had a kitchen so small that they couldn't even make French fries, just burgers and chips—the burgers seem wonderful in retrospect; could they have been so good?—but it hummed on a Friday night. The oldest SoHo places—Fanelli's and the Ear Inn—were still in place, and then there was Food on Prince Street, the best of the places that combined earnest Whole Earth Catalog health food with cafeteria service, a rich genre of eating places at the time, now vanished. What all of them had in common was that local clubbiness, and then, in the new places especially, an odd democratic spirit. What Bohemian villages always have in common is a certain camaraderie between the served and the servers. You can read the original *Scenes from Bohemian Life* and see the pattern, with the waiters and the waited-upon part of the same social class. In SoHo, too, the people who served were like the people who bought, out-of-work actors serving food to aspiring painters.

In another way, SoHo was unique among all the many Bohemias that the muse has visited since the Renaissance, and perhaps its ethic, which was above all one of virtuous labor rather than dissolute appetite, was attached to this fact: its architecture, though hidden away from view for almost a century, was inherently spacious and beautiful. This might not have been immediately apparent, grimy and rodent-infested as it was. And "dangerous": the residual fear of crime had in SoHo left a complicated sequence of locks on every door. To visit a friend, you took a service elevator and encountered a big moving lock, a Champion lock with a three-dimensional key, levers and gears and bolts more appropriate to a medieval keep than an artist's studio. It operated on brushed aluminum doors that would wheeze and heave and open.

But inside the spaces were beautiful—even when the lofts were chopped and jury-rigged and remade, as they were (since no one ever gives up a downtown home any more than anyone leaves an uptown walk-up). Here was a second bed suspended above a first bed, and a child's bedroom built, like Tarzan's tree house, in midair; all these still had a charm, a breadth, even a perverse kind of superior hominess, inasmuch as they broke out of the usual New York apartment tyranny of narrow snaking corridors and small air-shaft rooms. Already in the seventies, a parody version of the *New York Times* "Home" section showed how to convert an apartment into a loft. It was a joke, but also, like all good jokes, a social observation: a loft, even broken into improvised living quarters, had an enviable kind of originality and openness that the tenement studios and garrets of Bohemias past, in Paris and New York alike, had never quite achieved.

SoHo was also "picturesque" in a way that no previous Bohemian quarter in New York had quite been. The West Village has red-brick charm, but mostly in the older or, in its Bohemian phase in the late fifties and sixties, more thoroughly middle-class blocks. The folksinger Dave Van Ronk's descriptions of Greenwich Village life—when the folk clubs blossomed and Van Ronk stole from Reverend Ed Davis and Dylan stole from Van Ronk and everyone else—emphasize the tenements, the rickety stairs, the five-floor walk-ups, the tiny showers, the miserable-in-February bleakness.

SoHo *was* decisively un-green: there wasn't a park within walking distance, aside from the bleak green areas around Washington Square Village. But the streets were cobbled and coherent, and the cast-iron façades that filled block after block a genuine architectural marvel. Mostly built in the three decades after the Civil War, when New York was booming with Whitmanesque energy, the façades were cast in modular pieces that could be picked right out of a catalogue. The narrow wedding-cake fronts laid over the brick buildings imitated the forms and orders of classical architecture. There were cast-iron catalogue pediments and pyramids and windows framed by the classical columns, Corinthian and Ionic and the rest. Neon signs—aside from the few on old saloons grandfathered in— were prohibited, so the names of stores were indicated by billowing banners.

Two elements made those cast-iron façades of SoHo distinctly beautiful. One was that, needing to be repainted often to keep the rust away, they were colored—in soft blues, greens, reds, yellows— where conventional neoclassical architecture sought mostly pristine white. Not bright, for the most part, though occasionally some cheerful remodeler would paint an entire façade bright pink or acid green; still, the ivories and creams and blues and battleship grays gave the blocks a subtler play of all-over tones than New York streets, with their browns and white and occasional reds, usually possess. It even gave the blocks something of the color chemistry of a Roman street, those burnt and aged ochers and muted greens, seeming mellowed and aged. And, then, illuminated sidewalks still decorated the pavement below: these were long rows of small round translucent lenses laid in metal matrices into the cement, designed back before there was electricity to illuminate the basements of the small manufacturing businesses the buildings had been designed for. Useless now, enough of them persisted to give the streets at your feet a look of a virtuous nineteenth-century effort at efficiency and technological innovation.

———

The zoning and housing laws that had made SoHo a village of art were complicated. The name "SoHo" was a compression of "South of Houston," with a mordant pun on the London neighborhood buried in it. By the time we left, it was simply Soho, a neighborhood as old as time, as fixed as nature. As the story gets told, the neighborhood of cast-iron warehouses and small factories was saved, in the early sixties, from the grim hand of Robert Moses's expressway making by the doughty resistance of Jane Jacobs, the great urbanist. The entire neighborhood was saved only because it was to be torn down—and then, when everyone woke up and saw that there would be no downtown expressway bisecting Manhattan, destroying the old useless warehouse district, no one knew what to do with it.

But one thing is always true: artists are always searching for big spaces at cheap prices, and here they were. SoHo had never been intended for such uses—in truth, the buildings had never for a moment been intended for *living* in. But painters and sculptors and conceptual philosophers—Sol LeWitt–style large-scale minimalists and Chuck Close–style giant photo-realists—started camping out illegally in the factory lofts. Over time, reluctantly, the city government retroactively regularized the circumstance. The possibility of having your residence actually recognized with a "C of O"—a certificate of occupancy—was spoken of the way Colombian illegals (or Canadian ones) speak of getting a green card. To have one was to enter into a new world of legal uprightness. (And, like a green card, the C of O was accessible by more avenues than the simple letter of the rules suggests. People could spend years, decades, in a legal limbo, with their loft neither quite kosher nor quite not.) Once converted, however simply or, later, overelaborately, the loft spaces were large and inherently beautiful. Where once shirts had been sewn by lonely immigrant girls and candy made and paper boxes folded by their sweating immigrant brothers, now painters could work out their struggle between conceptual cool and expressionist angst in peace, working big all the while.

—————

Our new building turned out to be an odd warren of kinds, and life among the artists a daily—and sometimes a nightly—revelation. One Monday night, a year or so after we had moved in, I was lying awake at three in the morning, Martha in her usual state of deep, imperturbable slumber beside me, when I heard a funny noise. At first, it sounded to me like some small animal scratching. (All noises at night sounded to me like small animals scratching, because I had always been terrified that some night a small animal would get into the loft and scratch.)

I got up, without waking Martha (in those days, as in these, you couldn't), and, taking the flashlight that I keep by the bed for emergencies, which before that night had never arisen, I went to look for the source of the funny noise. I found it near the front door. Water was dripping through the ceiling, like blood in an old Vincent Price movie—dripping spookily down the wall in sheets and puddling on the floor. There was already quite an accumulation. At the age of thirty, I still didn't know what to do about such things. I didn't know what to do about anything domestic, really, and in the Blue Room everything had been so close together that to do one thing was to do everything.

I remembered that in an old *Honeymooners* episode Alice had taken a pail and put it under a leak. We didn't have a pail, so I took the copper stockpot that my parents had given us when we got married, and I put it under the leak. Then another part of the ceiling started to leak, so I got the ceramic pasta pot that we had bought over on the Bowery, at that time still a paradise of restaurant ware, and put that in place, too. Together, they worked pretty well. I was encouraged, until I realized that at the rate at which the water was filling the stockpot and the pasta pot I would be up all night emptying them. So I figured that my next move was to call the super. I called him up—he didn't live in the building—and, speaking softly but forcefully, tried to give him a strong, vivid image of what was happening: the water dripping down, the paint ruined, the beams rotting, mold forming. He said he would come over in the morning.

So I decided that it was my job to go search for the source of the leak. I went upstairs in my shorts—"sleep shorts," Martha called them, as though they were specially designed for the work of sleeping—and banged on the door of the artist who lived above us. She came to the door immediately; she was already up. She had heard the funny noise at the same time I did, and had discovered the leak, too. She was in her nightgown—a nightshirt really—and through the half-open door I could see some of her work, suspended from the ceiling. She was a sculptor, a very good one, and her name was—is!—Petah, Petah Coyne, then a beginning and now a quite famous second-generation conceptual-minimalist sculptor, a maker of objects. (In Paris, just a few years later, I would see her picture on the cover of *ARTNews*.) She made mobiles out of bundles of what look like lacquered twine. I had never seen her loft before. There was a wonderful wholesome scent coming from inside, which I couldn't quite identify. We figured out together that the leak must have been coming from the loft on the sixth floor (we lived on the fourth, Petah on the fifth), where a landscape painter named Marcia King lived. (Marcia, who has since passed away, had come all the way from Texas to try her hand at disquieting images of contemporary beaches.) We decided to go and wake her up.

A bunch of Marcia's canvases were propped outside her door. We called out to her, but there was no answer. "Maybe the air conditioning is on and she can't hear us," Petah said wistfully. Marcia was the only one of the artists in the building at that time who could afford air conditioning. (You need a big unit to air-condition a loft, and it costs a lot of money. In those days, although almost every uptown space, at least on the East Side, had an A/C, lofts didn't. It meant that SoHo was one place where, when a heat wave hit, you still saw people out on the street at night trying to escape it, as in a forties musical.)

We were silent as we imagined Marcia cocooned in the roar and comfort of twenty-eight thousand BTUs. Then, looking down, we saw a little trickle of water coming out from under her door, and Petah said, "Maybe the air conditioner has *exploded*."

We started pounding on the door. Suddenly, Petah put a hand to her mouth and gasped. "My hay!" she cried, and rushed back to the stairs. I followed her down into her loft, looked around, and discovered the source of the wonderful scent. Along the wall nearest the door, behind some of the mobiles, towered an immense haystack—a pile of bales fourteen feet high and about twenty feet long. The hay, I realized, was her material, her clay and plaster; it was what all the mobiles were made from. She wrung her hands. "Oh no!" she moaned. "If it gets wet, it's going to *fester*."

I didn't know what happens to hay when it festers, but the idea still appalled me.

"Get a ladder," I said, with a note of grim decisiveness that I had never before achieved with a woman. "We'll shift the bales."

I don't know where those words sprang from—some deep farm instinct, I suppose, or maybe just a scene in an old John Ford movie.

We sprang into action. She had a ladder—I guess she used it to get hay down as needed. I mounted it, and began grappling with the bales. I had always thought of hay as something silky and homogenous—something that looked and felt the way it smelled—but as I hefted first one bale and then another, I discovered that it was dense stuff, and as varied with incident as the meadow it must once have been. It was filled with thistles and burrs and small dried flowers, and scratched your hands as you gathered it. Up close, the smell was still good, but fatter and duskier than it had been at a distance.

Once we had shifted the highest rank of bales, my initial rush of adrenaline and determination waned. It seemed to me that I was likely to be restacking hay for most of the night. For one ungallant moment, it even occurred to me that the fate of my neighbor's hay was, after all, not my problem. But then her husband came down from their little sleeping loft, rubbing his eyes. He stood and watched us. I guessed from his passivity that he considered hay shifting in SoHo unusually delicate work—a specialist's job, to be left in the hands of artists and their explicators. I kept on with it.

It took us about an hour and a half to move all the hay from one side of the loft to the other and pile it up again. When we were finished, we stood together at the foot of the new haystack (the husband had gone back to bed) and panted in the heat. It was a pleasant, oddly intimate moment; we brushed some burrs out of each other's hair. Meanwhile, the flow of water had eased up. (We found out the next day that the tank of Marcia's toilet had broken—she was out of town—and all the water had sprung from that small well.) Just as we agreed that our worries were over, we heard a siren outside. A fire truck pulled up. You could see it, red and chrome, from the window, in the streetlights. The super, apparently, had done the logical super thing: he had called up the Fire Department, told them about our problem, and gone back to sleep. We shouted down to the firemen that everything was now okay, that we had saved the hay from festering. They gave us steady, opaque looks, and got back in their truck.

After that, Petah and I shook hands, a little formally, and, as we were saying good night, she told me, "My husband has a bad back, you know. He can't pick up anything heavy." That explained a lot.

When I got back downstairs, I looked at my watch. Five o'clock. I didn't try to brush off any of the hay that was still clinging to me. I was too tired. As I slipped back into bed beside Martha, all I could think about was how I would tell her in the morning about everything that had happened over the last two hours: my ingenuity with the pots, my forcefulness with the super, and the hour and a half I had spent, one floor up doing . . . *farm chores*. How pleased she will be with me, I thought, and how wonderful I will still smell.

———

But, then, art always reflects the spaces it's made in. You can feel the crowded labyrinth studios and blue-gray Paris light coming in the windows, the angular chaos of the view from the Bateau-Lavoir, somewhere in the background in every Cubist painting. You can sense the espresso and raw alcohol lofts of Tenth Street in the scumbled, midwinter nonfinish of the Abstract Expressionists in the fifties. SoHo spaces produced art big and sober and a little austere. The lofts lent themselves to scale—they provoked not the crowded grubby biomorphs of Tenth Street, redolent of espresso and gin, but the more spacious systematics of Sol LeWitt and then of Donald Judd. The expected scale of avant-garde art changed in tune with the accidents of these spaces, so that, when the avant-garde at last did return to Paris in the nineties, it was no longer to garrets and studios in Montmartre but to converted factories out on the edge of the city.

This made the basic vibe of SoHo confident and forward-looking, not embattled. Though there was as much unhappiness in lofts as in any other human abode, the sadness was the sadness you brought with you. The spaces themselves—tin ceilings supported by classical columns, floor-to-ceiling windows with warped old glass— were, in every way, cheerful. They made for a more confident art, an art in communion with *industry,* in every sense. Someone said around then that it was the work ethic, the religion of work, the constant talk of it, and the puritanical edge of labor that made SoHo unique among Bohemias. SoHo *was* devoted to an idea of work—in fact, "work" was its magic word; and though "work" meant art, it was important that art be seen first of all as work, with a residual sixties affection for a proletarian façade, however comical. (The first paper I wrote for was called *Artworkers News*.)

Largely stripped of that kind of spirit of play or blague that filled past Bohemias—there were lots of court reporters but no court jesters, lots of clerks but no clowns, SoHo of the seventies and eighties was a Bohemia without bohemianism—a place where sexual play and dissipation and all the other good stuff that avant-gardes had typically claimed for themselves had been pointedly, at times prudishly, replaced by an admiration for effort. I am sure there were as many affairs and as much alcoholism there as anywhere else. But the shoptalk of art was not of affairs and alcoholism. It was of effort and growth and the advancement of art—of "vocation" in that more priestly sense.

High ceilings make for happy painters. Beautiful spaces make for productive artists. Bohemian squalor produces sporadic poetic inspiration more often than productivity. Artists in beautiful places want to add more; artists in ugly ones need to drug the ugly away. Architecture inspires art inasmuch as it gives it a certain kind of space to fill. Big rooms may not produce big ideas, but large studios make confident art. When you have to back away to look at what you've made, you make something worth backing away to look at.

I see now that the spell SoHo cast lay in its being both a cathedral village, dedicated to the religion of advanced art, *and* a market town, devoted to selling produce of the true faith. The cathedral village was visible at night; the market town blossomed on Saturday mornings. A Saturday morning in SoHo in the 1980s was one of the most beautiful and moving and optimistic of New York rituals.

The galleries had first colonized the ground-floor spaces of the cast-iron buildings, and then begun to blossom upward into the upper floors. They became a demonstration of an eternal principle: nothing demonstrates the power of the free market more than avant-garde art made in its defiance. Art isn't betrayed by commerce; it begins there. In truth, the merchandise on sale, the works of art, *could* have been sold privately. (These days, they often are.) The number of walk-in purchasers at all those galleries lining the SoHo streets must have been tiny. But there were enough to let the business of showing the art matter, and then there was a genuine altruistic sense that sharing the pictures was a part of presenting them for sale. The surplus of good will that Adam Smith thought the essence of liberal market societies was present in SoHo then—Smith's point, still not sufficiently grasped, being not that markets make people free but that free people move toward markets; the instinct of sociability, allowed to flourish outside the suspicious watchfulness of clans and tribes, brings people together, and one of the things they do is buy and sell and share.

A SoHo Saturday morning was the best possible demonstration of Smith's liberal principle—though both the people making the art and the people who hated the art that got made were in vehement denial of this truth. The conservative critic Hilton Kramer loved freedom and hated command economies—but the SoHo art world he despised was an extremely good example of what free markets alone can make happen. People brought their wares to market; others chose to buy them; the order and reciprocity emerged organically from the intersection. Meanwhile, the crowd around the then influential post-structuralist magazine *October* loved the art that critiqued the system of commodification, without seeing that a system of commodification was exactly what had allowed the critique to emerge in ways it never could where commodification was prohibited.

This contradiction, mostly invisible to its participants, governed the intellectual life of the art world in the 1980s. The conservative cultural critics hated what they saw as the ingratitude and impiety of these things, without quite seeing that impiety is exactly what free markets in culture always produce. The radical critics, in turn, loved the "subversive" nature of the impieties, without quite seeing that only free markets in culture produce them. Radicals hated the system that forced avant-gardes into commercial galleries to be sold to rich people; conservatives loved the system that made avant-garde art, and hated the art that it made. Neither absorbed that the art and the system were the same thing seen at different moments in their propagation: A Jeff Koons was only possible under capitalism! And only late commodity capitalism could make a Jeff Koons.

———

Here is how a Saturday morning in SoHo would unfold in the middle years of the 1980s. You would take the 6 train down to Spring Street if you lived outside the neighborhood, or you would walk out your door onto Broome Street or Wooster, or one of those, if you lived nearby. Getting out of the subway, you would find yourself in an area still almost entirely Italian immigrant in feeling—Balthazar brasserie and the spread of French bakeries was still far off. There was a newsstand, a magazine stand, that only went out of business recently; the Italian immigrants who ran it were hockey fans, and liked to talk to me about the Rangers, at a time when there were still Ranger fans intact in Manhattan.

Crossing Broadway, still a strip of discount clothing emporiums and blank-faced brick buildings, with only an occasional cast-iron façade, you would cross over into SoHo proper—where the Cast Iron District began. Was it just my passion, or was it really like coming to the moment when you finally finish crossing the end of that blank stretch of the Adriatic, with the smell of gasoline and fish your only clue that you are entering Venice? Certainly, the first building that asked for attention was Venetian Gothic in style, complete with Lombard Gothic arches—the exquisite small palace at the corner of Spring and Mercer that (when did I learn this?) belonged to Donald Judd, the archdeacon of the minimalists, the most minimalist of them all. His simple shelves and boxes were so austere as to make Carl Andre's row of square concrete slabs look rococo, and the pale, pure grids of Agnes Martin seem like the work of a kitschmeister.

Judd was a hero of mine without actually being a favorite: I admired everything about him without much liking to look at his art. I recall the thrill of hearing him speak once, at a gathering of art history students, where he showed slides from the very beginnings of the museum in Marfa, Texas, devoted then only to his work and Dan Flavin's. "If you're interested in modern art you really have to come," he said flatly. "There's more modern art in this place than any other." And then he added, "Oh, I suppose the Museum of Modern Art has more *artists.*" And he meant it! The thrilling self-assertion of it: If you want to see modern art—pure, hard, and intense— look at me. Look at us! Don't look over there. What distinguished Renaissance men was not the range of their interests but the force of their obsessions. He had that. He had earned his building on Spring Street—a Renaissance palazzo in cast iron.

Then across Wooster on Spring (there was a café with Ben & Jerry's ice cream, still a rarity in the New York of Häagen-Dazs), until you finally reached the two-way, sunnier street of West Broadway. At number 420, you would always begin by taking the elevator up to the top floor, to the Charles Cowles Gallery, and from there you'd descend by the stairs to Sonnabend, then to Leo Castelli, and finally on downward toward the rookie Mary Boone. Each gallery had a house style, while strenuously denying it. At Castelli you saw blue-chip oldsters—Johns and the rest—from the most distinguished stable in the New York art world, along with a few decisive choices among the new. Uptown, Castelli had always been classy, and here he stayed classy by taking on the newly hot with an air of bemused European detachment that cooled the hot down just enough to make it seem sage. Castelli's ex-wife Ileana Sonnabend showed the friskier of the younger artists and the more demanding of the older. Big abstract canvases here, small sporty sculptures there—every eye was attuned to the arrival of the next thing, the necessary thing, and of course, eyes being eyes, made to recognize things seen before. We mostly landed on a variant of the familiar to stand in for the new.

After the trot down on the stairs at 420, you would inevitably bump into friends, eyes set professionally aslant from the work of looking, and exchange a warm greeting and a few terse words about the things just seen. "A one-line joke," you might say with a shrug, or, "It feels repetitive." It was another form of shoptalk that had its own decorum. "Good work" was a term of highest praise; "lovely" or "beautiful" was critical, with a trailing "but . . . ," the objection unspoken always at the end. ("It's beautiful, but . . .") "Original" was no longer a positive term, marking a breakthrough. No, history-minded values had subtly been superseded by the ethic of solitary labor: "What wise painting!" was the first sentence I heard about Eric Fischl's art. *"Wise," "strong," "sad,"* and *"solitary"* were all words of praise; *"nice," "new," "fine," "lovely,"* and *"powerful"* all words of dismissal. "It's just very strong and wise," was a fine sentence to say. There were, I was learning, always two dialects at play in a shoptalk, whether at a fashion magazine or in an art gallery. At *GQ* there had been a fancy language for our simple readers—"chiaroscuro chic" and all that—and then another among ourselves: "Taste is all white shirts." It wasn't double-talk in the usual sense, misleading speech. It was just a counterpoint of in-talk and out-talk. On the stairway of 420 West Broadway, "intriguing" meant unimportant, and "lovely" meant embarrassing. If you knew that, you belonged.

Then you would head west toward the galleries on the side streets: there were the two Barbaras, Gladstone and Toll. (I once spent a day at Barbara Toll's, watching a severe young Scottish conceptualist tear up hundreds of men's magazines—*GQ*, actually!—to make them into a Presbyterian-themed piece about the emptiness of commodity fetishism, the vanity of vanities. I kept virtuously mum about my connection.) Angela Westwater had the great Cy Twombly, whose scrawls and scribbles seemed potent with antique wisdom, and there one could also come across a late Philip Guston, as awkward and fatal as Samuel Beckett.

The social life of those Saturday mornings was at least as important as the chance for solitary looking. All art serves a double function, and the double function of American visual art by the eighties was as both a mark of generational identity and a luxury good for the wealthy. You recognized your generation's rage and secrets on a Saturday morning—the suburban guilt, the hunger for something less arid than a grid or a wall label, or just the truth that most of what you knew came from old movies and television—and then saw these become validated as things rich people owned and showed.

Of course, it was the second function that offended people.

=====

Something is always wrong with the art world, and the something that is wrong is always money. In the 1920s, the greed of the millionaires and the cupidity of the dealer Lord Duveen caused Italian churches to be looted so Fifth Avenue mansions could be filled, and for sums—half a million dollars for a Giorgione Nativity!—then thought to be unreal. In the 1960s, fury turned on the Marlborough Gallery for selling Rothkos for hundreds of thousands. The punch line is always the same: And they thought *that* was a ridiculous amount of money!

It was in SoHo in the 1980s, the story goes, that contemporary art was first made subject to the same principles of commerce— seasonal fashions, and "branding," and salesmanship—as any other product, while the auction houses, not accidentally, began to sell the avant-garde modernism that had preceded our contemporary kind, for absurd sums. Among everything else that has changed since, this hasn't. The market turned to the modern, and against the Old Masters, and the only way to feed the market became to make more contemporary art. Art was now available not to the merely wealthy but to the super-wealthy, to the tiny splinter group of rich people who have, since then, dominated it. Young painters like Julian Schnabel and Jean-Michel Basquiat became favorites of the dealers—that they were painters, makers of conveniently portable objects, instead of conceptual koans, was in itself part of the market mechanism—who then pushed their work on pliable museums and gullible collectors. The old values of art were overturned for the benefit of a new class of the hyper-rich, for whom collecting and investing were not only conflated but in principle indistinguishable. The market inflated new pictures beyond their intrinsic merit. Art was—though no one quite knew this at the time—mere kindling in the decade's bonfire, which was really not so much a bonfire of the vanities as a bonfire of the pieties, by which the vanities, made ever more fireproof, were permanently lit.

The tension between the role of art as the shared subject of a generation and art as so many baubles for billionaires was strange and constant. On the one hand, an Eric Fischl landscape spoke to a common intuition about life, real and rebellious—the drowning out of experience by imagery, the bad conscience of the middle classes. At the same time, it was a counter in an expanding game of chance, racing silks to place a bet on, a piece in a Monopoly game, a jaunty symbol the collector moved around the board. The mistake of the condemning critic was to think that, because the pictures were luxury goods, they possessed no other, more potent power; the mistake of the disillusioned artist was to think that, since they really were intended as *cris de coeur*, there was something wrong in their becoming commerce. They played both roles. They had to. Art is double, or it isn't art.

I figured out some of this on the run at the time, as we often do, some of it long after. Art always plays more than one role in a culture; it's playing many roles is what makes it art. (Poetry, in our time, is either something you read and write in a classroom or something you give to someone you want to sleep with.) Double use is a sign of pregnant meanings. Craft objects are meant to play only one role, opening bottles or turning with the wind; if they sometimes play more, it is because of a discerning eye that emancipates them from their original purpose. Art objects are meant to play many roles; if they play fewer, it is because of a limited eye that imprisons them from possibility.

═══

In the early eighties, everyone was waiting for the next big thing, the movement that would succeed repetitive Pop and spent minimalism. At OK Harris, the place where the photo-realists had gathered, a movement had emerged that, according to my own training in minimalism, looked very much like a heresy. A kind of still-rebirth of figurative painting had already taken place, including some excellent artists—Susan Rothenberg's horses had already caught my eye, and they have never abandoned it. But various micro-movements fought for attention: one gallery showed Pattern and Decoration, a sort of meek movement that seemed to be raising questions in halting American already answered by Matisse in luxuriant French.

These were sectarian stabs at a next step in history, the thing that would be achieved. No one was confident quite yet. The Italians appeared—Francesco Clemente, Enzo Cucchi, and Sandro Chia—like characters in Evelyn Waugh. But the truly new energy that was rising was, as new energy will always be, more acidic and impious than any academic quarrel between abstraction and illustration. The really new impiety turned on the question of push, of ambition and its manifestation as art.

Certainly, one cynical way to write the history of art in the eighties is as a transformation of the "work ethic" of the older generation into the raw ambition of the next, the austere seventies into the ambitious eighties. As Julian Schnabel and then David Salle and Eric Fischl and many more painters in their twenties had their first exhibitions, their readiness to rival big old "epic" painting using means that seemed almost to parody or, at best, approximate it—Schnabel was the most notorious, using broken plates to "animate"

a surface with angst, and black velvet to darken it toward despair—
enraged many, because it seemed so obvious, all push to be seen and
no accumulated practice worth seeing.

Ambition, everyone cried, had entered the art world—ambition
unashamed to name itself, ambition unalloyed with apology. Ambition! Of all the words of the city, it is the most shameful, somehow,
and yet, of all the acts of city life, it is the most essential. When E. B.
White writes of the boy arriving in New York with a manuscript in
his satchel and an ache in his heart, he leaves out that he was also
arriving with a drive in his belly, one that White, in his own discreet
way, certainly knew well enough. The eternal ambition of young
artists soon became a subject of momentary moralizing rage. Robert
Hughes, my own mentor among the older critics, led this particular
charge relentlessly and violently. They wanted money, homes; they
were happy hamsters on the dealer's wheel. And it was true, some of
it: they did want nice things. But no more than he did. And the previous generations of New York artists (and art critics and curators
and everyone else that trailed alongside) had wanted those things,
too, and had, in some cases, gotten them. To visit the studios of the
Pop artists, for instance, was to walk into townhouses bought in the
West Village when such things could still be had for forty or fifty
thousand dollars. The older generation had been more discreet—
but, then, generationally, they could afford to be.

The Blue Room effect that had been our first experience of New
York was, by other measures, still the effective principle: there were
too many people for too little space, and as the spaces got expensive,
the people fought harder to hold them. Bob Hughes would rant,
entertainingly, about the rancid ambitions of a Julian Schnabel,
unearned in his eyes. And some of this was righteous, but much was
merely real estate: Bob had bought his loft when one could be had
on a magazine writer's salary. Marx was not wrong about the essential thing, that most moralizing has its roots in money. People with
a lot scorn those without—but people who got in early hate those
arriving late, because things are getting crowded.

And then there was the more common allergy to ambition, to

announced ambition, that was perhaps part of the last American taboo. In the late sixties, when writers were breaking down taboos self-consciously—when the taboos still had power to enthrall and were pretty much begging to have things thrown at them— Philip Roth wrote about masturbation in *Portnoy's Complaint,* and the world was shocked and then thrilled by the violation. Norman Mailer, that same year, wrote about his vanity in *The Armies of the Night,* making the pious protests against Vietnam a theater of his own egotism, confessing that his vanity was as much at play at the Pentagon as his morals, that his competitive relation with Robert Lowell was as important as his condemnation of the war—and the world was shocked and then spellbound by the courage of the violation. But then poor Norman Podhoretz wrote *Making It* about his ambition, about how his place as a powerful book reviewer was the result of the same kind of ambition that had made other men stock-brokers and tycoons—and the world was shocked and remained shocked; even my friend Wilfrid Sheed was disgusted. It never let up, and the liberal Podhoretz had to change political clothes completely to start over. Sexual desire, vanity were acceptable frailties; announced ambition was still taboo. (Dick Avedon, being an openly ambitious man, I had seen, suffered from the stain, too. His efforts, perfectly sincere and utterly passionate, to depict the broken souls of ordinary people were often met by a resistance that suspected that he was depicting the broken faces of ordinary people in order to add more luster to his own name.)

Ego and libido were acceptable "bad" motives. But ambition was not. When the "sordid" motive of making money is joined to the sublime motive of self-enactment (masturbation may not be pretty, but at least no one *pays* you to do it), the economic basis of the arts becomes a little too apparent. The Expressionist who sold his pictures because he had to is a hero; the Neo-Expressionist who sells his pictures because he wants to is not. The action is the same, the aura very different.

So, in SoHo in the early eighties, ambition had to be sublimated into that other word—"work." Ambition was the vigorous impiety of the time. That it worked equally well to get you on the cover of *Vanity Fair* and into the museums may have been convenient, but it was also contradictory—and eras in art, a little inspection of its history shows, are defined by the fecundity more than by the purity of their motives. You reach into the sock drawer and pull out two completely different socks, and you know you are in the Renaissance.

———

An art village. Though far from a village atheist, I was becoming a secret doubter. I had been brought up in the church of the avant-garde art by my parents, true believers, who had when they were younger amassed a small but (for college professors) choice little collection of California minimalism and New York Pop. I had learned the catechism of the avant-garde with the same credulous comfort that Catholics learn theirs. "New" was good; "busy" was bad; "clean" was good; "strong" was, too—a single brushstroke was better than several, and there was something slightly absurd in those who spent their time drawing bunnies or, God help us, people's faces and bodies. This extended from the family catechisms to art movements that began and ended at the family dinner table. In the early months of our courtship, for instance, Martha had heard an inflamed argument my family was having at the round glass dinner table about the triumphs and limits of "generative art," and, curious and diligent student that she was, not having heard of this movement before, she vowed to find out what she was missing. At the library, she couldn't find anything about it, until finally she searched through some Canadian art journals, and discovered to her great chagrin that it was an art movement named, defined, acquired, and then excommunicated by the Gopnik family alone.

So I was in an odd position. I knew the faith by heart. I was able to instantly parse each rectangle of yellow as abstract rectangle, ironic abstract rectangle, neo-rectangle, camp rectangle, referential rectangle, post-ironic rectangle, or simply as the paint sample someone had left on the gallery wall. And yet I was beginning to harbor secret, half-spoken doubts about whether or not this faith of rectangles was *true*.

The truth was that, though my head was always engaged, my heart was only sporadically so. As a novice "critic," I was a believer, but fading secretly in belief—and the only good comparison I can find to liken this process to is with those Catholics I have spoken to who, having grown up within the Church, slowly peel away. There are conversion experiences, saints fall off horses, but de-conversion is rarely an epiphany. Bringing the horse back to the secular stable happens at a walk. Faith arrives at a gallop, but it leaves on tiptoe.

Still, those young Catholics—Bob Hughes was one of them— shared with those of us who "believed" in avant-garde art two things. First, there was our love for the indefinable aura of power that surrounded the activity. The proof of the value of the faith was the system each faith inspired. The light inside Chartres remains the best argument for Catholic theology, and the best argument for the continuing life of the avant-garde was the dense complexity of each Saturday morning in SoHo, where commerce, criticism, and crois- sants all joined in a vital compound. To say that the faith of advanc- ing art was a substitute religion, with history instead of heaven as its divine principle, is not false. And the particular people who had been charged by this belief in modern art—in its ongoing story, its unexpected twists, its constant forward motion, its modest losers revealed as saints and its heroes as prophets, the Van Goghs and the Pollocks—were filled with the light of faith, in a way no one else in the secular or academic world quite was. Even if they struggled with their faith, as believers must, they had a quality of moral intel- ligence that lent the academics among them a grandeur of vision greater than that of all the other academics I had known. The most impressive of them, Kirk Varnedoe, believed this right to the week of his cruelly early death: that a faith of skepticism, of nonbelief, kept the transcendence of the older kinds of faith alive in a way that gave life meaning.

Of course, modern art has always demanded a leap of faith, inas- much as it asks you to look at obvious and unprepossessing objects and invest them with transcendental power: the bread and wine of the Eucharistic oblation do not appear to become the body and blood of Christ any more than the bicycle wheels and black boxes of the Dadaists and minimalists assume new meanings except by the insistence of their creators. The skeptical Catholic, still wanting to believe, knew at some level that transubstantiation was all in your mind—but they believed that the reward for suspending disbelief was so large as to make skepticism seem fatuous and unworthy. After all, where else would it be *but* in your mind? And since everything else went on there, too, why was the cosmic cracker any less real than the desire or lust or ambition that played out there on other material objects? The girl or boy you desire might be a mammal that shat and spat, but love or paralyzing desire was not therefore an illusion. The bread you ate might be a Catholic cracker baked in Philadelphia, but that did not make transubstantiation less true. Belief is belief, not argument.

And even my professors, whom we would bump into touring the galleries, were capable of worldly action as academics usually were not. It seems absurd to say that studying advanced art proved its worth by the market values placed on its specimens, but we lived in this market economy and not some other. Robert Rosenblum, one of my teachers, soon became one of my good friends. He had bought Johns and Rauschenberg early, not as "investments" but as acts of friendship, of faith, and now found himself with treasures on his wall that would pay for houses and educations. He was puckishly amused by this fact, but a fact it was. Money, wonder, and glamour—the entire society had conspired to make the small gestures and decisions of the avant-garde resonate with value of every kind—and what better proof of faith could there possibly be than that? We build cathedrals not to enclose our beliefs but to let them resonate louder upward and out, as big public megaphones of our private mystical intuitions. When the intuitions echo so quickly and so loudly, how could one doubt being at the very center of the civilization?

Which is a grand way of saying that, though SoHo *looked* like a market village, it *felt* like a cathedral town even on the market mornings, a small place in touch with a cosmic principle. Of course, the cosmic principle may have been the illusion of its inhabitants—or the inhabitants might have been the comic bearers of the cosmic principle. Was the life of the art village essentially a comedy with cosmic pretensions? Or was it really a chapter in a great advancing story of the closest thing the century had had to a real faith, the belief in the open-ended development of avant-garde art? Of such questions, half comic, half cosmic, as Trollope knew, cathedral towns are always made.

———

The past was hidden, and yet all around. Sometimes it ran right to you. One night, two years or so into our residency, Martha and I woke up in the sticky air at around four o'clock to hunt for mosquitoes. We turned on the switch of the little Akari Light Sculpture on the night table, and as I stood on the bed, with a rolled-up copy of *ARTNews*, we both noticed that blood was dripping in sheets from the ceiling.

When I say "blood," I mean that it looked exactly like the stuff you find described in mystery novels and see in horror movies—something reddish-brown and thin and sticky, not the bright-rose-colored blood that bursts from a squashed mosquito but dark, claret-colored blood, the stuff that comes from deep inside a person. It was leaking down the wall around the heating pipe and turning into sinister-looking stalactites. My wife gasped, and asked if that could really be blood—what did blood *smell* like? As it happened, just before we went to sleep I had been reading an old John D. Mac-Donald mystery—a good one, with Bahia Mar, and a lot of deep thinking from Meyer—and had come to the bit where the broken body of the fragile young girl is found in the hold of the *Busted Flush*.

"It smells metallic," I said, remembering the way Travis McGee described it. "Like copper. It smells like copper."

She sniffed, and said, "Well, what does copper smell like?" Finding my trousers, thrown over the back of a chair, I reached into the pocket and got out a penny, and we sniffed that, and then we tried to sniff what was coming out of the ceiling. It was hard to tell whether they smelled the same.

For the next two weeks, the ceiling kept hemorrhaging. Sometimes we would wake up and find it dripping slowly, slowly. At other times, it would really be coming down, as though a whole new vein had been opened, or else as though—and this thought struck us both at about the same time—a new corpse had just been stowed away under the floorboards upstairs. Our neighbors above seemed like the last people on earth who would stow corpses under floorboards, but, then, the people who look like the last ones on earth who would stow corpses under floorboards are apparently the ones who sooner or later make a point of doing it. We thought of calling the police, of course, but we could imagine the cops telling us with a sigh that our "blood" was just some kind of New York gunk you're supposed to know how to deal with—a kind of gunk that is just part of grown-up life, like taxes. It was beginning to bother us, though. Fortunately, a meeting about the co-op conversion was coming up, and we offered to have it in our loft. We intended to confront our neighbors. On seeing the telltale blood, one of them might rise from his chair, like King Claudius.

Our building was always going co-op and never getting there. For the latest round of negotiations, we had hired a real-estate lawyer, who, like a movie star profiled in *Vanity Fair*, was tough and yet movingly vulnerable. His feelings got hurt easily. He had called the meeting to tell us how upset he was about something or other we had all done. Our neighbors came into the loft: Marcia the painter of Expressionist seascapes, who lived on the sixth floor; Petah, the sculptor who worked in hay, and lived on the fifth, just above us; the framer, Frank; the still-life photographer, Seth—the whole gang. Everybody sat down. Nobody seemed to notice the blood. The real-estate lawyer talked about everything that had hurt him recently: our failure to sign no-buy pledges, our inability to agree on what we wanted from the owner. We all felt guilty and inadequate. The ceiling chose that moment to open up a new vein. The blood was dripping. Nobody said anything about it. Finally, Martha decided to deal with the issue directly. "Can anyone here explain why there is blood streaming from our ceiling?" she asked Marcia, the Expressionist, looking up at the blood. "That's not blood," she said. "It's just *molasses*." We asked her what she meant, and she told us this story:

"Mrs. Franz"—the former owner of the building, who had sealed our lease with a double kiss—"warned me about it when I moved in, a decade ago. That the building had been a candy factory at the turn of the century, and that it still had odd oozes and memories. Anyway, one morning a couple of years ago, I noticed that there were long, pale drips coming from the ceiling. They were slithery and small, like the forms in a Morris Louis *Unfurled*. I got on a ladder and stuck my finger out, and then I tasted the stuff. It was sweet, as sweet as can be, like the sugar you use in a buttercream frosting, sweetness dripping from the ceiling.

"And then I thought, My God, that's it—sugar from the turn of the century! And I realized that when this was being boiled down, when they were making this right here in my home, I wasn't born, I didn't exist. It was thrilling, like the moment when they opened up the Dead Sea Scrolls and found them pristine. Sugar syrup from a century ago, bubbling out of the walls, and still so sweet." As we all walked over to the little alcove where our bed was, Marcia added, "The thing that's really mysterious is why up on the sixth floor we have sugar syrup while down here on the fourth floor you have molasses."

"I think it must be heated up by the pipes," our next-door neighbor, a cagey arts administrator, said. "They get hot, and that turns it into molasses. Well, it's not really molasses, although we've called it that for years—this problem has been going on forever, since we moved in. What it really is, is *caramel*. It caramelizes on the way down from the top floors to the basement. So down there, probably, there's a big puddle of caramel, like the base of a crème caramel."

I felt happy; I was living on the Big Rock Candy Mountain. But then Frank—the framer—pointed out that a vein of sugar syrup running through the walls probably wasn't so terrific from an engineering perspective. "It's a structural nightmare," he said. "Can you imagine the engineers' reports—what all that sugar is doing to the structure of the building? The way it's eating up the walls? It alarms me."

We all brightened: this might drive down prices, right to the bottom. (For the first time all night, our lawyer looked cheerful.) Everybody stood around for a bit looking at the syrup, like Vermonters at a sugaring off, and then said good night.

We were so relieved by this explanation that the strangeness of it didn't strike us until later. Martha shook me awake at two in the morning. "Why is there sugar in the walls?" she asked. "How did it get into the walls? Did somebody inject it in the walls? If this had been a widget factory, would widgets get into the walls and come tumbling out half a century later? What kind of an explanation is that?" At four o'clock, she woke me again. "Why did she *taste* it?" she asked. "Would *you* ever taste that stuff? Isn't that the *last* thing you would do?"

So the next morning, before coffee, I called up Marcia and asked her why she had tasted it. "Oh, I was hoping it was sugar," she said. "I had been hoping to find it ever since I first heard about it, years ago. It was so pure, so abstract—so *refined:* the past coming back to haunt you, only still so sweet."

———

Though SoHo proper was still filled with artists living in their studios, it was already ceding its primacy in art making to TriBeCa, a newer, sterner art village being forged from the old triangle of buildings below Canal. Its northern border was marked by a small triangular park—not a park, really, just a concrete space with benches, bridging the two neighborhoods. It was smelly and rat-infested, with rats the size of small rabbits. (There are rules for describing rats, as there are for tumors: the latter are the size of various fruit, the former the size of various other animals. A tumor is the size of a grapefruit; a rat always the size of a cat.)

This park was the most trafficked of places. It marked the border between SoHo, then "established"—ridiculous though it might seem elsewhere that an entire anthropology could be established in a decade—and TriBeCa, emergent. Artists would bump into one another there, on the way from studio to gallery and back again. The painter Eric Fischl tells of having a violent, friendship-ending argument with his rival painter, David Salle, on those very benches, exactly where Kirk Varnedoe, my mentor and teacher, who became chief curator of painting and sculpture at MoMA toward the end of the decade, and I used to meet at midnight and exchange papers on the meanings of their art. We were planning a great show to end the decade with, about modern art's relation to popular culture, and we spent year after year preparing for it.

Some of the SoHo artists became friends, including David Salle and Eric Fischl (even better friends now than then), and through my own friendships with many, I learned that artists are the most interesting observers of art there are, with a minimum of theoretical hobbyhorsing and the most alert attention to the actual content of what they've made. (The fight between David and Eric was about the autobiographical content of David's pictures, which he denied and Eric insisted was there, as indeed it was. Every love affair found its cognate in a borrowed image.)

The official story of eighties painting, by which one "movement" succeeded another, the baton passed mysteriously from apostle to apostle, persists to this day. It insisted that the dry Conceptual art of the seventies was replaced by a richer, image-laden Expressionist art of the eighties. The young painters whom I knew hated this cartoon history from the first, which they understood evaded a deeper and more interesting truth. The art they pursued was not "Neo-Expressionist"—"Expressionism" in its early-twentieth-century form they knew so vaguely that it was hard to be "neo" about it. If anything, it was movies, particularly American film noir, that haunted their imagination. They had come of age in cinematheques more than in museums, had been knocked sideways more by Hitchcock than by Max Beckmann. You could get bored looks descanting on De Kooning, but a single reference to the best Robert Aldrich picture would light up eyes and start tongues; you would get a flat reaction talking about Titian, and blank looks talking about comics, but could start a violent argument on the relative merits of Robert Mitchum and Otto Preminger. To get that strange American shiver of feeling—black velvet and massed violins, city streets at night and snowfalls in blinding chases—into their work was their aim, not quite articulated even to themselves.

The young painters were not at all obsessed by the "media image," by the standard demotic of the supermarket and the tabloid, as it was understood, intellectually or instinctively, by a Warhol. To them, it was the indiscriminate energy of pop culture that seemed to mark the Pop generation: the Whitmanesque taste for getting it all in. This was not *quite* fair; the appeal of this soup can or that romance comic to its appropriators was more personal and entangled than the critics chose to know. (Warhol loved his soups, and his choice of icons was Olympian: Elvis Dionysius, Aphrodite Marilyn, and even a grief-consumed Demeter in Jackie.) But it isn't false to say that the force of Pop Art lay in making you see a field of indiscriminate creative energy where you hadn't before.

The new generation in the eighties didn't see pop culture as a field of indiscriminate creative energy. They were connoisseurs of pop culture—those B-movies in particular, seen in grindhouses or, probably more often, in the still-thriving repertory cinemas—where Warhol's fandom was purposefully indiscriminate. The new generation had grown up as cinéastes. Discriminating fandom was their religion. Not as a camp alternative to the pieties of high seriousness, but as art forms that were self-evidently mature and manifold. Pop music, from Joni Mitchell to Dylan to the Talking Heads, wasn't a bracing alternative to concert music. It was all the music we knew. It rewarded us as art does, with metaphors for our own experience, allowing us to recognize it *as* experience.

This taste for B-movies was one that the art critic and, later, painter Manny Farber had first inserted into the imagination of the art world, and he, far more than the fashionable Frenchmen, was a hero to them. Having begun writing about art and movies for *The Nation* all the way back in the forties, he would have a much more profound effect than all the writings of Baudrillard. I sought out Farber myself, oddly, later on, thrilled by his commitment to the non-art sources of art. But all he wanted to know was why I never wrote about his paintings.

I had begun writing about art for various journals and soon learned that the relation between artists and writers, even when the artist is a writer himself, is like that between editors and writers. Editors are grown-ups; writers are children. (Even when the editor spends his daylight hours being a grown-up, he is still a child as a writer. I know.) Artists are angry supplicants, angered by having to ask for support. Writers on art are more often mystified by the artists' anger, thinking that it is the subtlety of their discernment that artists admire, not their capacity as advocates. This is a basic confusion, not easily or quickly cured. The artist wants the critic for the same purpose the accused wants a good lawyer—to win his case. The critic wants the artist for the same reason the judge wants an interesting accused—to show off the subtlety of his reasoning. This misunderstanding never ends, and costs more in hurt feelings and sundered relations than one can easily imagine.

Why Farber's paintings had so little of the quality of his writing is mysterious, or maybe no more mysterious than why anybody's work in the form they love is never as good as their work in the form they're good at. (Edmund Wilson's novels, Frank Sinatra's paintings fall into the same conundrum.) But the pictures had a dry, inventoried feeling, like a Wayne Thiebaud without the descriptive virtuosity or the unpretentious purity of spirit. I couldn't praise them, and praising him wasn't the praise he wanted. (Not long ago, David Salle, who knew him, too, had a good, blunt explanation: "Manny just wasn't a good enough painter to articulate his ideas.") The truth is that we are all what we are, and the effort to be another is the effort that unmakes us, as writers or painters or musicians. It is impossible to disguise anything. We are all naked, all the time. *Nobody* has pants on. I was learning that, too.

It was not that the young painters envied filmmakers—though almost all of them sooner or later made movies, or tried to, and it was no accident that the first complete poetic realization of the sensibility they shared was Cindy Sherman's mock movie stills, black-and-white staged images of imaginary moments from stock fifties movies, the young woman newly arrived in town. It was that they recognized that their emotions passed through the stylized light of the movie projector. Just as their predecessors among the café-concert painters in the French 1880s saw that some secret of their civilization could only be seen in limelight and gaslight, the eighties artists saw that some truth of the American psyche only appeared in the light penetrating from the projector in a grindhouse—not in the wash of television, which made all things look alike, but in the tempting thrill of the peep-show revelation. To get that feeling into their work was the battle.

The world had altered, but it wasn't money alone that was doing the altering. Entertainment was no longer sealed off from art, not because standards had "slipped" but because critical vision had sharpened. If you couldn't hear why pop music was as interesting as concert music, you couldn't hear. Artists expected to be auteurs. Selling out seemed a nonissue. Talking Heads emerged from RISD as an art project with a pop edge to become superstars and then, themselves startled, could spend a lifetime pursuing art. This turned out to be an illusion, too, as a generation of embittered musicians would discover when their record deals ran out; but for twenty or so years, from 1970 to 1990, it was a very powerful one. The eighties were the height of it. The good fortune of a David Byrne wasn't typical, but cultures aren't shaped by the typical. They're shaped by the thematically atypical, the extraordinary things that resonate with ordinary hopes.

"Presentational" was the most damning word the young painters I came to know used for all they didn't want their art to be.

Meaning, I came to grasp, the same thing that, decades later, when I wrote for the theater, I understood actors to mean when they condemned another actor for "indicating," or what playwrights mean by the word "expository." The art of the previous generation, they thought, in being "presentational," kept no secrets, made the subtext text. It wasn't supposed to. "What you see is what you see," the slogan of the minimalist Judd generation of the sixties, seemed not too simple but too much of a straitjacket, too solipsistic, too obvious. Even the art of Warhol or Oldenburg or a Richard Serra seemed to the young painters of the TriBeCa eighties "presentational" in just this way—all it had was "presence," telling its stories with no stories to tell. Its strength was its straightforwardness, and life was not straightforward. The irony was that the earlier generation had sacrificed everything—metaphor, story, even mood and feeling—for that effect, for a "what you see is what you see" in which the pure presence was the one thing that the work possessed.

The younger artists were certainly not torn between abstraction and the image—that was a trap for graduate students to fall into. What was going on in those streets was in truth one more romantic rebellion against a classical style. How could one register strangeness without falling into set patterns of Surrealism? That was their big question, and it was a question I recognized as my own, too, in another form: how to register the cracks and faults and flaws in a beautiful surface without becoming merely a scold.

It was easy to see, and to say, that what they ended up with was a form of Surrealism or Dada, as it had passed already into the American mainstream of art. But to say this—and I did—was to miss its urgency of feeling. In fact, if the art of the time could be summed up, it would have been in a simple and fatuous phrase: the young painters wanted to paint what they felt. Each of these terms of course was torturously complicated: What was it "to paint" in an era of mass imagery? What had you "felt" that wasn't part of some general feeling already cheapened by overuse?

One of the things they felt, of course, was the inability to feel— the way that feeling had been so crisscrossed and scarred with cliché and media images that even a firsthand emotion had become secondhand. Longing, needing, wanting, loving—each now had its set form. The hierarchy of emotions had become jumbled. Big things like weddings and wars and small things like celebrity divorces occupied the same space. The wisdom of Eric Fischl's work was the easiest for me to recognize, since it flowed from his writerly desire to tell stories, along with a desire to find a new angle to tell the stories from. I disliked Julian Schnabel's paintings—I still do, while admiring his movies—because they seemed so blatant, so farcically self-conscious in their desire to make a big picture by making a big picture. Energize the surface? Smash plates across it. Recover some of the aura of film noir? Paint on black velvet! But the first one over the moat to take the castle is rarely the safecracker with nimble fingers and fine tools. It is the guy with the big hammer, and skulls swinging from it. I recognized that there was a shiver of emotion there, a breaking through.

Theirs was a clash in the perpetual war in art between classical system and romantic rebellion, between mysterious enthusiasm and the lucid laying out of parts. "The spell of the mysterious image"— that could have been the title of two-thirds of the SoHo shows at the time. *My* one epiphany—the one epiphany I had brought with me from uptown, taking it with me on the 6 train down—was that there was something intensely new and significant about the way isolated individual voices did not have to be choired together to resonate in the huge incomprehensible emptiness of mass experience. Their art had none of the mischief or the "look at me" of Pop Art. Everyone had to speak for herself, and if you didn't you couldn't be heard. What I had learned from the Blue Room was, in the weirdest way, what I was learning from the downtown art world. But it was the same thing: big towns amplify small voices. The experience of the Blue Room was the experience of the time. The analogies between the new art and the writing I was beginning to dream of doing seemed remote, but not entirely remote—because what I wanted to bear witness to, the one thing that I thought was mine, was that the distance between small spaces and big spaces was now so large that the emptiness had become resonant. All of the old middle ground of New York, all the intermediate institutions—from cafeterias to argue in, to art that people like my parents could afford—were being stripped away. This didn't mean that you couldn't be heard; just the opposite. It meant that the space between the Blue Room and the Big Store, being larger than ever, was more resonant, more likely to echo than it ever had before. Small shivers made big sounds. In an abandoned concert hall, press the sustain pedal down and a single finger on one piano key fills the room.

I wish I had seen and said this more clearly then. But the things we know to be true we are sometimes reluctant to say. Or perhaps, inevitably, I was competitive: uncomfortable in the role of critic, essentially a storyteller, I didn't want to cede too much impulse to my peers. I was right, I think, to mistrust art as political propaganda, or the attempts to "radicalize" the art world—not because radical polemics are unworthy but because the art world is the most hopeless place to make polemics live, much less make real politics happen. You *could* radicalize the art world, but it was like radicalizing the circus: even if the clowns might be made to frown and the lions to eat the lion tamers, a circus pushed to the margins of behavior is not a circus reformed. A circus made marginal is merely a sideshow.

And anyway, I had come to think that one can be a thoroughgoing elitist in the arts and a thoroughgoing egalitarian in politics. The two are not only not restrictive of each other but in a real sense dependent on each other. It's exactly *because* we recognize that talents are unfairly distributed that we want to be sure that the necessities of a good life are not. But I also felt sure that, whatever its slogan, betting against new art is always a fool's errand, not because all new art is good, but because somewhere in it lies—like it or not, believe in it or not—the psychic image of its time. Art traps time. It just does. The mood of a moment can't escape the shapes of its chroniclers. To say that it's the wrong art is to say, unbeknownst to the speaker, that we feel we are living in the wrong time. But, then, we always are. And then you will look back, and there will be the time, trapped in its art. Art reflects life by reflecting light. Jeff

Koons's bunny had exactly the same shimmer as the small face of a CD of the same period; the light in a David Salle is the light of the movies of David Lynch. I had figured that out inside, I think, but hadn't yet found a way to say it. It required more independence— more lightness of mind—than I had yet acquired.

<hr>

Two men, wildly mismatched, most fully recall those streets for me. One was the critic Robert Hughes, the other the artist Jeff Koons. They existed at opposite ends of the village—Bob in a loft he had bought on Prince Street in the early seventies; Jeff at restaurants and galleries along the Gold Coast of West Broadway, and then in his studio on Broadway itself, along the border of the Village. They despised each other—well, Bob despised Jeff; I doubt that Jeff knew enough to despise Bob, and anyway, despising people didn't seem to be in his arsenal of emotions. But they were the alpha and omega of the period: one the perfect embodiment of pre-ironic man, infuriated by anything that seemed merely outré or mannered as violating the righteous passions of art; the other the first embodiment of post-ironic man, enraptured by the outré and so enwrapped in the mannered that he couldn't know it as such. In the mid-eighties, knowing both, I tried to navigate, or triangulate, my way through the decade with the two of them, a north and a south star, each giving opposite information about the ocean.

Bob Hughes I had admired since college, intensely, for the authority of his art writing in *Time* and even more for *The Shock of the New,* still, almost forty years on, by far the best synoptic gospel of modernism—though it had been far from admired by my avant-gardist family. Bob's essentially pessimistic view of modern art—as a failed attempt at Utopian transformation that left many lovely things along the unconcluded way—was not ours. It was scandalously skeptical. We met on the street at Dean & DeLuca; I recognized him and screwed up the courage to say hello, and he, in turn (as of course I secretly hoped), allowed he had heard of my early efforts, written though they were in a tone of strenuous midget exhortation. After what was becoming a familiar look of slight surprise—I was younger and smaller than my juvenilia's tone of having all the bases covered and all the goods in the shopwindow out, and every allusion already fully alluded to, might have suggested—he offered me his hand.

Realizing we were near neighbors, he made an instant invitation to dinner, which he quickly accelerated to an invitation to come out fishing at his place on Shelter Island that weekend, to carry on the conversation. There were family from Australia arriving; it would be a colonial party! (He knew we were Canadian.) "Nothing like a boat and a sunburn to carry forward the exegesis of Die Brücke," he said, laughing his whale's laugh, chin turned way up, revealing his oddly stubby baleen teeth. I accepted, of course, and then, to Martha's great relief—fishing boats being her idea of hell, and fishing boats with hard-drinking Australians her idea of its final inner circle—he called on Friday to apologize. Victoria, his very longsuffering wife, had a hideous headache; could we defer our plan for a week or so? And meanwhile meet for dinner at a Japanese restaurant around the corner? I needed no special insight to recognize that Victoria's headache had been contrived—though certainly a husband with an urge to invite total strangers for an already overpacked weekend party was one who could induce headaches at will. Over the years, we received many more strenuously impromptu Wednesday invitations to fishing weekends, invariably canceled at the last moment by Victoria's headache/streaming cold/migraines and beyond. Martha felt for her.

But we did have dinner that Friday, and then many compensatory, post-migraine Friday-night dinners after, either at Omen, a Japanese restaurant he loved, or else at an Italian place farther down the street whose name I can't recall, perhaps because whereas, at the Japanese place, you could sip the warm rice wine politely, the nameless red Italian wine at the Italian place was too good not to swallow, glass after glass. Like all ambitious Australians—Clive James was another—he was a natural Italophile, and my Francophilia, then and later, left him uneasy. The fussiness of the French seemed tiresome to him rather than fastidious; the openness of the Italians to pleasure unmediated by too many rules chimed with his New World sensibility. Over the years, I came to know Clive—his exact contemporary and equal as antipodean *homo universalis*—even better, and was fascinated by the way in which both of them seemed to have swallowed Western culture whole, like the Chinese boy who swallowed the ocean in the fable. The almost absurd absoluteness of their erudition was a form of generosity; they had swallowed it all to spit it out elsewhere. (They shared an admiring, officially friendly, deeply competitive wariness of each other's existence—with each, I always felt, secretly suspecting that *two* antipodean *homines universales* was one more than the world quite needed.)

Red-faced and so resonant of voice that other tables would stare over at our table with looks of varying annoyance and indulgence— one of those people who can achieve the effect of a debating team at table while sitting alone—Bob spun conversation that drew effortlessly on an inner well of aphorism, insult, opinion, snatches of Australian folk ballad, and a limitless reservoir of modern English verse. He reached down with the bucket of his argument, and there, always, was the apropos instance. He had memorized more poetry than any man or woman I have ever known, and long stretches of it would come pouring out of his lips between the imprecations: he knew all of Larkin by heart, so thoroughly that you could have saved yourself the cost of a paperback copy of *The Whitsun Weddings* just by prodding him into reciting it, usually by first getting a few lines wrong yourself. He put it down to his Jesuit education. "They beat verse into you with a stick," he said, and I sensed that the beatings had produced more than just verse. A Johnsonian air of sexual torment radiated from him after the second bottle. He had been an angelically handsome young man, I knew, and drink and salt air and a sedentary life had plumped him out more roguishly, until he looked like Robert Shaw playing the part of a canny Australian sea captain in a movie. The kind of cultural omnivorousness that he displayed was, in the Village, slightly embarrassing—one choice line from Kristeva or Deleuze carried more weight in the art world than the whole Book IV of Pope's *Dunciad*. He didn't know that—or, better, didn't care.

He hated irony in all its forms save his own favorite ones. We would argue, sometimes late into the night, running over the same material, remaking the same debate. It was an ongoing argument about the artisanal in art, the significance of craft to inspiration. He had come to hate, rather than merely discriminate among, the current generation of artists. I worried sometimes that his insults sprayed into the air would bring immediate (and understandable) retaliation from a stray subject of them who happened to be hanging around nearby—"Call that drawing? Chewing gum made two-dimensional." Or, on Koons: "All the fully articulate emotion of an autistic child banging his head against the corner wall, and getting paid for each drop of blood produced." Or, on another occasion: "Write for the *Times*? Write for the *TIMES*? Mate, it's like sticking your dick in a Cuisinart."

But he honored the great Johnsonian distinction between wit and mere abuse, and he had a serious, developed argument in mind. The great modernists, he insisted, had been masters of the full range of visual craft, men and women who saw and drew and *chose*. Each decision to "break" the describing hand—to be honestly clumsy, to draw "badly" rather than well—was a choice, fully conscious and realized. Each rule violated was a creative discovery knowingly dared. "Artistic choice is now autistic compulsion," he intoned. "The good guys drew as well as they needed to; this generation couldn't draw better if they tried, mate. I won't say that they couldn't draw better if you offered them a million dollars. Because they *have* been offered a million dollars not to draw well, and have taken it, thank you very much."

I argued back, or tried to—he could aphorize after two bottles, while two glasses had me blotto, with Martha discreetly reaching out to put my glass beyond the reach of a repour—that the important thing was not that Matisse and Picasso could have done "better" if they chose—that was true of any number of other forgotten painters—but that they *didn't* choose. The broken hand might be whole and sometimes might not be, but its accomplishments were freely made, whatever the technical acquirements. Technique was a value, not an absolute virtue, and only one value among many others, including originality of vision, intensity of communication, and a grasp of the historical moment. It was comforting and reassuring to see that the modernist masters could have done otherwise, but not doing otherwise was the whole point of what they did do.

Irony, he argued in turn, is a toxin to the imagination, formaldehyde, killing the butterfly even as it fixed it down. Art made of secondhand experience, things held in quotation marks and borrowed sincerity, betrayed the material of lived experience. "Lived experience" was a holy phrase for him. "The unexamined life is not worth living, and the unlived examination not worth looking at." I learned from listening to him something else, that the real gift and goal of criticism lay in the capacity—half knack, half skill—to tell what is genuinely contradictory in art, and thus rising from the intensely lived poles of a specific human personality, from what is simply muddled. Being a good judge of art lies in having the ability to tell vital contradiction from vitiating confusion. Since all strong art is contradictory—the contradiction between piety and physicality being the most common kind in religious art, beautiful flesh denying the flesh—the critic must be double, too. Matisse is nothing but contradictions: childlike drawing and North African color, voluptuous sensations with an ever-anxious touch, rising from the complete personality and whole of a French bourgeois who wants to touch, fears being touched. Late Picasso, on the other hand, is nothing but confusion: decorative and human and narrative and storytelling all crowded together with logorrhea expected to do the work of eloquence.

Bob could see in a second the vital contradictions in Francis Bacon—the play between despair and décor, between all that melodramatic scenery and the genuine core of angst it enclosed. He could perfectly articulate the contradictions, the fruitful, life-giving tensions, in his beloved Bob Rauschenberg—obscenity and transcendence, the goat and the De Kooning touch. But the very same kinds of contradictions articulated in a remarkably parallel manner in a Salle or a Koons enraged him. They were simply not the contradictions he knew in his own character, and so he could only perceive them as confusion. He knew what it was to drink hard, consume poetry like pasta, and enter into rivalry with the great Mediterranean traditions. Fishing for tuna off Montauk and talking about Henry Moore were continuous for him, life-enhancing complementarities. But he could not know what it was to eat well, love B-movies, accept popular culture or the "media image" as a normal rather than threatening part of visual experience, or, for that matter, at the same time to like big outsize suits and suave, tightly wound paintings. The new set of contradictions looked to him not just like confusions but like deliberate contempt for the older set, which by now were no longer known to him as contradictions, merely as another truth.

The paradoxes of our own personalities get entangled in the art of our time, and then tangle and trip us up. Critics date not because our eyes fade but because our sense of the living contradictions grows stiff. Bob knew this, even in the midst of his damnations. After a body-and-soul-breaking automobile accident in 1999, he would give up writing about contemporary art, for what had become for him the more felt subjects of cities and the civilizations they induce. The contradictions of Rome seem eternal, which they were.

———

To what degree, or how entirely, did I believe the case *against* craft and skill to be true even as I made it? The truth is that I struggled every day, all day, not just to get the right words but to get the words I wrote in the one right order they desired. All that I admired in writing was pure craft, the fiendishly hard-acquired skill of sentence making: those ten right words in that one right order, the difference in weight between Latinate ones and Yiddish ones, the single short closing sentence of monosyllables that could have the wit and authority of a winning drop shot in tennis. To be single-mindedly devoted to a classical craft standard in writing while using that same craft standard to deprecate craft standards in art seems to me now a slightly self-consuming activity—even, in a way, an absurd one. The realist painter who could get one leaf of one tree down right I patronized, even while I knew how insanely difficult it is to get one leaf down right in writing. I like to think that this was a pregnant contradiction. But it may not even have been a hopeless confusion. It may have been no more than plain hypocrisy, held up by village blindness, as so many village values are.

If Hughes was a man of fertile contradictions, Jeff Koons, at the very opposite end of the era's sensibility, was an artist who seemed to have set in play contradictions that no one else had been crazy enough to know could exist—like a mathematician who, multiplying negative numbers, somehow discovers a whole new world of positive ones—or maybe just like the games counselor at a summer camp who somehow organizes a tug of war between two teams on either end of the camp, with one made of zebras and the other of leprechauns. You couldn't deny the accomplishment, or, at first, see the purpose, or then, finally, understand how he had found the forces and put them all in play. If you bumped into Jeff Koons on the street of SoHo in the eighties, it was always surprising. He had a kind of sweet but slightly cartoonlike face—the kind of face you see more often on character actors, than on wary, sly creative people. His smile seemed one size too big, his eyes too open in wonder or surprise; the expressions seemed plastered on rather than simply articulated. It wasn't at all the vibe or feeling given off by most artists, who, though they no longer cultivated a "bohemian" black-turtleneck vibe, certainly had a style that was meant to feel artistic, distinct. They wanted to seem cool. Jeff no longer wanted to seem cool. Cool didn't matter. Cool is a way of defending ourselves against seeming too purposeful. He was all purpose.

I had seen his famous chrome bunny of 1986—a polished silver balloon blow-up child's toy rabbit, a bulbous carrot clutched in its hands, ears long and erect and yet molded, curved, cast in polished stainless steel, hard and shiny—at the Saatchi Collection in

London, in an early show of what was then called "neo-geo" art, meaning neo-geometric, filled with a dour, punning awareness of abstraction's resemblance to the logos and brandings of corporate culture. Most of the neo-geo art was diagrammatic; Koons's wasn't. Soft and hard, gleaming and repellent, at once a joke (I thought) about Brancusi's streamlined Platonic animals and an assault on the whole tradition of "displaced" objects that had marked twentieth-century art. Since Duchamp, artists had been taking bicycle wheels and urinals and Brillo boxes and bringing them into museums and announcing them as art. In that way, anti-artists had been violating the sanctuary of art for a century. Koons was the first to see that you could violate the sanctuary of *anti*-art—that the displaced objects of Dada and Duchamp and Pop could be treated not as intelligent jokes but as visionary statements, so that your bunny was not merely a blow-up balloon bunny but a blow-up bunny transformed (by other hands) into a sleek streamlined sculpture, a shining luxury object, an empty, borrowed object that was borrowed from the deepest recesses of your imagination.

The displaced ordinary object was, so to speak, now ready for its close-up—it was ready for its shrine, it *shone;* the joke was on those who thought that art had come to an end when Warhol announced a soup can as art. The announcement, it turned out, had actually been a herald, not the seventh trumpet; with the museum open to anything, anything could come in, not as jokes but as private fetishes, even as luxury goods. Warhol had made something of tabloid images, so that what looked at first like simple ironic displacement actually revealed itself to be a picture of American mythology—divine Marilyn and grief-stricken Jackie and Elvis, doubled, tripled, and even octupled. In the same way, Koons had, with minimal means, made something that became a maximalist mirror. The bunny looked like its time. It glowed like a CD. It was rounded like a Nike. It was shining like Trump Tower. It was, as Charlotte the spider would have written, *some bunny*, and one of my very rare prescient moments as a critic was to say so, and recognize that Koons was less philosophical than, in his own strange way, inspired.

This was one of my few good guesses in the decade, and the conviction only increased when, after I'd written about him, we sought each other out—as artists and their admirers will—and I discovered that "weird" didn't begin to capture it. He knew less about art than a graduate student might have, the obviously expected comparison of his bunny with a Brancusi seal got a slightly baffled, cautious response. But he had a long, absorbing soliloquy on himself and his art and its place, one that I did not so much respond to in conversation as dip into at various moments across the decade. "I am asked to lead, but not prepared to lead—chosen and yet somehow unready . . ." "The essence of my art is its formality. When I say formality, I don't mean this in the sense of formalism." He would look at you as though the distinction were transparent, hyper-lucid. "I'm a formal artist. Everything in my art has to do with forms. I mean by that their formation, not their form." I groped to understand. "People keep saying my art is rich in images. I think of it as being a study in forms." Well, that made sense, of a kind—every artist asks you to admire the forms, even if what is shown is a blood-curdling murder. "I'm much closer to Morris Louis than to Superman," he would conclude, and you wouldn't know what to say—what Morris Louis had to do with it, or where Superman had come from. The soliloquy was at once so earnestly delivered that you were sure it must have content and yet so arbitrary in elements that you half-suspected it of being what used to be called a put-on. "All of my interactions with you have been pleasurable and inspired by integrity," he said at the end of one coffee.

One memorable night, at dinner, he politely and enthusiastically asked Martha, "What *is* irony? People keep telling me that my art has it, and I really don't understand what it is." She stumbled, taken aback, "I don't know, Jeff, I think *you* should tell *me*." To her non-answer he responded with an opaque and perplexed silence. He really *didn't* know what irony was, and was hoping, politely, that someone would tell him.

Through the mists and abstractions, a truth emerged: he was serious. More than serious, he was sincere. All of his formative experience of art had been ironic. The put-ons had been his pieties. Duchamp and Warhol, the borrowed and appropriated image—they weren't anti-art to him. In a world where everything was ironic, nothing was. Once, over a plate of Terra Chips, he said: "Why did the potato emerge from all of these chips as the champion? Why not this beet? Why not the sweet potato? There was no logic. Was there a logic? I don't see a logic. The potato was called. I'm the potato." In a world where *everything* was held at a distance, in inverted commas, how could you tell irony from its opposite? All he had ever known as art was already ironic—it was suspended in quotes, demanding comment, and misunderstood if read too literally. He had seen the same yellow rectangles that I had seen.

But though you were meant to become more sophisticated through this process, he had become the opposite. If everything was ironic, then nothing was, and what used to be called your buried, inner life—your sexual obsessions, your sexual dreams, your pet fetishes, long-remembered television series—could come bouncing out into the gallery, crafted by Italian artisans in the forms of manufactured kitsch, counting as art, sincerely your own. Inner life and outer life were one, a seamless web of kitsch images and adolescent appetites. In a way, the greatest transformation of the period came the moment when Koons was sued, successfully, by a terrible photographer for appropriating his postcard images. In the past, high art had poached on common experience freely. Now common experience was back with a lawyer. The post-ironic lay in that battle, the new world of imagery. For what was called "kitsch" in his work was not the knowing quotation of a borrowed demotic; it was the unmediated—and extremely expensive—creation of a naïve pantheon of personal symbols. The bunny was everyone. *You* were the bunny. He worked like Warhol and thought like Joseph Cornell. It was a compelling American mix. Wilfrid Sheed had once said that he wondered what would happen when kids grew up for whom the parody version was the only version they knew. And now we knew.

So here, in one ten-block area, could be found three kinds, at least: pre-ironic man, passing away, with his love of Rome and wine, his sexual torment and social-democratic politics; post-ironic man, just coming into being, with Terra Chips and philosophizing and hedge-fund money; and between them mid-ironic man—not only unprepared to lead, but with no one asking, a mixed-up bag of chips if there ever was one. Mid-ironic man, me, was still hostage to the old values but prepared to entertain new tastes, to embrace even the loony if it promised to lead us forward in a final parody of avant-garde advance, and so embody the age. Pre-ironic man, post-ironic man, with mid-ironic man (and woman) standing between the two, in doubt and wonder and worry.

———

Art traps time; but food traps manners. The art lasts. The food rots. This makes it a much better bet to invest in the art than in the food—and yet, when you want to re-create the manners, the food, and its offering, tells more than the art can. So: the restaurants of SoHo at that time were a map of its hungers. The desire to eat well and act wisely—it was my generation's particular contradiction of kinds. The generation before ours thought that eating well was a form of showing off. We thought that eating well was a form of acting wisely. The next generation, who take eating well for granted and want at all times to be fair, not privileged, think that eating really well is a way of enacting virtue.

But at that time the restaurants in SoHo and nearby, though they may not yet have defined a new ethic, certainly defined a new aesthetic. "Yuppies" (a term no more useful for understanding the time or class than "rednecks" is for studying people in Mississippi) spent money on exotic olive oils and eating out as their one purchase of luxury; they were still unable to afford the apartments their parents lived in. There was the empire of the McNallys already taking shape in TriBeCa, a new kind of restaurant that was themed—more a branch of show business as dining, with big spaces, crowded tables, slinky servers, and good food. This was part of a New York tradition, the same one that Joe Baum and Restaurant Associates had started with The Forum of Twelve Caesars and even The Four Seasons. The difference, crucial and typical of the time, was that these new themed places were designed for the young and newly affluent rather than for businessmen—for artists, or dealers anyway, to dine at, rather than for Madmen to lunch at. Opening with the decade in 1980, The Odeon, down on West Broadway, was a restored cafeteria that created the new condition of crowding—where being packed in together with the right people was a good bit of what was being sold. The Odeon, over time, would give birth to Balthazar and Pastis and many beyond.

The Odeon was famous, I discovered, for the drug activity in its bathrooms. It's an embarrassing admission, but in all those years when everyone was trying cocaine, I never tried cocaine. I don't think I was even *offered* cocaine. Or maybe I was, and was so dim that I didn't know it was cocaine I was being offered. Our tipples were older, coffee and champagne and red, still then mostly French, wine. This was partly a backward-looking habit, but it wasn't really from falling into an older crowd. Our best friends preferred champagne, too. It was a sort of counter-programming from the other side of a generation: not smoking weed but drinking Rhône Valley wines instead was a way of rebelling against our own parents' too utilitarian approach to intoxication. We didn't want to turn on and then tune in. We wanted to tune in *before* we turned on. We wanted a system of values reflected in a set of choices—this small bottling, this out-of-the-way peasant vineyard—so that, after the intoxication was over, you had still mastered an idea. It was another way of turning the dissolute into the disciplined—of making art, work.

═══

Closer to my heart, and more tenderly typical of the era's aspirations than The Odeon, were the still-lively and possible smaller restaurants of the neighborhood, still expressing the dream or ambitions of a visionary owner, or a single chef, or, most touchingly, a couple conjoined in the religion of eating. Of all those places, the one that best captured the time and the place was the little restaurant that

David and Karen Waltuck opened in 1979 on Grand Street. In the late seventies and early eighties, some small ground-floor room in a store on an obscure street on the southern fringe of SoHo was transformed—overnight, it seemed—into something new and beckoning. What had been one more dark corner suddenly seemed to glow, day and night, with the spell of the new. You could glimpse pale-apricot walls as you walked by, and read the italic menu penned in Karen's extravagant calligraphy. It became a wonderful pilgrimage to walk over and see what was on the menu that night. For those of us who couldn't afford the extravagance of dining there, it was enough to read the italic menu and imagine.

What Chanterelle represented was several contradictions of the period, all of them fruitful. One was the attempt to reconcile a love of luxury with an aesthetic of austerity, minimalism with maximal pleasure. This was accomplished in many ways, some subtle, some obvious. The signature seafood sausage, all white on white, announced itself as a sausage while withdrawing the bad conscience of the pig from it. It was white, right through. The subtlety was an attempt, unconscious or reverent, to outdo French luxury traditions with American ones, or replace them—no register, no bar, no bottles on display, and no window into the kitchen. Commerce was extinguished even as luxury was celebrated.

Dean & DeLuca persists, in all coffee bars across Manhattan, but I would have to explain to our children that the art gallery apparatus of it—the steel shelving and track lighting and handwritten spice cans of brushed chrome—these once *meant* something, when they were new in the eighties. An earlier generation's ideas of luxury persist even after the originality of what they celebrated has vanished. Fortnum & Mason in London, now quaint and touristy, once represented the sheer bustle, the imperial reach—from Chinese tea to Madagascar chocolate to Turkish delight—of British commerce. In my own doubtless cockeyed view on the next generation, a certain kind of funky functionalism inhabits the cheese stores of Bushwick and Williamsburg—hand-lettered signs and ironic department heads. Their point seems to be that caffeine only fuels irony, and that luxury, being available only in small doses, should be inherently apologetic. Our forms of luxury apologized for nothing. They claimed their space. It was the most beautiful room in New York.

———

I see that I have lost track of my heroine among these dense thickets of art theory and food memories, having shown her, after finding our loft and spotting the molasses, only asleep, and then putting a hand over my glass, and bouncing back a question to Jeff Koons. In truth, Martha was happy and busy. We had room to look at each other—no treat for her, it was for me. After almost three years when we had been on top of each other in every imaginable way, we now had what felt like vast savannas of space between us. I am blind to her in the Blue Room years—scarcely a single isolated memory of her eyes or smile or even clothes remains—because we were so close. I could not always separate my eyes from her face. Now she had rediscovered her best friend from teenage years, the novelist Meg Wolitzer, and they would have rapt, malicious phone conversations about New York people every night, sending Martha into paroxysms of laughter, while still trying to be "kind."

She now had a canvas to work on, and made our place even more beautiful. White was her signature, white with poetry of a slightly whimsical cast. Lights of white fiberglass fabric made by my mother glowed from floor to ceiling; a mosquito net—there of necessity but looking ghostly good—covered the bed; a single midnight-blue sofa and a white rug with two sober hares looking out from it. I still think it was the most beautiful place to live. I tease her today, but it's true that she always spent every penny we both made, and we always lived beautifully. We have always been in debt, and always in the midst of lovely things. Someday the debts will overwhelm us, but the memory of beauty will, I hope, remain.

She graduated from Columbia to work as an assistant film editor on a Balanchine documentary in an editing room of the Maysles brothers. There is a pleasure in watching someone you love doing something well that has nothing to do with your love for her. The husbands of singers marvel at their reaching notes; I once saw a great professor of Shakespeare see his inamorata give a lecture on John Donne, and his eyes popped out of his head. It isn't surprise; it's that when we love someone we really do love them whole, for who they are, and what they *do* seems a bonus, an extra, undeserved.

Her hands had a second life on the deck of the Steenbeck, where she would trim away obnoxious traits—I once spent six hours watching her remove an over-hearty laugh from an interview with a ballerina, while still preserving the continuity of the sequence, with side shots and inserts so subtly introduced that I'm sure no viewer could tell that it was anything but one continuous interview, barely touched by an editorial hand. (I learned, too, that movie critics have as little understanding of movie mechanics as, well, art critics do of drawing: what is praised as exciting film editing is almost always already in the camera when it comes to the editing room, and what are praised as great performances are often crafted by the woman with the Steenbeck. Editors win best-actor prizes for actors, and screenwriters win best-editing awards without getting them.)

I see her now mastering her craft, and I wonder as I write this whether this was not the larger, truer, overriding point of all the smaller SoHo points. Admiration for artisanal craft is one of the few surviving universal emotions—it has survived even the loss of the artisan class. Invariably, when someone did do something well—a dessert beautifully plated, a wicker rocker well re-caned—it was the source of amazement even among those critically committed to believing that craft was an old-fashioned hobby and the well-made object a sentimental diversion for art. Human beings can't help admiring something well made. It occurs to me now that what I made well may have impressed her, too—indeed, may have been the only impression there was to make.

Our excitement over the artisanal may be a displacement of unconscious dismay over what has happened to our art. The critic with a microbrew in his hand is praising, instinctively, something well made, demanding, and delicious that could only have been pro-duced by years of craft, hard-learned and delicately applied. The more artistic our art—the more imaginatively free and indifferent to traditional skills—the more artisanal we ask our objects and products to be. The artistic and the artisanal are always in a strange zero-sum game: when artistic acts of unbounded imagination rise to the top, the artisanal finds a form to return in everyday life; when high art is again artisanal, carefully crafted. The nineteenth-century academic masters, the great ones, Ingres and Delacroix, would eat happily from standardized recipes and took pleasure in the advance of industrial agriculture, or were indifferent to it. They had all the craft they needed right there on the canvas. (Champagne, the great product of the nineteenth-century Bohemia, is a remarkably standardized, high-tech product.) Even the Impressionists at their cafés never asked where the coffee beans had been grown or whether the absinthe was double-distilled.

But as art flourished in France in the late nineteenth century above all, it depended on genius more than talent or skill—so that an amateur like Rousseau could hold his own in naïve poetry against any academician, and a master like Cézanne could depend more on the right placement of every touch than on the dexterity with which the touch was laid down. And so craft rose again in daily life; William Morris and the Arts and Crafts movement blossomed around the same time to re-inspire lost technical skills (bookbinding and luthier work). When genius takes over our walls, craft takes over our tables. When virtuosic skill is onstage, we eat . . . whatever, with whatever kinds of plates and knives are at hand. (One of the last places where sheer skill, pure craft, counted for everything was in rock music, among electric guitarists—and, no surprise, rock musicians lived on fast food and M&M's.) The multi-generational turn toward the artisanal—the raw milk cheese from a single cave, the bourbon from a single barrel—may have always been a reaction against the turn of our art away from craft.

Was this perhaps the real argument? The argument, foundational to the time, which we could not see because, like all foundations, it was holding up our feet and all the furniture? SoHo in the eighties was the place where the final battle between the artistic and the

artisanal began—between commodifying the acts of wild imagination and efforts at reviving lost craft tradition—the artisanal routed
the artistic on the ground, the artistic routed the artisanal at the art
auctions. (At a trivial level, it was reflected in the space between
the handmade, signed artifacts across the street at Zona, an early
Southwestern household-goods store where, for the first time, each
craftsperson was named and credited.)

Yet the art that "won" the decade economically was less the
handmade, hard-wrought, soul-fought expressionist glimpse of the
mysterious moment. It was the stuff that floated. It was the shopped-
for, thought-through, ingeniously fabricated cold acts of the often
cynical imagination. (Of course, being cynical was the point, as
being ironic had been before.) It was Koons and Damien Hirst and
Mike Kelley, and not David and Eric, who set the tone for what was
to come. Yet the appetite for the awkwardly handmade could not
be extinguished. Jeff Koons became the rich man's bullion; micro-
brews became the daily currency. Starting in the SoHo eighties, we
ended up with what we have today: art that no hand has touched
that costs billions, and chocolate bars that boast of their handcrafted
origins and cost ten. In between, life goes on, as it will. We lived
within the doubleness. We live there still.

======

One big question still lingered, unresolved: How did we get into
this amazing village? Why had we been given the golden ticket of a
small but beautiful loft, and with a stabilized rent, too?

It took time to figure that out. We had been in the building for a
year or two before Martha and I went with Petah, who had become a
real friend, for dinner to a good Mexican place down the street. She
ordered a burrito verde and the kind of Mexican beer you drink with
lime, and began reminiscing about her first years as an artist in New
York, back in the late seventies, and about all the people who had
lived in our loft before us. She asked us if we had ever met someone
called Jerome. We said no—who was Jerome? She looked genuinely surprised. Hadn't we taken over the lease from Jerome? We

said no, we hadn't. Oh, she said. Then she leaned way back, took a sip of beer—a subaltern in a Kipling story, about to tell a tale—and at last we heard about Jerome.

———

"This all began in the early 1980s, just after I started working with dead fish," she said. "I used to go into Chinatown, and I would see all these beautiful dead fish—carp, I guess they were, gold and aquamarine, and they seemed sacred or holy, somehow. I was so drawn to them that I would spend all my money buying them, and then I would bring them home. I painted my walls black, so that the fish would show up better, and I hung the fish on the walls, like reliefs. Mrs. Franz used to invite me for tea sometimes—she was so sweet to me—and I could see that she was a little puzzled by something: the smell coming from my place, I guess, though from the outside you weren't getting *half* the smell.

"The bad part started when Lamar, my husband, seemed to be going blind. He woke up one morning with a horrible eye infection, and I persuaded somebody at the NYU clinic to look at him. The doctor asked us if there was anything unusual in our home environment, and I said yes, about two hundred dead fish. The doctor thought I was being fey, and he gave me one of those NYU-clinic smiles—you know, silvery—and then I had to insist that I was serious, there were two hundred dead fish in our home environment.

"The chance that Lamar might lose his sight made me think a little about getting rid of all the fish. But the doctor wasn't sure that my fish were responsible, so I didn't do anything right away. It was just around then that Jerome began practicing with his punk-rock band every night downstairs. Jerome lived in the loft where you live now. He had been there for about five years, I guess, and he was the son of ———." Here she named a man who, back in the early sixties, had been a very successful comedian. "I suppose he had some money from his father. Anyway, he was always searching for himself, going from enthusiasm to enthusiasm, and was living in a pretty squalid, interesting way down in your loft. The thing about Jerome was that he wasn't just one of those people who pass from enthusiasm to enthusiasm. Jerome passed from enthusiasm to enthusiasm and was still enthusiastic about the previous enthusiasm. If you went down to visit him, you would find him smoking opium while doing tai chi, and at the same time he'd be singing Gershwin songs. By the early eighties, his enthusiasm was punk rock. Well, it was really punk-rock revival, but if you lived upstairs from it, it just sounded like punk rock. He would bring a pickup band home every night from one of the clubs, and they would play until four or five in the morning. I used to pound on the floor, to beg them to quiet down. They never did. I guess they thought we were joining in.

"I don't think I would really have gone downstairs to make a fuss, though, if Lamar hadn't hurt his back. This was while he was recovering from the eye infection. One day, he was just walking across the floor and he collapsed. We know now that it was a ruptured disk, but then all we could afford to do was call up the clinic again. They told me not to move him. I think now that they meant don't move him *a lot,* but I thought then that they meant don't move him at all. I left him there, right where he had fallen, like a warrior. So Lamar was lying there on the floor, and the big *thump, thump,* of the bass guitar coming from downstairs bothered him. I went downstairs to talk to Jerome about it, but as soon as he let me in I sort of got distracted, because all over your loft there were these cages full of rats."

Seeing our reaction, she said, "Oh, they weren't from the loft. He had brought them all there. He got them from some laboratory supply or something. Not black rats or anything. White rats. They still made me uneasy, but Jerome was very cheerful about it all, and he told me he had become convinced that it was his vocation to become the . . . I don't know, sort of the rat savior of New York. He explained to me that he wanted to perform a magic ritual of some kind that would summon all the rats of New York into your loft—bring them cascading in from the sewers and the warehouses and the refuse piles. He showed me a book he had been reading— something about Javanese ritual—that had a rat invocation in it.

He had made some kind of altar, and he showed me where he had pounded holes through the baseboards under the front window, so that the rats could all rush in and be welcomed.

"I went back to my loft, and it suddenly occurred to me that Jerome was crazy. It came over me like a hard, simple fact: This is not some sort of interesting Beuysian performance. Jerome is crazy. So I went down and told our landlady, Mrs. Franz, and she let herself into his place while Jerome was out at the club. She saw the whole scene—the rats in cages, the holes in the baseboards, the altar—and somehow she got an emergency eviction order, or whatever they call it, and stuck it on his door.

"About four-thirty that morning, I heard a sound that wasn't so much a scamper as a kind of low *whoosh* with gravel in it, like water breaking on pebbles. At first I thought it was the radiators, but then I remembered that it was the middle of July. It was a terribly hot night, and I didn't have anything on, but I went to the back door and opened it, and there, pouring up the stairs in this white wave, were all Jerome's rats, coming to eat my fish. Apparently, Jerome got home at about four—back from CBGB, or wherever—and he saw the eviction notice, and I guess he thought, Well, okay, they want me out, they want my stuff out.

"The first thing I did was to slam the door, and then I ran to the closet and put on a pair of stiletto heels that I hadn't worn since high school back home. My husband couldn't get up, of course, and a lot of the fish were on the floor. I realized that the rats must be attracted to the smell. I didn't know what to do. I started throwing dead fish out the window. One at a time at first, and then more and more. I've often wondered what everyone down below must have thought, being rained on by all those beautiful fish.

"Well, of course, all the commotion woke up Mrs. Franz, and she came out in her nightgown and saw those white rats flooding out of your loft and racing up the stairs. Naturally, she thought of me, and she ran up the front stairs and let herself into my apartment. She was sort of thrown back by the smell, as if she'd been punched, but she recovered and came on in, and saw me standing nude in red stiletto heels, over Richard's body, throwing carp out of the window onto the street.

"It took almost a week before things were back to normal—before all the rats were trapped and everything. I decided that I really had to find some other material to work with than dead fish, so I took the fish that were left and went uptown on the subway and put them in the trees in Central Park. They looked very beautiful there, too. The next week, I started working with hay. And a week later, when I bumped into Mrs. Franz, she said she was going to rent the loft to the most normal, meekest married couple she could find. And a week later you two moved into Jerome's loft."

Now we knew that, too.

———

A few months ago, I went back to see the Judd house—the one on Mercer and Spring that I always passed by on Saturday mornings on my way into SoHo. Now it is the "Judd House," kept up by a foundation as a sort of domestic museum of the period, with a small portion of Donald Judd's scintillating collection of objects—his own and the other Minimalists'—kept within a solemnly enshrined and maintained home, left just as it was in 1984, with parental beds and kids' puppet theaters and kitchen counters.

Stunningly beautiful—even the windows have been restored to give them nineteenth century irregularity and waterfall shimmer—it was a reminder of the absurd good fortune artists had, falling into these inherently beautiful spaces: there are still the high ceilings and the broad windows and the unbroken views of SoHo, looking out onto decorative cornices, so unlike the normal hedged-in quality of Manhattan streets. What was stunning to us, though, was that everything within it, though warily watched by the twenty-something guide to be sure that nothing was touched or even microscopically dislodged from its place, were simply the things that had been unthinkingly part of a normal SoHo household in 1984. By the sink there were Dean & DeLuca copper pots, of the same kind that we had owned, and there were Wüsthof knives from Broadway

Panhandler, and almost round off-white plates from Ad Hoc House-wares, and empty but still piously conserved bottles of wine from SoHo Wine, where you stepped past a large, sleepy dog.

All of them were now locked and held, solemnly and in proper place, as though domestic artifacts from dynastic Egypt. There was a mattress on the floor, on a floating platform—albeit one only three inches or so from the floor. I couldn't help think of how every loft building of the period was infested with mice and rats, and how they must have dealt with it. (Martha noticed a box with knives right by the edge; but it was Lucas Samaras art object. Maybe it played a double role.)

The line between the improvised and the institutional is so rapidly breached in New York! All the things that were just part of the commonplace civilization of 1980 were now part of a tightly conserved archival past. What was just the way life was thirty years ago had become . . . . The Way Life Was, to be archived forever, with that young guide tumidly instructed in the dogma of the house, watching warily lest a visitor pick up one of the Wüsthof knives, touch a paperbound copy of *The Shape of Time* microscopically dislodge a pot.

I noticed at last, on a low shelf, in a nook, a Russian rabbit-fur hat, of exactly the kind that they sold around the corner on Prince near Elizabeth at a little import bazaar, and which everyone wore in the winter of 1985—even John Gotti's thugs wore them, I suddenly remembered, when they shot Paul Castellano outside of Sparks Steak House that winter, wearing the hats above white trench coats to confuse witnesses. (Gotti's clubhouse, the Ravenite, had been only a couple of blocks farther east. They must have bought them at the same little store.) We produce a constellation of objects made from haphazard decisions—we buy this knife, this hat, this pot— and before we know it, we turn back and see ourselves as part of a fixed era in time.

The Biblical story has it wrong: it wasn't Lot's wife who, turning back to look longingly at her home, turned into a column of salt; it was the city that turned to salt when she turned back to look at it.

Look back at SoHo or Sodom and what you see is a frozen fossil of what was. We had hoped the past would stay labile in memory at least, that you would still be able to go back and see it bouncing. But it doesn't. Facing front, looking back—it's all hard, whichever way you look.

9

————————————
————————————

Writing

Though I spent my nights in SoHo writing about art, I spent my days in midtown thinking about words. After two years at *GQ,* I had been hired, in a fit of generosity on the part of its editor-in-chief, to work at a publishing house, a good one—the very same one, in fact, that has its name on the spine of this book. (I was happy at *GQ* and anyway still working on my Ph.D., so I might never have left, even for so tempting an offer, had my good father not come to town and told me that I was crazy not to take it. The insecurity I was underestimating, he pointed out, in *this* case was my own. I was ready for a bigger stage than cuffs and moisturizers.)

Oddly, or maybe not so oddly, I was as ill-suited to the fine-detail work of book publishing as I was good at the fine-detail work of fashion journalism. But, then, fashion copy is instant and ironic; it needs only the brisk cooperation of a handful of conspirators to appear. Books are serious, sincere. Someone's life is at stake each time a book is published. And books are big. They take time and the intersection of many schedules, whereas I can barely keep track of my own.

I *was* good at all the smaller writerly tasks—writing flap copy and catalogue copy for the sales force—that publishing demanded.

Here I found that the trick was to reach not for the note of alliterative insider's swagger that had helped "sell" at the fashion magazine. Instead, one learned to cultivate a note of high sentience, of plangent urgency, that would suggest to merchants and salesmen, not to mention readers, that *this* book, despite the tedium of its subject and its author's long history of disappointing reviews and unearned advances, was not just a good book, but an essential book, one of the books that would be talked of and argued over when it, at last, appeared. You achieved this effect with a small roster of imperative-sounding adjectives: "urgent," "taut," "intense," "unforgettable," "delightful," "galvanizing," "important." (Good writing is done with verbs and nouns; "copy"—advertising, of whatever kind— with adjectives alone.)

I was lucky to spend time in publishing, too, because there was a small boom in books in the eighties. Not perhaps for the first time, but certainly for the first time with so much, well, oomph, young writers with a first novel or a book of short stories enjoyed a shower of celebrity, even glamour. It was almost the last moment when writers not specially blessed by fortune or Pulitzer Prizes could still somewhat realistically hope for upward mobility. Since then, writing has retreated into the colleges and universities, and become a kind of perpetual self-help program, rooted in weekly "workshops" and summer seminars. (When I have "taught" them, my primitive bleats about form and structure and sentence shapes were drowned out by the intelligent and unconditional support each student gave to all the others—the point of taking a writing class, I had to learn, is *to be in the writing class,* to be lifted up by—or to—the common identity.)

Writing for a little money and some fame was not a new thing, of course. One of the editors I got to know best in that building was the legendary Joe Fox of Random House, who would take me out to dinner (he had his eye on a book about American art, my very own *Anatomy of Art,* eventually signed up, though still undelivered as of this writing). Over martinis (!) and a bottle of red wine and a porterhouse (!) he would—and here's a chance to use that odd verb properly—regale me with stories of writers from the fifties, some of them "his." Ellison and Capote and Salinger and Baldwin . . . The heft of what they did was obvious to the world, and, as he believed, not so much against the evidence as alongside it, proof that that world continued on. An "important" book on a significant subject was destined not just to sell but to end up on the cover of *Time* magazine, to become the subject of heated dinner table conversation, to matter, to *count*.

That no good writer would ever again appear on the cover of *Time*, that "counting" now counted in a different way—that *everything* was a niche, and that what was not "niche" was a parade of oafish grotesques, a parade one could parody or join or both but never now overcome with some other, better parade—was the secret shared knowledge of our generation. Fame came in smaller bits, and money in smaller chunks—and yet it did come. This was so even though a "boom" in writing could hardly be heard over the thermonuclear explosions of Wall Street, or even the continual snap and crackle of the art world. Art world paydays made book world paydays look like no paydays at all. Visual artists hunted for golden tickets, and when they got one, they were set. Good pictures in the art market—a market that has never stopped booming in all the years since—buy estates in the Hamptons. Even large royalties in the literary world (the handful—no, fingerful—of truly "commercial" writers aside) bought small apartments in the upper reaches of West End Avenue, and then in Park Slope—no small or bad thing, but not the same thing.

Yet, for someone interested, as I was, in continually making little comparative anthropologies of things, it was fascinating to experience firsthand the difference between the booms in the literary world and art world. Each month, it seemed, a new writer—a David Leavitt or a Meg Wolitzer or a Mona Simpson or a Lorrie Moore—emerged from the fiction programs or creative-writing classes with a collection of short stories or a first novel and became celebrated, talked of, the "flavor of the month," occasionally even the bouquet of the season. Resentful and envious observers—i.e., all older writers—exaggerated both the money and the celebrity won. Still, the difference between the lives and livelihoods of the Delmore Schwartz–Randall Jarrell generation, which Eileen Simpson writes about so movingly in her memoir *Poets in Their Youth*—with the writers scuffling from one part-time job to another, a sinecure at a liberal-arts college teaching freshman composition being the most golden of tickets they ever got—and our own was plain.

There was still no "real money" in writing, but there was a kind of play money, Monopoly money, in it, different from the true no-money-at-all of earlier times. In retrospect, of course, this was only the briefest of pauses on publishing's way to the bottom—like the moment when the *Titanic*, having sheared in two and seen its bow entirely sunk in the ocean, saw its remaining, rear half rise and rock steady in the water, giving a brief illusion of horizontal stability before it, too, filled with sea water and headed for the bottom. There was only one way, and direction, the boat, or serious writing, was heading. But for the passengers on board, that momentary pause must have seemed, if very briefly, hopeful.

What was fascinating about the literary world in the eighties, as against the art world, was that the literary world ran on the myth of no masks, whereas the art world ran, at the same time, on a belief in ever more complicated masquerades. In the art world, the young painters and collagists and video makers I was coming to know all believed as a matter of uncritical faith that everything you made had to pass through the prism of another manner. It could be the borrowed manner of commercial art, as in Barbara Kruger's parodies of advertising, or that of greeting-card platitudes, as in the glowing signs of Jenny Holzer. One might put on a big suit to parody the bigly besuited, as David Byrne did, trusting the audience to know the difference between the mannered and the meta-. But everyone in the art world accepted masks as naturally as mummers do. Everything still worked on Jasper Johns's simple, telling formula: take something, do something to it, then do something else to it. The artists I knew were always doing things to things done to—and the job of the art critic was therefore to undo them, unravel the tangled skein to show the impulse inside. Sometimes this could be enlightening, as when Bob Hughes took apart the famous Rauschenberg combine, a stuffed goat skewering a real tire, to show its many sources and erotic resonances. At other times it could be merely comical. It became the set piece of that moment for an artist to take some utterly self-evident claim—that homelessness was wrong, say—and then to encode it so obliquely that only an art critic could decrypt it. The "work" came to consist of the obvious statement, the encryption, and then the decoding, all in one neat and often expensive package.

But the literary world still believed in naïveté. The young short-story writers who clustered around the charismatic Gordon Lish were full of faith that you could make art just by being honest. Even doing something to your truth was, well, dubious. Authenticity, direct speech, unmediated urgency, emotional candor—that was still the goal. Lish taught them to fear the mannered words of mere social presentation—"restaurant," "haircut," "commuter train" were all, it was rumored, verboten. (I got to know him well, mostly as a genial relater of old Jewish jokes, good ones, about Mr. and Mrs. Shmuelovitz, such as the one in which, after interrogating Mr. Shmuelovitz to the point of revealing that he has killed his wife, the ladies by the pool at the Fontainebleau have one final question, "So: you're single?") Since I loved comedy of manners as much as, if not more than, the articulation of raw emotion, the eliminations seemed sad to me.

The direct manner produced countless stories written in the present tense (of the "Joan is driving the station wagon to the strip mall" kind—the present suggesting instant presence). It was in its way a style more connected to the method acting of the forties and fifties than to the B-movies that often featured that acting, those same B-movies the painters so loved. Something of pure voice and no manner was the heart of what the time wanted from writing. Raymond Carver's artless-seeming—though obviously very artful via Lish—stories were a model, and so were Alice Munro's plain-

Jane (but actually Jane Austen made plainer in Ontario)—seeming stories.

Martha had been utterly right about that—about her extreme and prescient admiration for Alice Munro, I mean, offered on our first date in Montreal. Martha had become a bemused, polite spectator of the art world that we lived within—worried, I always sensed, that the entire thing, with its absurd jargon and opaque objects, was an elaborate Sky Masterson con being played on her husband, a face card squirting cider every day directly into his ecstatic ear. But she loved the company of women writers and novelists. It was my own involvement with the young writers that had allowed her, on a rainy, memorable Friday, to re-meet Meg Wolitzer. Meg was then a bright light of that literary circle, and now, two young women in their twenties, they reunited, became enraptured with each other all over again—fifteen forever, a rapture that has not, as yet, lifted. I would come home from the office—the very words had a thrilling ring, "I am coming home from the office!"—and find Martha plopped on the Eames sofa that she had retrieved in ruins from someone's studio and had restored, her pretty legs tucked beneath her, helpless with laughter at some parody Meg was doing at the other end of the line.

It was instructive to witness the *depth* of women's friendships, how they can exist outside time or worry and remain purely uncompetitive, how they exist outside common pursuits or common "interests," exist purely and for their own sake.

But she was finding a life, without knowing it entirely, as a support for other people—me chiefly, but others, too—and had I been more alert I would have been more concerned about her self-abnegation, her losing herself in other people's cares and quarrels and pages.

═══

I played a tiny role in this small writers' boom, writing the flap copy for the younger writers, liking the shoptalk and the small duties of editorial work, different from those of fashion copy or even art criticism. There was a *magic* in the commodification of literature, making it a much happier event than the commodification of art, in large part because you were just *hoping* it would become an object for sale. Whereas in the art world the worry was that the object would be degraded by reproduction, the idea of limitless reproduction was, in publishing, the whole improbable fantasy. The terrible fate of art imagined in Walter Benjamin's seminal essay on "The Work of Art in the Age of Mechanical Reproduction"—the art object robbed of its aura and turned into countless simulacra of itself—was exactly what you *wanted* to have happen to a book.

There was a lot more wishful thinking, dreaming, and hoping injected into the process in the midtown office than there was in the SoHo village. Once one had made it to a gallery wall in SoHo, the picture would certainly sell to *somebody*. It would become an object for sale and covetousness if anyone saw it at all. In the book world, the flap copy and the catalogue copy, the copies sent out to reviewers and for blurbs, all of it managed to put an overlay of optimism on what was a process statistically almost certain to disappoint all around. No one quite *covets* a book the way she covets a picture. If a book got launched as a commodity, it was a wonder. If a picture didn't in those days, it was a mystery; you changed dealers. If the book failed, you just hoped someone would let you publish another.

I loved editing, though I was never really any good at it—too absorbed in my own sentences to really superintend other people's with the care they deserved. The really great editors are monastics at heart. They love the self-abnegation that comes with editing, and though they may write from time to time, they prefer the sanctified celibacy of not writing. And, of course, they derive power from their abstention: by not writing while knowing all about writing, they achieve exactly the same power that the great monks do. They are worldly but not of this world. Monks bake bread and make cheese, and they savor the smells, but, finally, they are there to serve food, not eat it.

I had, and have, none of those self-abnegating gifts. But editing is also a form of caregiving, particularly when one's "patients" are older, as many of mine were; for me it was a kind of accelerated way of growing up. I became the editor to such hugely distinguished older writers as Wilfrid Sheed, the great critic and fine satiric novelist, and later Whitney Balliett, the matchless poet-chronicler of American music, and became aware that, despite the differences in our age and stature—and for all that I could scarcely offer a useful word about their finished sentences, being still so narrowly in pursuit of my own—I was helpful simply by wearing an editorial mask, as absurdly as one might wear a Groucho mustache and glasses. If you are the object of transference from a seventy-year-old master, you assume the manners of an older man. Since assuming manners is pretty much the only way there is to learn them, it works out well. I was a grown-up by virtue of being an editor, because, important corollary, all writers are children.

As with most roles, playing it becomes being it. Having to be strong for them made me stronger than I was. The bond of editor and writer is comic but intense in a way that no bond of artist and critic, much less artist and dealer, can be. What all psychoanalysts seek—that "transference" whereby the patient ascribes to the therapist limitless stores of wisdom, parental care, and far-seeing attention—editors earn with indecent ease from anxious writers.

It was a reminder of what the art world had already taught me, if only I had paid attention and enlarged its lessons: everything that looks like a formal transaction in the arts is really a psychological one. People make pictures, not "periods." Editors only secondarily shape sentences or even structure books; they more often serve as surrogate fathers, reassuring their oddly adopted and often elderly foundlings that they can climb the jungle gym all the way to the top. Even the most famous interventions, like Gordon's on Raymond Carver's stories, where whole pages got excised or remade, and endings reimagined, are possible not because the rewrite looks better to the writer—"No *good* writer ever really likes being edited at all" was the emphatic aphorism of one of the best—but because the transference has taken place so completely that the writer feels naked without the paternal approval that the interference suggests.

If he won't change my work, he must not care, the writer thinks. The editing may benefit the work—taking clotted and overworked material and simplifying it so that, as Shakespeare didn't say, slow, not-so-bright things come to clarity—but the transaction is moved more by the writer's primal scene than his ambitions for the finished "product."

———

Something else I saw then: writers' lives were not tutelary in the way that artists' lives so often were. Richard Serra could be an ornery hero, Jeff Koons a strange local saint. Writers lacked that kind of vividness. Lonelier and sadder for the most part, they endured long stretches of absolute isolation, not the isolation of the painter's studio, which is almost always intensely social at either end, with fellow students at the beginning and then, later on, assistants. (Not to mention the ever-comforting presence of materials, beautiful in themselves, that must be bought and stretched and lined and sharpened.)

Writers' work really is solitary, and there is no *"donné"* to it. A painter starts with four marks, the four sides of her canvas, and makes a fifth. The writer starts with nothing—staring out into the abyss of language, where any sentence might be made, any word order attempted, however ugly—and must find the one right string of words there, with the additional torture that words are never in themselves beautiful, as the marks may be, even if sometimes strings of sounds may become so. As a consequence, writers live alone even when they live in company, turning sentences over and around in their heads, as artists can't turn images. Artists *work* their images, of course, and rush back to the studio to do more. But the image still exists outside the head of the artist.

The visual arts, for all their occult obliquity, are *real.* Half the effect of an art object is in its pure thingness. It's big, dark, polished, and dense; it's small and shiny and weird. The object exists here, and now, even when it attempts to represent some scene or place. Writing, no matter how vivid or accurate, is reflective. It has no material life outside the materials it embraces. Brushstrokes are both the things they indicate and the thing they are. Words are just what they mean; reduced to mere sound, they become nonsense. We talk about the beautiful sounds of certain words or phrases—"summer afternoon" or "Christmas music"—but in truth robbed of their reference they are just more mumbling in the mouth.

In this simple sense the writer's sentences have no existence at all, their place on the page being a mere illusory resting place before they rush from the head of the writer into that of a reader—if any readers are out there. The writer's work really doesn't exist outside of the head of the reader, and readers are rarely present in the writer's immediate world. We shout out sentences to spouses, and the spouses invariably pretend to listen, but, robbed of their context, the sentences as we shout them make little sense. Sentences are like the cat in those quantum diagrams, existing only when they are at last perceived. Before then, they just jump around inside the writer's head. In there, they can't be abandoned or even put down for a minute, like a colicky baby. (Perhaps this is why writers like writing about child rearing: they already know what it is like to have a charge that never really rests and occasionally smiles.) The painter's "lonely" is merely pensive; the writer's lonely is truly alone.

——

I had begun to find my sentence shapes. While the possibilities of songwriting seemed to have snapped shut—we still hadn't heard back from Art Garfunkel; still haven't, actually, Art—my ambitions had focused more narrowly on writing, and write every day is what I now did, or tried to, even as I boosted other writers' fortunes. I was torn between two manners: the argumentative, thesis-driven one of the art critic, full of dubious saws and hypermodern instances, and the simpler, almost faux-naïf one that I admired in the work of my heroes, Thurber and White. By day I would thunder about simulacra and the semiotics of the sign; by night I would sing, or try to, the modest beauties of the MoMA garden in the snow at dusk.

I wasn't ready yet to bring the two together. My own natural ambit, I discovered eventually, was somewhere where the two manners met, in a kind of aphoristic prose, filled with neat epigrams, placed on the page like shiny ribbons on a present—funny in parts and touching in others, with a few passionate political views trailing along behind. That was the way I ought to have written all along. But I didn't. The voice we search for is the voice we have, but cannot hear for all those other voices in our heads.

I agreed with the Lish doctrine as to voice being everything; disagreed inasmuch as it seemed to me that every voice is choral and polyphonic, in its true articulation. If you're speaking from the heart without significant redaction from the head, you're not talking whole. And the head includes restaurants and haircuts as much as sex and blood. Bits of experience ripped out like gobbets of flesh intrigue me, but bits of experience where the flesh comes off to reveal the clothing beneath intrigue me more. The lure of the plain fact, the one-beat phrase, the same note struck first and then struck twice and then struck for the third time—it *is* a good way to write. But just as the sounds of notes in music are made from the overtones, the parts the ears fill in, the sound of a writer's voice is made from the overlying ironies and unexpected turns and curlicues for their own sake that make for beautiful sentences. Sentence shapes contain those tones, and are what a writer needs for disguise just as much— and in much the same way—as the stripper in *Gypsy* is taught she needs a gimmick and a stage name. The writer's sentences allow for the appearance of naïveté, as the stripper's gimmick—the Bo Peep outfit, the neon girdle—allows for the illusion of nudity. Both are designed to give the appearance of complete candor to what is in fact an act of elaborate guile.

Yet, beyond the playacting of "editing," I knew that there were secrets about writing that transcended the comedy of transference and the little duties of "copy writing." I was at that time a man in search of secrets. I believed in secrets—a secret to coaching hockey, to stealing bases, to making spaghetti sauce, to writing. That the only secret to any of them is the same dumb process of breaking it down into small steps and building it back up hadn't been given to me to know.

Secrets to find and hear—and now I need to flash forward, as in an *X-Men* sequel, where the chronology gets kicked around but the sequences remain completely unchanged in style, to when I started, just a year or so later, to write and edit at *The New Yorker*. For six years, I had continued to slip those pieces under the door, and they kept coming back to me. Finally, thanks to a piece I'd written on baseball and art history and its sudden wary embrace by Charles McGrath and Roger Angell, and then, once again, thanks to the generous forbearance of Robert Gottlieb, I was let inside, to edit a little and to write "Talk of the Town" a lot.

It was, for a young writer, like opening the windows on the most extraordinary and eccentric Advent calendar that had ever been created. You would open a door and there would be Brendan Gill—or Whitney Balliett—or, getting closer to Christmas, Roger Angell. (It was Angell who came upon me with my fast friend the writer Alec Wilkinson around that time, experimentally trying on a jacket Martha had chosen for me that Alec thought of imitating—we had decided, rather pathetically, to become Well-Dressed Men—and who then gave us what is technically called a withering glance. "Writers around this office used to *drink*," he said sternly, and shut the door.)

There was one door on the Advent calendar that was closed, though urgent sounds of typing clattered from inside. I asked Alec whose door this was, and he replied, almost reverently, "That's Mr. Mitchell's office."

It's easy to know Joseph Mitchell's work now. He has become an American classic—even played in the movie adaptation of his masterpiece "Joe Gould's Secret" by Stanley Tucci, and is richly back in print for good after decades missing. But at the time there was something utterly mysterious about him. He was a secret within the Advent calendar of the magazine. His was the door that didn't open even as Christmas came closer.

Alec, I knew, had modeled his own elegant and taciturn style in part on Mitchell's, a manner even more impressive to a naturally garrulous stylist like me. Alec had introduced me to Mitchell's precise, cumulative, oddly mysterious writing—oddly because the enigmas were made with minimal means. There was only an accumulation of precise descriptive sentences and unbroken direct quotation to achieve the effect. I read "McSorley's Wonderful Saloon" and "My Ears Are Bent" and "Joe Gould's Secret," the then unknown but now famous story of how a Village character, famously at work on a huge, encyclopedic "oral history of our time," turned out, upon his death, to have been writing, over and over with manic obsessiveness, the same sad story of his mother's death. It seemed like a warning to all writers, and a truth about writing, too: no matter how large or "objective" the canvas we attack, our marks are always personal, and usually the same, again and again.

One day I bumped into a distinguished elderly gent—a very distinguished-looking elderly gent. I realized with a start that it was Mitchell. After a few seconds of introduction, he looked at me and, turning his head, beneath an old-fashioned man's hat, asked a question, intently. "Do you like to read the *Russians?*" he demanded. He had a beautiful soft North Carolina drawl, all the sentences leaping up at their ends, like dolphins.

"Yes, of course! I like to read the Russians," I said. It was true, though not as true as the way I said it suggested it was true.

"Do you like to read that *Gogol?*" he asked, pronouncing Gogol so quickly, almost as a variant of "go-go," as in the style of sixties dancers, that for a moment I wasn't certain what he meant, but then the context supplied the answer.

"*Love* Gogol!" I said enthusiastically. In truth, I hadn't thought much about Gogol since I had lost my pants and become one of his characters. My tastes since had run to more optimistic and romantic French and American writers.

"Do you read that . . . Tur*genev?*" he said even more enthusiastically. We might have been exchanging the names of old families from Carolina we were both related to.

"*Love* Turgenev!" I said, and thought for a microsecond—the egocentrism of young writers at work—that there might be a reprimand looming here. My own published stuff, such as it was, ran more toward melodramatic effects than to the straight descriptive integrity of Turgenev. (Of course there wasn't; I'm sure he had no more awareness of what I'd written than I do now of the newest twenty-something I share space with. But a young writer who's been paid any attention at all quickly becomes paranoid about . . . any attention at all.) He was, I feared, urging me to simplify my work. He wasn't, of course. He had no idea my writing was too fancy and in need of simplification. But reading Turgenev is a good plan for anyone, and so I did.

A few days later, I went up and knocked on his door in order, God help me, to praise Turgenev. We had now, after all, Turgenev in common. And then I had the courage—of a kind I hadn't called on since asking Martha out on a date to hear *Die Winterreise*—to ask him out to lunch. And to my surprise he said yes, and suggested that we go to the Saloon of the Oyster Bar in Grand Central. It was a place I knew and loved already, and had the right aura of old New York and the right hums of the living city.

I had a chance to observe him as we walked the few blocks from office to station. He was naturally elegant, in a startling, old-fashioned way. Alec once said that Mitchell was the most stylish man he had ever known, which was funny, because Mitchell looked as if he hadn't bought new clothes since around 1941. But it was true. He had the natural elegance of the self-possessed, the true style of someone who has a completely integrated self projecting forward in a completely natural way, even if the costume is eccentric. It's the kind of elegance Roman Catholic priests have, the kind of elegance the Hasidim have, the kind of elegance the Queen's Guard have— people who are completely as they present themselves, even if the way they present themselves might seem mannered or calculated in a more self-conscious man. A woolen vest, an old-fashioned overcoat, always a plaid necktie, and a crushed felt forties kind of hat. (I recall asking myself what the name of that kind of hat was—and realized that my hat vocabulary was hopelessly impoverished. A Stetson? A Borsalino? A *derby?*)

We walked the four blocks to Grand Central and I saw the city for the first time through his eyes. He was always looking upward. Walking along the avenue (he said later), if you looked up at the second-story windows, you saw the real city. If you took your eyes away from the pavement you saw ballet classes, detective agencies, tailors—you had a wholly different sense of what New York is.

I had gone on many pilgrimages, but more than anything I wanted to understand the secret of his work—how he and the gen- eration of writers, of whom he and Phil Hamburger were the last representatives, had pulled themselves together. You can't ask a priest or a mystic the secret of what he does. That was the lesson of "Joe Gould's Secret." The secret that people tell you isn't the secret they're keeping. But I tried to paw at his secret anyway over the red- checked tablecloths of the saloon and the oysters, to pry the secret out, like opening an oyster.

"Boy, I love Joe Liebling's writing," I said. "How did he go about—what were his days like?"

Mr. Mitchell looked at me, "Mhhm," he answered, noncommit- tally. "Well. He often would be willing to eat a bad clam." Then he was silent. Okay: dubious shellfish might have something to do with literary greatness. A month or so later, we would make the same slow, stately walk from the offices to the Oyster Bar, and I would try to lever out the secret again. He didn't have any desire to share it. He would simply listen and say, "I know! I know!," as though the recognition of the question were the same as the answer. (His other secret, why he hadn't published anything in so long, I was wise enough to know was unaskable.)

I learned, though. I realized that, above all, he was, as a writer, a *listener.* He listened beautifully—head cocked and, with that slow, sympathetic murmur of "I know! I know!," always on call. It did make me, by contagion, a better writer. Writing "Talk of the Town," I learned to listen, to understand—what my experi- ence with the Maxies of the world should have already taught me, if I had paid attention—that everyone has his story, and everyone wants to tell it, if he feels safe in the presence of the listener. The most secretive people in the world are not really secretive. They would pour their hearts out, if they could be sure that the listener would never make a mock of them. It was, in itself, a good lesson, and I found myself, notebook poised, for five years listening to self-made eccentrics—table-hockey champions, and women who wrote "slash" fan fiction, a new thing then, and slack-rope walkers, and even a man who taught thirteenth-century fresco technique. Stories poured out from people, and you took them down, and that, to a decent extent, was what writing was, *all* writing was, its secret: listening to what people said, making lists of what they made and owned, taking notes and distilling the results into an aromatic essence. So I learned *that* secret just from being across the saloon bar from him. You just go places and you listen to people. That is the secret of writing, or a reasonable part of it.

But one day at lunch I pressed him more about the secret.

"I so love what you write, and what Liebling wrote and Thurber and White and Gibbs—what was it that all you guys shared? What was it you had in common?"

And he looked at me and he said, "Well, none of 'em could spell."

Okay, I thought. And he looked round almost guiltily, as though the ghost of one of his old colleagues might be looking on, tasting an oyster pan roast. "And none of them really had any sense of *grammar* at all." *There* was a myth he was glad to dispel.

Then he looked off into the distance.

"But each one . . . each one had . . . had a kind of wild exactitude of his own," he concluded.

And I thought, There it is! That's the secret! And I wrote the words down on a card, "A Wild Exactitude," and kept it over my desk. I do still. It seemed to summarize for me everything that I valued in the tradition. You wanted to catalogue, to inventory, to love the word for its facticity and record as much of it as you could. To *listen*! But that would only produce a parody of that high style unless you had some other element that was extravagant, that was willed—that was wild, that was even a little bit crazy. Flat descriptive sentences describing an absurdly vivid character, simple inventories of impossible objects—that was the end! Good stories were strange stories told straight. Unless you had an appetite for the exact, precise thing, and an equally large flair for the strange and the eccentric subject—balancing those things in every paragraph you wrote and even, if you could, in every sentence—you would never be much of a writer about anything. And it seemed to me that he had given me the secret, and it's a secret that's stayed with me: A wild exactitude! I still can't imagine a better title for a book about good writing.

———

But there was another, sadder secret buried in that secret, which I was still too young to understand. And that was a secret about silences. Why had he had been silent for so long? I was too shy, or too sensitive, to ask him directly, but at one of the last of those lunches he raised it himself.

"People wonder why I haven't published in so long," he said abruptly when the check came. "But I'll tell you why." His gaze leveled. "My sentences didn't run out," he said as he smiled, crookedly. "They ran away."

He didn't add anything more, but I knew at once what he meant, or thought I did. Mitchell didn't have anything new to be wild and exact *about*. It wasn't just his sentences that had run away; his subjects had. He had experienced his subjects, as writers will, as sentences. The New York he had so matchlessly evoked was not the New York he sat within now. The flat declarative descriptions got their energy—their wildness—not from his exactitude alone. They got it from shared knowledge of the world he described. Making sentences match scenes looks easy. But it is hard. Rubbing one against another is the friction that makes them wild. The readers do much of the work. So his silence wasn't a mystery. It was a rational response to his situation. Subjects just ran out, taking your sentences with them, and if you weren't watching, yours might, too. Subjects pass like the names of hats.

When you're a young writer you think that style and energy will get you through. If you have an engaging—a vivacious!—style, and enough energy, then you can accomplish anything. Publish and publish, make yourself felt, and your voice heard. But as you get older, you discover that energy and style don't make writing. No, writing is made by their opposite, sentences and circumstances. Painters depend on their materials more than they admit, but writers depend on their circumstances more than they know. Writing involves a lot of bumping into people. It's essential to be exact, but to be wild is hard, because we can only become wild about common objects. The objects worth being wild about decrease with time, or at least our ability to detect them decreases.

Joe Fox explained something similar to me over dinner, insisting that Truman Capote had finished his lost book, the novel *Answered Prayers*—and then destroyed it, leaving readers with only those chapters that had already been excerpted in magazines. "He had lost his talent, which was always indeterminate," he said. "But he never lost his taste. And his taste told him that his book was terrible. It was the only part of his talent that survived." Writers run out of subjects, being subject-bound, and their talents are time-bound.

Writers aren't silenced. Writing *is* silence, unless it is turned to speech in another head. We catch our subjects on the run. Sometimes they run toward you. Sometimes they run away. Painters are their marks and their time, which they can't explain; writers are their sentences and their circumstances, which they can't escape.

10

Sleeping and Talking

One night, sometime in the late eighties, at around eleven o'clock on a Friday, I looked over at the bed in our loft and saw that Martha was sound asleep. Now, one of the things about Martha—I think it's one of the reasons we've been able to cohabit so happily for so long—is that she can sleep through anything. She is, as I've said, a champion sleeper, one of those people who fall asleep at nine at night and wake up at eleven the next morning and have breakfast and then take a nap. She loves to sleep—actively enjoys it, finds sinking inside slumber a pleasure somehow deeply sensual. Her sleepiness coincides with her huge consumption of hyper-strong coffee, a combination that puzzled me until, years later, we went off to her ancestral home in Iceland and discovered that everyone there drinks coffee all day and sleeps as much as they can or want to. There must be a recessive gene for poor blood circulation splashing around in the tiny Icelandic gene pool, as they self-medicate with caffeine and then succumb to their chromosomes with instant unconsciousness.

I was awake in part because I am always awake—a world-class insomniac, I wait hours for sleep to begin its normally minimal drugging—and also because I had promised her to stay awake to watch for mice. Essentially, what we were doing, by leaving the Blue Room for this bigger room, was leaving insect life for rodent life. The loft in SoHo was overrun with mice. You would see them by the baseboards on dark nights, even hear them creepily scuttling in the kitchen in the dark. But in the same Canadian way in which we had thought a piece of plywood would protect us from the roaches, we believed that the mice could simply be warned off from invading our space. We used to stamp our feet upon entering the loft and shout, "Mice, go away!"—and we believed that they therefore would, we were confident that they would *listen*. But Martha could still fall asleep securely only if I promised to stay up and watch for the mice as long as I could. Why she could not go to sleep without a mouse-watchman—though she could stay asleep while I slept, too, when the mice presumably were free to express themselves as they chose—was mysterious, in the way of the mysteries of marriage.

It was just around that time that I had started to find work talking to people at night for money. I was beginning to write art criticism—though I had been hired to write "Talk of the Town" stories at the magazine, I had been persuaded to write art criticism, too. (No one will believe this, but I really didn't want to do it: escaping from art criticism was the whole point of having a job writing "Talk" pieces.) That small notoriety was beginning to get me gigs as a speaker—small-time gigs, triple-A gigs, a lecture at the Drawing Center around the corner, or across the street at the Knitting Factory. Not as grand as MoMA, but at least I was no longer working the lunch shift. Occasionally, I'd even get an out-of-town engagement to lecture at one of the smaller museums, in Richmond or Salem or Baltimore.

I enjoyed it. I liked speaking, I liked being listened to. I liked making sense. I probably liked being listened to more than I liked making sense. But it wasn't a time for sense. I tried the many approaches there are to public speaking—with a set text to read, a set text memorized, notes on paper, or notes on three-by-five cards, or notes on yellow legal tablets, alongside a list of slides, as we called them then.

It took me years to learn the simple speaker's truth that the best way to deliver a talk is . . . by talking. You study your subject, get a sense of what you want to say in the order in which you want to say it, and then you stand up and say it. The preparation is like packing a parachute—it has to be done carefully, and only you can do it. But then you jump out of the plane and there you are, skydiving. You almost can't help doing it well, since doing it well just means surviving. There's almost always a haystack to land on. The worst that can happen is to land on a lesser haystack. And if you miss the haystack you don't actually die. It just feels that way for a moment.

I looked over at Martha, as I did so often in those days. I liked watching her sleep; she did it so . . . completely. Our bed was placed in the far corner of the loft, in discreet isolation from the rest of the loft's doings. I say "discreet": loft life revealed that the discretion of the bourgeoisie, of which we hear so much, turns out to be almost entirely spiritual, induced rather than instantiated, more a matter of space quietly implied than divisions firmly made.

The discreet bourgeois dispensation played out traditionally in two places—the bedroom and the dining room—and we had neither. The bedroom was, in proper nineteenth-century apartments, supposed to be the segregated place of married love—what they called connubial bliss—and the dining room the locus of family life: a piano, a long table, candles, and blank and baleful looks passing among the participants.

The eighties loft was a blended space, one very big room, where our bed, under a mosquito net—put there for the most practical of purposes, as we had mosquitoes to go along with the mice, though the mosquitoes, we convinced ourselves, were coming from New Jersey—created the false air of an old Marlene Dietrich movie, where everything takes place with six or seven occluding veils. The little two-person dining table, carried over from the Blue Room, could become a big one for Thanksgiving, owing to a plywood extender with a Venetian tablecloth laid upon it.

The blending of spaces, though, didn't realize the old dream of modernist architects, a single space for living, where everything would blend seamlessly together and the old, cold middle-class dispensation, which unnaturally divided the organic unity of life into chilly compartments, would be warmed, and thaw—where we would eat and love and sleep and celebrate our flexible and open lives in a flexible open space.

That can't happen. The divisions of life are, if not natural, then necessary, and what actually happened in lofts, even still-childless ones, was a kind of strange construction of invisible walls. The area around the bed became "the bedroom." Where you ate became, "Beauty and the Beast" style, magically, a dining room. Emotions and appetites flowed in neat, fixed currents around the spaces, stopping somehow right around the edges of the action. Visitors were reluctant to cross into the bedroom, even though it was five steps from the "living room." Once the Thanksgiving table was up, we might have been living in Concord, Massachusetts, with the March family in the mid-nineteenth century. Even in more crowded and child-filled lofts than our own, the same strange rule applied: space, in a slightly Einsteinian way, curved around the activities chosen, closing them off in their own gravitational fields, rather than enveloping them all in one cozy blanket. When I visit friends—I almost wrote "younger friends"—today in their *Cabinet of Dr. Caligari*, diagonally cut spaces on the third floor of an old tenement in Crown Heights, I recognize that they are making the same accommodation. Life needs rooms, as love needs dreams, and makes them out of airy nothing when no other material presents itself.

———

Bedrooms contain beds, and space wrapping itself around them, and, with Martha asleep on ours, I see that I have now the strange and slightly panicked duty of writing something about SoHo sex. This is an already much-sung subject, at least in its more obscure and aggressively original corners. Transgressive sex and substance-assisted sex in that time and place have all been beautifully memorialized, by Nan Goldin and Chantal Akerman and others. The duller and more familiar form of love—our form—though, has not.

They sang "The Ballad of Sexual Dependency." I sing that of

"Sexual Domesticity," a quieter number, though not without its own little tang of transgression. For married love, as I have written, is the last taboo, and talking and writing about long-married erotic love taboo even to the long married. Why it should be so is a mystery. Why is writing about wanting your wife too much so weird? That's the question. Wanting your *lover* too much is romantic. And wanting someone *else's* wife too much is the stuff of epic. Even a wife gone, the widower's plight, moves us to license erotic memory.

Perhaps it's because you *have* your wife or husband. The happy ending is priced into the tale, and you are, so to speak, boasting past the point that the market will bear. You sold the stock at its peak; don't make us watch while you count your profits. Lost love is longing, but long love is crowing. All tales turn toward "And they lived happily ever after," but a single detail of what they so happily did for so long after ruins the fable. Uxoriousness is a form of hubris.

And, then, we all know instinctively what science shows in fact: that those long in love are idiots of a kind. The best science we have about romantic love suggests that its perpetuation depends, to put it more bluntly than a scientist would, on stupidity. There is, we're told, a region of the cerebrum known as the ventromedial prefrontal cortex, which is the bit of the brain that specializes in negative judgments of others. The ventromedial view is always that the others are all smelly and repugnant—it is a way of keeping the other tribe out of our tree. It's why we ventromediate, so to speak, even our family members who stay for more than three days. "Natural selection has long favored those who responded negatively to the one malevolent intruder, rather than positively to myriad friendly guests," one neuroscientist writes. In long-married couples, the ventromedial prefrontal just shuts down—you can see this on an MRI!—or fades out, and refuses to accept the (accurate) information, apparent after seven years to most normal people, that the spouse *is* a kind of malevolent intruder. We would like to believe that the long married see more; our instinct tells us what science confirms: they just see nothing.

And to the normal embarrassments of long-married blindness are added, for a writer, the extra embarrassment that the subject of the misperception, far from being the lost love of another time, is still present—sharp-eyed and in possession of a querulous prose style of her own and the promise of a bitter memoir yet to be written. "I don't want to be exploited and exposed," Iseult says to Tristan after they have actually gotten away from King Mark and rented a little place in Brittany. ("It's not too large, but cozy.") And so: no poem.

Well, out with it—I was infatuated with her, with the fact of her dressing and undressing so casually in my presence. I wanted her so much when we were in our twenties that if I could turn back the clock it would not be to make love to her again, but to make up for all the chances missed.

My desire for her was the engine of all my ambitions. In fact, by an odd alchemy refined in New York, if not peculiar to it, anxiety, ambition, and desire had all compounded together into a kind of life fuel. I wanted to succeed to keep her coming home. I wanted to do well to continue to intrigue her. I wanted to bring her home the scalps of defeated enemies—even if the enemies, in this case, were no more than art critics with mildly differing (and just as hard to follow) views about the significance of this scribble, the historical potential of that appropriated ad. I wanted to succeed in order, in every sense, to keep my eye on her. (And, of course, the perpetual sadness of marriage, she really wanted none of these things. She was content for us to be at home, and happy, and sex for her was not a thing "earned" or "won" in any way but merely to be enjoyed—a participatory sport in which all must have prizes, rather than a competitive sport in which someone might triumph.)

In the Blue Room years, as I've said, it was different. I can hardly recall her face, my eyes were so close to it. We were always on top of each other, in every sense. We became a blended person. Though we were as unlike as two people could be—one graceful and one awkward; one neat, one messy (no prize for guessing which); one sleepy and one insomniac—in that tiny compressed space, either we would come together or we would blow apart, and we came together.

Only in the loft, our new room, did we step far enough apart for me to see her again, as I had seen her when we were teenagers. I was on a lazier schedule in those days—nowadays it's all I can do to keep my eyelids from popping open at 6:00 a.m., but then, after a night's insomnia, I would sleep for a few hours past 4:00 a.m., and my publishing, and later my magazine, employers were kind as to arrival hours. She would get up to get to the editing studio, and I would watch her get dressed—underwear and tights and asymmetrical Japanese tunic—with hooded eyes and dry mouth. The image stayed with me all day as I worked, and simplified my purposes to a needlepoint. The irony was that it was Martha who played the traditionally "male" role in our relationship—getting up every morning to go to work, and coming home exhausted after a day at the office, in this case the office of the Maysles film-editing studios—while I, transforming from hybrid editor-writer to full-time scribe, stayed home and, well, baked cookies, and braised short ribs, getting dinner ready every day for her exhausted return. (And it was up to me to say, "How was your day?," since writers don't have days, but always the same day, again and again.) Her being the daily wage earner also meant that she was, without willing it, the strip-tease artist in reverse, her getting dressed being as titillating as getting undressed, my rose gypsy rather than my Gypsy Rose.

She was, in every sense, my learning curve. My learning curves. Sex in marriage, I learned, doesn't exhaust itself, but it does mutate. When you start out in married life, sex goes from being an event, an arrangement, to being something always available. And so it becomes at once routinized and ritualized, with the two balanced on a knife's edge: We can put it off, make it a pleasure we must choose. We can also put it on when we want to—perform it, like a play! The routine becomes . . . routine: the chances not grabbed because there will be another chance, the rest or reading indulged in place of sex because the 3:00 a.m. possibility is no longer the only possibility the week presents.

And then I don't know of a couple who have not, pressed to be honest, retreated—or is it advanced?—early in marriage into some kind of playful shared infantilism, where they inhabit a pair of hamsters, or become the family dog chatting with the local cat or impersonate imaginary children. And that I am more loath to confess this than I would be to confess group sex with a zebra is in itself proof of my point—that sweetness is the last taboo, and the universal truths of coupledom almost forbidden to speak.

But the routine of sex, however it may be postponed by those who have the luxury of postponement, when it *is* finally engaged takes on some of the sacredness of ritual. The whispered fantasy, the girl at the end of the bed slowly (and a little unwillingly) undressing for show, the intoxicating combination of the touchingly ordinary care she showed (her eyes on her buttons, her head cast down, never flirtatiously looking out; the clothes counted for too much), and the extraordinary image she presented—the oyster-opening shock of her body, the curve of her hip and indentation of her waist, the surprising throw of her upper leg, the perpetual shock of nudity. (Over time and children, these hours become whittled down to mere moments: she comes into the study, where her dresser is, to dress, and I say, "My one good minute of the day." And, sadly, it is.)

In a *very* long marriage, lovemaking eventually gets to the point where you explore less than you enact. Eventually, you start to *re-*enact, so that the couple become a bit like those Civil War reenactors, the ones who put on Blue and Gray uniforms and fire disarmed old rifles. That they know the actions, the uniforms, the climax, and the casualties before they start the excitement doesn't diminish the pleasure they take in the exercise. The pleasure of long-married sex, like that of a scripted reenactment of Gettysburg, lies in the combination of furious action and complete predictability.

———

But in SoHo she still stands there at the edge of the bed and looks down at the buttons on her blouse, watches the snap of her jeans, studies it before she takes them off.

Married lovemaking collapses into a pattern, so that what remains with me are not really moments in the loft—as I do recall the moments in hotels when we traveled in those years, the boats rocking outside our hotel near a gondola station in Venice, her breath quickening, and the transformation of her face above me, the sound of the boats playing behind her sound. No, what remains is the pattern, unvarying, as though Peter Pan threw his shadows, one after another, into a pile in the corner, and we made out one consistent shape through the occlusion of so many.

Perhaps this is just a fancy way of saying that, though all I can recall from that time is unending erotic desire, I can't recall a single erotic act. Or is it that I only care to try to recall them now? They weren't subjects of memory then—just objects of life. Perhaps the true shape of desire only becomes apparent to us as we age. When we're young, our ambitions are mixed in with our appetites, so much that we can hardly tell them apart. As we get older, our ambitions are either achieved or else permanently eliminated as possibilities: you ain't never gonna be President now. So the anxieties of ambitions recede but the appetites remain, and have their way with us, and in our memory, perhaps, the appetite becomes simpler than it was. Lust, which seems like appetite in its constant recurrence, resembles anxiety even more in being anticipatory—our fears are much keener before things happen than when they do, and we desire a body much more than we can quite credit we did after the act is over. Thus one appetite consumes all the others, and is still standing and swooping after the other appetites and anxieties have been relieved.

Afterward, I would always sleep. Perhaps it is because anxiety and appetite are so mixed together in your twenties and thirties that the momentary reassurance of love produces a beautiful self-induced bloom of poppies in the bloodstream. Anyway, that's the way it was for me. It remains the only time in my life I *have* slept— after making love in SoHo—the way that people are supposed to sleep, the way the heroes slept in the spy novels that engrossed me as a boy: "he found himself helplessly slipping out of consciousness"; "suddenly, without warning, he was asleep"; "when he opened his eyes again, it was morning in Istanbul." My sleep today is again pitifully fitful and light, sporadically aware of each night as it passes.

But then I slept. Romantic love always ends with an exit, adulterous love with an exit and a murmured excuse. Married love alone always ends in sleep. The proof of its success is the silence it induces. Ah! Maybe *that's* why you never hear about it.

═══

So this story opens with Martha asleep—sound asleep, for reasons pure or illicit or compromised, I'm not sure—when the phone rang. I snatched it up immediately, not wanting to wake her. As I say, it was nearly eleven at night.

The man on the other end introduced himself as John, and then he said, "We're all so looking forward to your keynote tomorrow morning at the Pluralism and Individualism conference."

Now, I had no memory of agreeing to giving the keynote at any conference, much less a Pluralism and Individualism conference, but it was entirely within my capacity to have totally forgotten something significant that I'd agreed to do. So I said, "Oh, of course, just a second, let me get my book"—I had no book—and then I said, "Oh yes, you want to run through the details with me one more time, just to make sure that they coincide with what I have written down?"

He seemed more or less reassured by these signs of hyper-conscientiousness at the other end of the line. "Of course. It's at the Doral Inn Hotel tomorrow morning at eight-thirty, Fiftieth and Lexington; we're expecting a full house and, of course, keenly looking forward to it."

Of course, what I *should* have said is "Sorry, this just does not ring a bell"—but how can you say such a thing to someone who believes he's a mere eight hours away from hearing your keynote on Pluralism and Individualism? So I said, "Great, see you then!" and I hung up the phone—Martha was still asleep—and I immediately began to weigh the consequences of my actions. Certainly, ambition might involve the simple urge to get attention—but there is always lurking in that urge the possibility of getting too much attention of the wrong kind. That's a complicated way of saying: Seek attention stupidly and you will fail, and you will make a fool of yourself. In the early morning, no less.

And then I realized that I was trained as an art historian—and if you have studied art history, you will know that all of modern art can be neatly slotted into one of two categories, pluralism or individualism. You have the alienated self-portraits of Van Gogh, and then you have the scary city scenes of Ensor. You have the isolated single figures of Giacometti, and you have the frightening crowds crossing bridges in Munch. You can pretty much grab a handful of slides of modern paintings at random and—bang—you have a lecture on pluralism and individualism. And so that was exactly what I did, grabbed a handful of slides and put them together.

I'm not sure what motivated me to do this. The sound, or sane strategy—"I'm sorry, I wasn't aware of this engagement, and so can't do it"—calls out to me now, as our follies of youth seem so simply corrected in middle age. Some part of it was the sheer embarrassment of absentmindedness—a reluctance to admit to my still-frequent amnesia about obligations—but some part, too, was about those scalps, those prizes, that engine of anxiety and appetite driving me forward. I loved the idea of doing things for her while she slept. It was a form of fictive sex, of extended eroticism. Her sleeping while I took the subway to go speak was another way of making love.

The next morning, while Martha slept, at around seven o'clock, I got up and dressed, suit jacket, jeans—still jeans, no replacement suit trousers—and sneakers, my usual mufti, and I went off to the Doral Inn Hotel at Fiftieth and Lexington. I got on the subway, the 6 train at Spring Street, and went on up.

You may remember the old Doral Inn Hotel; it was a little piece of Cincinnati in the middle of Manhattan. It had Cincinnati architecture and Cincinnati lighting, and it even had a place where you could pull the car up on a circular drive, the way you can in Cincinnati.

I went in, and there, in the lobby, in the half-light of eight-fifteen in the morning, was a well-dressed, nervous-looking young man. John! I deduced quickly, and so it was.

He shook my hand. "Oh, we are so glad you're here," he said. "We're ready for you to go on."

He opened the door immediately, and we were in an auditorium the size of a large movie theater, though, as I recall it, much wider in articulation—four or five hundred seats, spread out panoramically across the room. And all the seats filled with these incredibly well-dressed people. All the men had on jackets and ties, and all of the women had on skirts and stockings, and there was a giant banner that said "Pluralism and Individualism: '85."

Who are these people? I asked myself. Are they Scientologists? Are they libertarians? They're certainly enthusiastic about the ideas of pluralism and individualism, to have come out at eight-fifteen in the morning. And though it might have been their "keynote," they seemed not bleary-eyed but primed—keyed up already!

So I got up and I gave a lecture that would have done Professor Irwin Corey proud. "We must always remember that, when we consider the nature of pluralism in modern society, it inevitably breaks down into the collisions of individuals," I intoned. "And when considering the role of the individual as he or she realizes him- or herself in our world—we must remember that they cannot help but become plural, by their very nature." On the one hand, I explained, individualism segregates and atomizes. On the other, community and cohesion—call them pluralism—bring the individualized individuals back together. Between the individual asserting his—or her—individuality, and the plurality of human kinds accepting their inexorable multiplicity and, to be sure, plurality, we would ever find ourselves defining each term—in terms of the other.

I couldn't have done better if I had been spouting it at MoMA, or writing it for *October* magazine.

After keeping this up for twenty-five minutes, and getting what I still choose to believe was a warm hand at the end, I stepped down, walked back out, and found John waiting for me outside the auditorium. And I'll never forget what he said; it sticks to my mind, like "it fit good." He shook my hand and said, "Thank you, that was very healing." And then, in the time-honored manner of conference organizers toward impecunious speakers, he passed me a white envelope that I suavely, or as suavely as I could manage at eight-forty-five on a Saturday morning, slipped into my inner jacket pocket.

I waited a decent interval, until I had turned onto Lexington Avenue, and then I opened the envelope. The check was for five hundred dollars, an enormous amount of money for us in those days. I cheerfully put it back in my pocket, got on the subway, got off at Spring Street, and walked back into our loft.

Martha was still asleep. By now, it was about nine-thirty.

I took off my clothes, I got back in bed, and slept for another hour; then she woke up. I told her, "You will not believe what happened while you were asleep!"

I showed her the check. And I insisted that we use the money for a celebration, for a blowout, for one more effort to try to scale Scott Fitzgerald Mountain. With this mad money, our windfall of five hundred dollars, we would do something truly glamorous and carefree, the eighties equivalent of jumping into a fountain. We would take this money and go out and have one great dinner. We would go to a wonderful French restaurant and we would have champagne and wine and brandy and all the things Scott and Zelda would have had, and we would truly enjoy ourselves. It was, I suppose, on an impossibly Lilliputian scale, the same dubious instinct that the money men of the time, the ones who wore yellow suspenders and worked in the then new business of hedge funds and private equity, insisted on: I have earned, and now we will spend.

And, damn it, we did. We took it and had a great meal—a wonderful meal at Chanterelle, the restaurant around the corner, the most beautiful room in New York, apricot walls and silver-and-white linen cloths—and we came home drunk and happy, and I opened the door to our loft and turned on the light.

There is nothing in the world that will sober you up as quickly as hundreds of mice dancing in your home. The scene inside our loft looked like one of those old thirties cartoons where you see a little barnyard and the mice are playing string basses and fiddles and dancing. Maybe there were ten mice, but it looked like a hundred. Even twenty mice is enough to sober you up. I pushed Martha back and out and said, "I think we ought to go someplace else to sleep tonight." Now, this was in the days before ATMs, it was in the days before a taxicab would take a credit card. And we had spent every penny of that five hundred dollars at the restaurant. We had one dear friend who lived up on Seventy-fifth Street, and we knew that we could always stay with him—but the only way that we were going to get there was to walk. We turned around on Broome Street, and we started the long march at one in the morning, up to Seventy-fifth and First.

And yet the night held a sense of epiphany about it, at the same time. The oscillations of inside and outside, of up-high and down-low, of suit-buying elations and trouser-losing deflations, that had been the rhythm of our first five years in New York seemed more settled, almost touched the edge of the serene. Because I suddenly realized what I had failed to in all that time in New York. And that is that we are the mice. The mice (or the cockroaches, or any other pest) are not the invaders—we were ourselves the country mice who'd chosen to come to New York. No one asked us here, no one had shown us in; so we simply have to struggle and fight for our little crumb of comfort, as the mice do. We would never escape the mice. We might never scale the Fitzgeraldian mountain. But we were here. We were here as the mice were here. And I knew, at that time, that I was never going to find my trousers again. I also knew that, if the mice had our loft, we, in some way that could not now be taken from us, now had New York. We didn't sleep that night. We walked—no, we scurried—up the avenues, like mosquitoes fleeing New Jersey, like mice coming home.

11

Wanderings

When you first come to New York, you hardly notice the change of seasons: spring flows into summer and the gray autumn into grim winter and then back to spring with scarcely a mark, a flutter, in your mind. You're too busy, and too driven, to sense the seasons, whose simplest signals—the accumulation of fallen leaves on the sidewalk I knew from my childhood in Philadelphia, the accumulation of white snow on the streets I knew from our youth in Montreal—were anyway hardly to be seen.

Gray streets under gray skies through gray months in gray weather. I used to joke that they called the clubbiest restaurant in town "The Four Seasons" because it was the only way a certain kind of New Yorker could be made even marginally aware of what the seasons *were*—could even tell that there were seasons at all. You looked at the menu, and it told you.

"The world here looks gray now because it *is* gray," Martha would say to me, stubbornly, when I grew melancholy at the change. Yet, as life in the city went on, you *did* become more acutely aware of it—the length of the summer, the dreary year's beginning, which stretches from January to April and the first stirrings of baseball season. That first week of January, when all the Christmas trees in the city are thrown, denuded of glory, into piles in the gutter, like plague victims, waiting to be carted away. There's something inhuman and chilling about the ritual. All of these beautiful evergreens that scarce three weeks ago had been the centerpieces of parties and festivities in every apartment and loft in the city, so that you could see them in every window, taking Joe Mitchell's rule of the second story and extending it out to Epiphany: look up and where, in the normal run of the year, everything seems clouded, there was a tree, with its own cloud of lights upon it. And then, suddenly, every one of them just tossed aside: stripped, denuded, disgraced, discarded. For the first five years, when the trees must, in truth, have been piling up on the street outside the Blue Room, I didn't notice them. When they must have cluttered the curbsides where I searched forlornly for my pants, I didn't see them.

But now I did.

And you began to register those darker notes—small ones at first, but then you saw that the city was filling up with larger ones. The "homeless crisis" was now impossible not to see every day. We were told by the experts that homelessness reflected medications untaken and shelters unvisited as much as poverty unrelieved. Nonetheless, you recognized, with what humanity you had, that it was deeply wrong that a city that celebrated wealth to the degree that this one did should be able to endure so easily the presence of so many people who had nothing at all.

One bitter cold February night, when Martha and I were walking home from a movie theater on Houston Street, we noticed a man opening the front of a newspaper vending machine. Then he curled himself up into a ball inside and shut the door behind him. It was an act both of contortion achieved and of comfort sought, apartment hunting in another dimension of desperation. We had lived for three years in a place not much bigger by local standards, but this was different. It was an image, once seen, that could never leave you. Those images began to crowd all around.

Toward the end of the decade, I felt for the first time, among all the lights, a certain sadness, even a kind of darkness in our own

days. Our darkness was not the good melodramatic darkness so useful in fiction and films: needles and knives and betrayals and affairs.
It was a smaller darkness of compressions and anxieties and the
sheer exhaustion attendant on doing more things than the day can
quite bear. The twoness that had been our unquestioned faith—the
easy double faith that no room was too small to share, no city too
big to conquer—began, not to *fade,* no, not that, but to tear a bit. It
frayed around the edges of the hem, as happens to pants worn too
long, if you have them.

For Martha this absence was more painful. I had not been
aware—or had not chosen to be aware—of how much she missed
the garden of the house where she had grown up in Montreal, how
the grayness that I still sometimes reveled in, street upon street,
seemed oppressive to her.

Work divided us, and the things that united us—going to dinner
parties, attending openings, all that—divided us, too, in another
way, since it broke the spell of shared fantasy that had supported us
in the Blue Room, the belief that, by willing an imagination alive,
you could will a world into being. It was not that there was less
love in the room, but there was more static in the signal; the purity
of emotion that we had sought and found, however ludicrous and
absurd and even delusional, was passing.

═══

The one analgesic I found was walking through the city, over
and over. The two great technological gifts of the eighties were
the Walkman and the hyper-developed sneaker, which, together,
turned walking into an all-encompassing emotional activity. For a
long time in the 1980s, I seemed to do nothing but walk around
Manhattan. The modern sneaker, rising from Nike and Adidas,
constructed with more architecture inside than most apartments,
now allowed even the flat-footed to stride, Hermes-like, on what
felt like cushioned air.

And then the Walkman made every block your own movie. Just
as the period of the first flâneurs falls exactly between the rise of gas

street lighting, which opened the city to twenty-four-hour idling, and the onset of the automobile, which made cities loud again, so walking in the 1980s lay right between the invention of the Walkman, which suddenly neutralized the noise of the cityscape, and the onset of the iPhone, which replaced isolation-booth serenity with our now frantic, forever-on-guard-ness.

I had my Walkman plugged into my head everywhere I went, listening to Paul McCartney (the soft Paul McCartney of the time, when he would put out a new record every year that had two good songs among a flutter of fill) or Stevie Wonder or, most often, James Taylor and Sting. A few years later, in the early nineties, when Bret Easton Ellis published *American Psycho*, it was disconcerting to discover that the cold-blooded Wall Street serial killer had the same tastes in music I did. Ellis's point, I think, was that "soft" music was the soundtrack to hard passions, that, whereas honest-to-God death metal was at least honest, and so purgative, in its violent message, the Phil Collinses and Stings of the world kept their murderous rage beneath a façade of sweet tunefulness. I didn't believe it. The sweet is often simply sweet, and though sweet and bitter together are a better solution than either apart, when forced to choose one or the other, only the distraught take the bitter.

You could walk anywhere then. Saturday all day, Sunday all day, I'd tramp through the Lower Manhattan neighborhoods. The differences, architectural and social, between TriBeCa and SoHo and the Lower East Side, to name only contiguous areas, were distinct and vivid and nameable then: cast-iron buildings shading off into old industrial egg- and paper-carton factories sweetly interrupted by small triangular parks, and then, edging over, as you walked east, into poor-law tenements, the new frontier being reclaimed by painters. Saturday mornings I would set off and walk all day, and achieve a feeling of happiness—which is, always, some kind of unearned release achieved unawares through absorption—in a way that I haven't felt before or since. SoHo in the eighties was the finest place for walking there could have been, not only architecturally beautiful but, by accident, still beautifully composed: illuminated sidewalks still functionally illuminated the basements beneath, while the pioneering businesses were as chic but widely spaced as rocks in a Japanese garden—a single one-room restaurant with a hand-written menu outside, a block of old businesses, the odd charcuterie, a sole Korean deli for the whole neighborhood. At twilight you walked, so to speak, from campfire to campfire, with beautiful darkness in between.

I loved those walking Saturdays, began to look forward to them with an intensity that belied their simple aimlessness. I would walk up Mercer Street, the most beautiful and mysterious of SoHo streets—optically, if not actually, bounded on either end by the exclamation points of the two most romantic of all New York skyscrapers, the Chrysler Building at the far northern end and the Woolworth Building to the south. My official reason for walking so often and so long was to get to the gym: I had joined a "health club" that had a slightly sad mirror-and-rubber-plant décor, "like Cheryl Tiegs's last marriage," Martha said. Like every other member of our generation, I biked and I lifted and I steamed and I showered after. But I used the gym merely as a destination. I liked to walk up Lafayette Street for its own sake.

What was I searching for on those walks? What *was* it? Sometimes I could start walking at ten in the morning and not come back until six or seven at night—though my arms would always be filled with beautiful food that I had found at the Union Square Greenmarket, just coming into its own then, or at Dean & DeLuca. I would cook, and on Saturday nights we would listen to Sid Mark's four hours of Sinatra on the FM radio. (He, and it, had become the subject of my first "Talk of the Town" story for *The New Yorker*, eccentric obsessions proving their value.) There was still something so different, so perturbed about that moment in our New York evolution. And all I could think was that I was still trying to do what wiser and older walkers had done, too, and that was to reconnect to my own aspirations through the simple hard physical act of perambulating, trying to remember what things meant by walking past where things were.

I began, graduate student that I still was at heart—Chekhov says somewhere that he spent a lifetime knouting the peasant out of himself; I have spent the same lifetime flogging the graduate student out, but he always comes back, as did Chekhov's peasant; he's his own Lopakhin—to read about walking in New York even as I was walking in New York, to define the peculiarly New York contribution to the meanings of walking. There was Alfred Kazin—whom I actually met once, and didn't know whom I was meeting, fool that I was; had I met him only a few years later, I might have gotten something as useful as what I took from Joe Mitchell. (It isn't whom we meet in life that matters, it's when we meet them.)

Rereading the great New York walkers, you find one note that eluded the cynic-contemplatives of Paris: in New York, walking, even without companions, can still be an expression of companionship, of expansive connection; a happy opening out to an enlarged civic self rather than a narrowing down to a contemplative inner one; a way of scooting toward the American Over-Soul, in high-tops.

It starts with Walt. Whereas the Parisian poet-walkers of his time walk to take it all apart, dissect the scene, find the skull beneath the street lamps, Whitman walks to take it all in, see what's up, get the life of the city right. Walking in New York, Whitman says, leaves him "enrich'd of soul—you give me forever faces." Whitman is always walking *through* the city. "Brooklyn, of ample hills, was mine," he tells us of his walks, and then that "I too walk'd the streets of Manhattan Island, and bathed in the waters around it," which says something about the state of the waters then. Making his way down the streets, leaping into the Hudson: those are Whitman's promenades. He seeks not a glimpse inside his own mind but *connection:* "Manhattan crowds . . . with varied chorus . . . Manhattan faces and eyes forever for me." This makes him a man of boats and bridges as much as of boulevards; his New York is as much Brooklyn as it is Manhattan. (And there's his ferry, connecting them.)

Kazin, whose 1951 *A Walker in the City,* heavily haunted by Whitman, remains, I discovered too late to tell him, the best book ever written about New York on foot, is all about going somewhere.

Kazin uses walking as a metaphor for ambition and escape; his is a study in how ambitious kids can ascend on foot from the provinces just across the bridge. He was walking all the time because he was getting the hell out of Brownsville, and couldn't afford a taxi. You *could* take the subway—Moss Hart in *Act One* writes of taking the subway—but Kazin prefers to walk, because the subway is one of the chief things he is escaping from. (When Moss Hart escaped from it, too, he took taxis, Broadway hits being more helpful in that aim than *Partisan Review* pieces.)

As Whitman is walking *through*, Kazin is walking *to* and *toward*. He's going somewhere with every step. (When he retreats to Brownsville, it is to see how far he's gone.) Yet we find in both Whitman and Kazin a note of simple delight in the pure chance of walking in New York, what Kazin calls the walking that supplies "a happy, yet mostly vague and *excited* feeling." Whatever else we walk to accomplish, we always walk in New York to randomize our too neatly gridded city existence. You go where your feet take you. Buses take routes and even subways have schedules, but everyone on foot goes where they want to.

———

Sometimes, those Saturday walks could be joyful. I went on long walks with Dick Avedon, a champion walker, who loved to set goals, ambitions. Once, he called me on such a morning, when Martha was away in Iceland with her mother, and suggested that we "walk the length of Manhattan, and look for masterpieces."

Dick didn't, it turned out, really mean to walk from Spuyten Duyvil to the harbor, but just the length of Fifth Avenue from the Metropolitan Museum to Washington Square—the navigable river of commerce and art on which most of his sixty-odd years had been spent.

Dick, planted in the middle of the cobblestones on the park side of Fifth, with the traffic going around, flowing around him, seemed to be watching the parade of buses on the avenue. "Do you know," he said, looking east, "I grew *up* over there. At Fifty-five East Eighty-sixth. And my father and I always used to ride the double-decker buses together right here on Fifth Avenue on Sundays. I remember once we were on the bus and I had my autograph album with me. I always did in that period; I was maybe twelve. My father suddenly looked out the window, on the upper deck, and said, 'There's the mayor's brother!' Of course, it was the sort of knowing thing that fathers are supposed to say. Mayor La Guardia was fat, so another fat man had to be his brother. But I thought, The mayor's *brother!*— and *leapt* from the upper deck, down the stairs, and *jumped* out onto Fifth Avenue, with my autograph book. I twisted my ankle as I landed, but I kept going, limping terribly as I raced after this poor, anonymous fat man." Dick became for a moment his own younger self on the same pavement—crippled by his leap, dragging his wounded leg, autograph book still gamely held out before him, like a pilgrim's cross. "I held out my autograph book to the fat man, and he looked at me in amazement. Of course, I eventually had to limp back to the bus. It was the sort of overeager thing I did that embarrassed my father.

"My God, how I loved autographs!" he went on, as we began to walk south along the park. "I had the most amazing collection of autographs. I had a whole section called 'Great Jews and Great Judges.' Rabbi Weiss, Governor Lehman. I had Oliver Wendell Holmes and Chief Justice Hughes, who signed on their beautiful Supreme Court cards. George S. Kaufman wrote on a blue card, 'For Richard Avedon, and very glad to do it.' I had Rachmaninoff and e. e. cummings. The only movie stars who interested me were Toby Wing and Lyda Roberti. No one has even *heard* of them now. Lyda Roberti introduced the Gershwin song 'My Cousin in Milwaukee' in a movie musical, which I thought was *major*. I had them both. Today, whenever anybody asks me for an autograph, I always send it back and write 'signed with pleasure.'

"Let's make a day of masterpieces!" he said suddenly, emphatically. "We'll look at nothing but masterpieces. When we moved to Eighty-sixth Street, I practically *moved* into the Met. I would visit all the time when we lived near here, to look at certain things—the

Fayum portraits from Egypt. The Modiglianis. The Soutines. And those figures—the Etruscans with their tiny waists and hips and their smiles. The Modiglianis and the Etruscans, above all."

As we approached the Frick, Dick peered down Fifth toward the Empire State Building. "Avedon's Fifth Avenue. Did you know that that was what my father's store was called? It was on Thirty-ninth and Fifth. I used to go into my father's room, after he lost the store in the Depression, just to look at the stationery and the envelopes and the sales slips and smell the carbon paper. Diane Arbus and I both came from department-store families—there was still a myth of the department store in our time.

"There was a certain kind of Jewish Broadway world of the period just when I was born, back in the twenties, that for our parents was a sort of an ideal. There was a family called the Strunskys—Simeon and English Strunsky. I think Simeon was the editor of the *Times Book Review* or something, and related to the Gershwins by marriage. I always heard about the Strunskys—the reach of the Strunskys and the depth of the Strunskys and the style of the Strunskys. I wanted to be a Strunsky, not a Dick. Years later, I was in a lonely little inn on Cape Cod and saw the most elegant elderly couple, gravely waltzing by themselves in Hyannis. I suddenly thought: Strunskys! They must be Strunskys. And they were!

"There was a certain Strunskyite ideal that governed my childhood; it's hard to describe, and I've rediscovered it only fitfully. It was Gershwin and O'Neill and Dorothy Parker and crossword puzzles and Moss Hart and George Kaufman playing cards. The Marx Brothers when they were still in New York, and my mother couldn't stop talking about them."

We went into the Frick. Dick first took in a Memling portrait of a young man. "It doesn't really work, does it? The trick with portraits . . . It has to be serious, to keep the romance of the surface—and deepen it at the same time. It's those Germans: all that rigor and precision. It stays on the surface, though. It doesn't look romantic at first, but it's far more romantic in its materialism than—I don't know—than Fragonard. Fragonard is all spirit."

He walked a little farther into the next room and was stopped cold by a pair of Gainsborough portraits, a man and a woman. "My God, what doesn't he know about aristocratic people! The silver hair and wigs, and the mismatch of the black eyebrows on her. It's not the technique he employs, though it's a perfect technique. It's what he knows about that man, and that woman. Gainsborough comes close to certain Goyas—to Goya's Condesa de Chinchón" (a touchstone for Dick). "That same kind of freedom, and welcoming contradiction. Gainsborough is as close to Goya as anyone, though you're not supposed to say that."

He made a quick inspection of the other faces in the room, dismissing the Lawrences ("too much flesh; nobody's cheeks are that pink") and the Hogarths, but being moved by a Reynolds portrait of an elderly lady with an elaborate wig, plaited with hanging silver ribbons. "What you can do with a hat—the pathos of the perfect hat against the aging face . . ."

We turned, and Dick pretended amazement at entering the room of Fragonard's *Progress of Love*. "What doesn't he know about movement!" he said. "What he can do with a kind of sexuality, constantly translating it into perfect controlled movement and yet keeping the nervous edge of it alive always, not simpering or posed. Real movement, rising from inside the lovers. You get past the chalky surface and the pastry in a half-minute, and then everything just takes off, he goes so *far*." Dick approached the surface of the panel in *The Progress of Love* where the girl flees the boy, her arms spread straight out. He peered intently into it.

At last, we reached our destination: the central hall of the mansion, lined with Mr. Frick's choicest pictures. Dick walked immediately over to "it"—Rembrandt's *Polish Rider*. He stood still in front of it. "My mother would bring me to see it when I was nine, and for a long time that picture meant everything in the world to me. I was that young man, and I was in love with him—with myself, my idealized vision of myself, what I might be. I saw him as me, that possibility in life—everything lying ahead, and not yet knowing it, not looking at the road, but out. It sounds so grandiose, I know, when you say it, but the sense I had was so *strong* that someone else, Rembrandt, had felt everything I was feeling. I was so *reassured* by that picture. Everything I want for my work is still in it—in that contradiction, the beautiful rider and the broken-down horse." Then he added, with a smile, but more softly, "I *was* the rider. And bit by bit, I've become the horse."

Dick slowly disengaged himself from the Rembrandt, and walked up, peeked at the Piero, and then turned left, to look at the shiny blue satin Veronese, *The Choice of Hercules.* Hercules in Veronese's picture is a slight, weak-chinned, aristocratic Venetian boy in a ballooning white silk suit, looking pettish as he is pulled between the two imposing, pneumatic goddesses. "Veronese was in the *worst* kind of bind," Dick said. "But we've all experienced that. It's one of those things. The guy said to him, 'Paint me as Hercules. In my white suit.'"

We turned off past the Frick and into the park. Dick looked down. "It's funny, about portraits"—he was still back at the museum—"how the best portraits are always emperors or postmen. People who are all self-image, or people who have no self-image at all. They come with a kind of dignity to the camera."

Then on through the dark underpass that leads to the children's zoo. As we approached it, we came upon an odd, familiar little park personage—the button man. An ageless, white-bearded man, a figure right out of Joe Mitchell, wearing a heavy, stained overcoat covered, studded, with a thousand photo-buttons—Polaroid snapshots of passersby who have come to him to have their pictures taken, wrapped in plastic, and laminated to a tin lapel button: you can wear a picture of yourself.

Dick looked at the photo-button man with a combination of awe, curiosity, and possibility. He sized him up.

"This might be just the thing," he said at last. "Don't you think? For Martha? A photograph of us, enjoying a day in the park? She can wear it all over Greenland." I didn't correct him as to Martha's homeland.

He walked up to the button man, who, in his long, studded overcoat, proudly surveyed his domain. He looked like the mayor of Munchkin City, and seemed magisterially unconcerned by the lack of custom.

"How are you?" Dick said, walking up to him, hand outstretched. "Have you been doing this for long?"

The photo-button man in turn sized up the famous photographer. "Awhile," he said, as one not inclined to give away too much too quickly.

"We were thinking, actually, of having a button made." Dick said this gaily, affirmatively, eagerly—but with exactly the right inflection of tentativeness and uncertainty to make it clear that he, the *patron,* was willing but that it was, in the end, *in the final analysis,* up to the artist—the button man—to decide whether or not this portrait made sense in terms of his mood this morning, and in terms of the corpus of his work.

Understanding this, the button man played his part. He turned and slowly looked over the two men—both schleppy in jeans and T-shirts—gravely. At last he sighed, as one whose gifts are consistently wasted on inadequate material, and said, "Sure."

Dick and I stepped up. "Stand over there," the button man said, gesturing to the brick wall of one of the outbuildings of the zoo. His camera was set up on a tripod facing the wall. "The light," he said shortly.

Dick considered these words with immense gratitude, and looked up, melodramatically, at the hazy overcast sun, as though he had never before considered the possibility that light might affect a photographic portrait, and then allowed himself to be positioned, mug-shot style, against the wall.

"Do you always use this background?" Dick asked. The button man, a little exasperated, stopped just short of rolling his eyes.

"Yeah," he said. "The *light.*"

"Oh," Dick said. The light was, in fact, coming right into their eyes, causing both men to squint a little as the button man returned to his tripod and slowly settled on the shot.

"You're using a flash?" Dick inquired, in spite of himself.

The button man looked back up, warningly. Dick subdued himself.

"Let's make it a really . . . natural, easy, candid snapshot," he murmured. "No hysteria in the smiles. We'll just make a nice . . . candid snapshot." He sounded, though, a little dubious about the approach. Then he assumed his idea of a natural, easy, candid look, which was vaguely sinister in its guilty, not-quite-anything-ness— like the smile of a footman who has been caught in the hall closet with the second-best parlor maid.

The button man snapped the shutter, the flash went off in the middle of the park, and then he stepped back. "Let's try again," Dick said. Now he assumed another "candid" look: studied, severe, and unsmiling. The flash and shutter went off again in mid-expression.

"Okay," the button man said wearily. Again the quick little tongue of the Polaroid darted out of the camera, and the button man carefully laid the second photograph on a nearby stone balustrade alongside the first.

We crowded around to watch the two images develop. Dick characteristically thrust his jaw out at the two pictures, as though willing them to become deep and human and extravagant. In fact, one made us look like a couple of nervous lounge lizards in mufti; the other, like a pair of Nebraska convicts caught after a father-and-son killing spree.

Dick looked the two possibilities over. "The second one, don't you think," he said at last. "It has a certain gloomy authority that may appeal to her. We look tragic and lost without her." He handed the image back to the photo-button man, who expertly wrapped it around a blank tin button so that the two men's heads, unsmiling, candid, were all that was visible, and trickily covered it with clear plastic, using a little hot iron extracted from the depths of his coat to seal it. Money was exchanged. Dick looked at the button happily, but a little dubiously. Then he shook hands with the button man again, and began to walk on, toward the bridge leading to the zoo.

"This is no good for Martha. It's unthinkable that we send this to

her!" he said at last. "We have to go back and make a *real* button."
He turned violently around and began to trot back toward the button man, I following at his heels.

When he got there, he shook hands once more with the still-bemused (and business-less) button man in his overcoat.

"Listen," he said, "now, you and I are going to get to work. What you have here is something *amazing*. The possibilities of what you can do with this technique are endless. You haven't begun to scratch the surface of everything that's in *this* technique, and that's *in you to express*. We're going to work together and push the stick forward for your craft. Let's make a button that's a button." The button man looked a little bewildered but game.

"We need models for the shot . . ." Dick said, and then stepped forward into the traffic of people coming up along the red stone walk. A stream of young women walked by: girls in bicycle shorts, girls with small children. Dick looked them over, his head bobbing back and forth like a wary boxer's.

Two young black girls appeared, impressively cast in leopard-skin tops and tights. "Don't you think?" he whispered. "Girls," he said, stepping forward with a planted, man-at-work smile set on his lips, "I wonder if you could help us out . . . I'm . . ."

The two stepped a solid step out of the way, disdainfully, and walked on by. Then another two, and still two more. "Girls . . . could you . . . I wonder if you'd . . ." Dick sputtered a little as the stream of femininity rejected its interpreter.

Finally, Dick gathered himself together. Two rotund women, dressed oddly alike—white blouses, the kind of high-waisted pants that cry out to be called slacks, fastened with woven leather belts—were nearing. Both wore glasses in the shape of hearts—valentines, tinted pink. "Ladies," Dick said, "I wonder if you'd work with me for five minutes." He held out both hands pleadingly. "I'm working on a picture over here with a friend; we're making a kind of comical button to send to his wife." Dick put into "wife" a virtuous, hands-off, "no pickups around *here*" quality.

The two women, a smaller and larger version of the same type—mother and daughter, clearly—looked at each other, giggling and shrugging.

"You must be sisters," Dick said, throwing dignity and truth to the Central Park winds.

"No," the mother, as she obviously was, said. "This is my daughter, Michelle, and I'm Shirley."

Dick feigned elaborate disbelief, all the while stepping back with tiny steps, drawing his subjects into the little charmed circle where the button man in his studded overcoat and I waited. "That's amazing. What brings you to New York? Is it a vacation? . . ."—keeping up a steady, innocuous patter as he drew them in. His body had taken on the shape of unthreatening virtue: eyebrows raised, arms close in to his side as though bound there, palms out; a man fastened by his own rectitude—unthreatening as a leprechaun.

At last, he had lured Michelle and Shirley, still giggling and shrugging, into the cameraman's *light*. He looked around intently, judging angles and backgrounds. "Let's use *that* as a background," he said, pointing to the back of a gray dumpster. It was, apparently, the nearest thing he could find to a white no-seam. "If we use that we can make it work."

"I wouldn't try it," the button man said, professionally.

"Well, let's experiment for a moment. We'll set up over there, and then . . . we'll see." He began to block the positions of his little company. "Now, Michelle, dear, can you put your arm around Adam, and then, uh . . . let's bring Shirley in. . . . Right . . . Now, everybody . . . *leer*." The three subjects, all intensely embarrassed, tried to leer.

"That's not a leer," Dick said. "We've been picked up! *Leer*."

He clasped them in and stepped forward to demonstrate a leer—Groucho Marx come to life, bent over double with aching lechery and desire.

They tried again. Still, no leer. Now, instead of insisting, Dick dropped his voice, and, with the intimacy of a teenage boy making a picture of his girlfriend at a Fotomat, just repeated their names: "Shirley. *Michelle.*" The intimacy of the intonation worked, and their faces passed from self-consciously coy to high-heartedly seductive. Dick nodded violently to the button man, and he hit the shutter.

Dick, almost dancing with joy, took three quick tap-dance steps of pleasure. "Mmmm, I think this is going to be something," he said, and he thrust his jaw out and looked at the picture. "Now, that's a picture." He held it in his palm and showed it to his company. Michelle and Shirley and me.

Michelle and Shirley, who were beginning to enjoy themselves, relaxed as the button man walked over to the balustrade and began to laminate the picture onto a button. He finished and handed it to Dick, who cupped it in his hand.

"You know," Dick said, happy, and wanting, obviously, to enrich the experience for them—to make it into a moment—"it's funny. This is my work," he said conversationally. "I'm a photographer."

"Isn't that nice," Shirley said, with barely contained irony.

"No! Really. I mean photography is my work," Dick said. "No, really. I do all the covers for *Vogue.*"

Shirley's face, which was cast in a smirk of indulgence, now fell back into alarm. "Uh-huh?" she said, cautiously.

"No," Dick went on, oblivious. For he had spotted the problem: they weren't *Vogue* readers. "I do all the covers for *Mademoiselle,* too," he explained. "And for *GQ.*" He thought for a moment, as though digging something up from the back of his mind. "I'm *Avedon,*" he explained—cheerfully, benevolently. Suspicion turned to panic. Michelle and Shirley, scarcely pausing to say goodbye, turned on the madman with the Polaroids and the delusions and made off into the park, like squirrels.

Dick watched them go. "Ah, fame," he said. He seemed hurt. But then he looked down. He had the button.

=====

It was the same constant lesson, even if it came from different teachers: the means of art was just ceaseless labor to get the button right.

You took as much trouble on something that no one would see, or know was yours—a single sentence in an anonymous "Talk" story—as you did in the big stuff you hoped to show the world. And the subject of art was always contradiction, an uxorious young husband exposed in casual flirtation, smirking at Shirley while claiming to be sad. Even if you had to invent the contradiction out of passersby in Central Park.

But such happy encounters were rarer than long solitary wanderings. Walking on streets, walking through neighborhoods—Martha was even launched one night on an odd walk of her own. In 1990 we went to a party, the very last dinner party of the period, where one of the art dealers filled his townhouse with every imaginable figure of the art world and the money world of the period—Jeff Koons and Carl Icahn, Julian Schnabel and Peter Brandt, side by side. It turned out to be a party for a strange occasion—one of the billionaires was going off to prison the next day, and this was his farewell to New York. There were toasts raised to his bad fortune; the unfairness "of what's called justice in this country" was cursed; the persecution of the very rich (!) defied.

I was, perhaps, not in the best mind to take the evening in equably. The big show that Kirk Varnedoe and I had been working on for years about the entanglement of popular imagery and modern art had opened, and been much attacked. Nowadays, when I am on the road, it is the single thing that young curators cite most often and approvingly from all my work, proving once again the odd and unexceptional and rather Kiplingesque point that success and failure are so intermingled that they are distinct only at specific, not successive, moments in time. (Rather like modernist art and popular culture, come to think of it.)

Still, all of the nastier elements of the eighties did seem to have condensed into one storm cloud that night. Everything that was turning ugly in the time was there. The entanglement of art and money was one I could look at with a certain aplomb when I considered it historically, but not so much when I saw the relation between a business culture that had increasingly come to value only what you could grab and exploit, seated side by side with an art culture that had become addicted to the drug of money. You knew that even if there was no definable difference between this relation and the relation of the Medici—who were certainly no more ethical or admirable than the rich people in that room—to the artists of the Florentine Renaissance, still, there was something overheated and weird about it, something that boded no good to anyone, something imbalanced, something fatal, something that no amount of historical perspective could wish away. Something new. Something strange.

Martha said to me afterward—and I made it the basis for the first work of long fiction that I had ever succeeded in writing, a novella called "The Children of the Party"—that it reminded her of nothing so much as the dinner party at the end of *Through the Looking-Glass*, that gibbering, nightmare banquet, where everything turns from amusing nonsense into a wild phantasmagoria of appetite and absurdity, the creatures colliding with one another in a completely chaotic atmosphere of formalized horror.

Alice gets out in the end, back through the mirror in the living room and fireplace. But there was no way that Martha could see of getting out, back through the mirror, going home to the fire and kitten. She got tipsy, which I had never seen happen to her before, and wandered the room. I watched her small figure, in a yellow Alaïa dress, circle the tables—officially, simply looking for the bathroom, but pressing ahead, *touring* the room, taking in the strange flat conversations and nervous eyes of the guests. At the end, she told me later that night, after she had grown too sick to be in a taxi and I had taken her into a little ATM room on Fifty-seventh Street to recover—one of the little glass cash rooms that had seemed so touching, so thrilling, a New York invention at the beginning of the decade and had now become a place only to escape into, a shelter from the larger storm of money—she had had, through some collision of champagne and chaos, a kind of vision, a waking nightmare.

She had seen, she said, all of the artists and all of the billionaires, impaled like insects on that hideous, small-town snowflake that had been suspended, a few years before, above the previously pristine and thrillingly efficient intersection of Fifty-seventh and Fifth. (We didn't know then that it was Donald Trump who had, by legend at least, helped engineer the ominous snowflake, so gross in its proportions and so nakedly needy of its ugly wire supports. It's hard now to believe that Trump would have spent the money. But it hung, certainly, a piece of gargantuan and essentially suburban ostentation, outside his house.)

When I close my eyes now, I can still see the vision she communicated to me, of revolution and chaos, the sanctuary defiled, the world gone wrong, and wonder if, in her yellow Alaïa, she had not been given the gift of prophecy by a small and fashion-conscious God.

═══

But smaller disquieting signs than that large prophecy also appeared. As the eighties turned into the nineties, there came new creatures walking above our heads. After the mosquitoes had come the mice, who raced along the floorboards and squeaked in the walls and, on that one memorable night, suddenly ran out, in formation, from corners in our loft that we didn't even know were there, sending us in flight from our home.

With each of these infestations, we had passed through the same emotional stages: first, panic and dismay; then impotent, beseeching phone calls to the landlord; then long nights of one-eyed sleep; the purposeful phone calls to a small exterminating company; and at last—as the traps began to snap on little gray bodies or the poison began to reveal, on the bathroom floor at night, flipped-over brown insect carapaces—an exhausted, vengeful satisfaction.

Still, nothing in the past had prepared us for the arrival of the rats.

It happened on a Sunday night. At about twelve-thirty, Martha called me into the bathroom. From high above, in the ventilator shaft, came the sounds of scratching and breathing and animal motion. A few moments later, the sounds migrated, skittering along above the stamped-tin ceiling toward the back door; they included, unmistakably, the sound of confident scrabbling feet—a sound of weight and certainty.

We spent all of Monday in quaking denial. But on Tuesday morning we called up the other tenants and found out that the people down on the second and third floors had been hearing similar traffic in their walls for a couple of weeks. The city, I should add, had been tearing up some nearby streets for about that long, as part of a protracted and, given the city's circumstances at the end of the decade, rather loopy project to re-cobble a section of SoHo in order to restore the neighborhood to some imagined condition of nineteenth-century charm. Then, on Wednesday morning, one of our neighbors woke us at around seven. "I *saw* one!" she wailed. "It was the size of a *cat*. It ran into the bathroom in the middle of the night, and when we finally worked up the courage to confront it, it was gone, but one of our sponges was torn to pieces." Other sightings were reported throughout the day. "It was running down the hall," another neighbor said grimly. "It just walked right down the center of the hall. Big as a dog." Martha and I tried calling the "management agent," but he was unresponsive, and then we tried calling the city, but the Department of Violations passed us on to the Bureau of Infractions, and it said that we needed to get in touch with the Commission on Intractable Problems, so we finally just called up the exterminating service, which I'll refer to as NRN, and asked it to send a man over.

NRN turned out to be an oddly intense, high-morale little business. When we had mice, NRN first sent Paul, a melancholic West Indian man, who told us (with what reliability I can't say) that he had been the minister of agriculture of a good-sized Caribbean island nation "before the coup." Then he gravely scattered packets of poison all around the loft, with the air of one conducting a sacred ceremony. The next day, to our surprise, Sam, the boss of NRN, arrived at our door. "I'm worried about Paul," he explained. "He's a very good man, but sometimes he's thinking sugarcane when he should be thinking apartment." Sam turned out to be a Method exterminator. He stood stock-still in the middle of our loft, head

bowed, for what seemed to me a disturbingly long time. "I'm thinking like a mouse," he whispered at last. "I'm thinking, If I were a
mouse, where would I go? Where would I feel safe, trustful in this
space?" He even wrinkled his nose from time to time. Then he laid
traps and stuffed steel wool in all the crevices he found. We never
saw another mouse. Lee Strasberg would have been pleased.

———

But when I called about the rats I noticed that even the people at
NRN, who were usually pretty breezy about pests, seemed to
have a disturbingly healthy respect for them. Ginny, the woman
who answered the phone, said flatly, "We'll have to send Gilbert."
Gilbert turned out to be a gentle, extremely tall man with a dry,
pawky sense of humor and a soft, almost lilting voice. I got the key
to the basement from the super—we figured that the problem was
originating in the basement—and let Gilbert in, and then retreated
upstairs. About an hour and a half later, Gilbert came up. "Yeah,"
he said. "You got them, all right. You got the *big* boys. You got the
super-rats."

"What do you mean, the super-rats?" I asked, brilliantly imper-
sonating a calm person.

"Well, let's put it like this." He thought for a moment. "These
rats, if you see one, they look at you like *you* the problem."

Gilbert set some traps in the empty loft next door—huge traps,
with wooden backs the size of racquetball paddles—and pumped
poison under the floorboards. "Yes," he said cheerfully. "You won't
be troubled by no mice now. They can't coexist with these boys.
Nobody coexists with these boys. Yes, you got the big boys now."

I didn't want the big boys. Gilbert turned to me as he finished and
said, "Now, you shouldn't be seeing them, but you may hear them at
night. They eat this powder as they run along the beams, and then
they cry with fear to their mates when they find that they've been
poisoned." He imitated the sound of a poisoned rat calling out in
lament to its spouse. "Now, that's a good sound, for you," he said.
"It means we're turning the tide. You hear that sound, you remem-

ber, that's a good sound for you." I tried to meet Gilbert's eyes, since I suspected that there might be a certain amount of Schadenfreude inflecting his professionalism, but when I did they seemed completely earnest. "The one thing is," he said as he packed his equipment into his cart, "I think you ought to come down the basement sometime. I think if you're taking responsibility for these boys you ought to see the basement." All week long, people in the building kept calling for Gilbert's services, and eventually, he and I became friends. He showed up almost every day to solve one problem or another—somebody had a dead rat for him to remove, or somebody had found a crack in the ceiling on the first floor—and I would follow him from loft to loft. We would talk rat talk and rat lore. "There is the same number of rats in the city as people," Gilbert might say as he sealed up a rat hole with steel wool and putty. "Same number. You see one of the big boys—maybe that's you, your rat. It's a weird kind of thought." Each afternoon, he ended his work by saying, "I really think you ought to come and see the basement," or "I'd like to show you that basement," or just "Someday, we'll go down to the basement together, and then you'll understand about the big boys."

Then, coming home one afternoon, I saw a brown-snouted creature patrolling outside our building like a sentry. It was the size of a Miata. I watched it march into a crack in the building's cast-iron façade. Two women, strangers, were walking alongside me. "Did you see that?" one asked the other.

"That's my home," I burst out. "That's my *home*." I don't think I'd ever been so upset. That evening, I went to see my formidable German psychoanalyst. "So what about rats—what does it mean if you're afraid of rats?" I asked impatiently.

"Nothing," he said calmly. "Rats are not symbolic of anything. They are a fact. They must just be coped with."

Facts to cope with. This seemed like useful advice, so the next morning I hired a welding crew to close the crack in the façade; I insisted that the super come along a little later and seal the holes in the bricks in the side of the building with putty; and I called up Gilbert to get him to cast an eye on all this work. When Gilbert arrived, pushing his neat, well-ordered little cart, I showed him everything: how the welders were welding the crack together, how I had the super stuffing the holes. "I think we're coming along here, Gilbert," I said.

Gilbert smiled. "I *really* want you to come down and see the basement," he said. I shrugged—I had welders to supervise—and he disappeared. An hour or so later, Gilbert came to get me. "Now you gotta come down to the basement," he said. "You *got* to."

I looked at Gilbert. I realized that we were entering heavy, *Iron John*–type territory here. I was scared, and so I said, simply, "Gilbert, will I see dead rats?"

"No." He laughed. "I got them in bags—body bags." He seemed full of an odd kind of gaiety. I screwed up what courage I could, and followed Gilbert down the dark basement stairs.

What was I expecting? The word "basement" summoned up for me, I suppose, the picture of a rec room—knotty-pine walls, and shag carpeting, and a humming dehumidifier. The basement of our building, though, was right out of the second act of *The Phantom of the Opera*. One huge room—one huge *chamber*, really—followed another. Each had a high, vaulted ceiling, supported by a set of vast, imposing cast-iron columns with gloomy Corinthian capitals. "Piranesian"—that is the word I am looking for. Our basement was Piranesian. What could Elisha Sniffen, the architect of the building (his name is in the AIA guide), have been thinking of?

Gilbert took me on a tour of the labyrinth, and after a lot of twists and turns we came to what I realized was the space just under the sidewalk—I could hear the welders buzzing away, still at work outside. A black Hefty bag was standing on the floor. Gilbert waved his flashlight toward the bag. "I got some one-pounders in there," he said jovially as he picked up the bag; it sagged with the weight.

"Now, look," he said, pointing toward the space under the sidewalk, and I did.

The space was simply open, below street level, to the underside of the whole street. You peered out and you could see pipes and ducts and the underside of asphalt. You could hear the N train running, over on Broadway, three blocks away.

"You see!" Gilbert said with uncharacteristic emotion. "That's why you had to come down to the basement. That stuff, that *welding*— that is a *joke*. This place is open to the world! They're coming in and going up there, and there, and there." He pointed his flashlight at the top of the basement walls. "Nothing's been done here since the nineteenth century. My family was *slaves* the last time somebody come down this basement." It was an exaggeration, but I got his point.

"What you're telling me, Gilbert," I said finally, "is that there's nothing to be done. That everything I'm doing is not going to do any good." I felt sick.

"No. I am *not* telling you that," Gilbert said. "I'm telling you that there's no *solution*. You can't keep the rats out of your building. It would take twenty thousand dollars' worth of masonry—it would take a century's upkeep that somebody forgot all about—to keep the rats out. I'm telling you there's no *solution*, but there's a *technique*. Did I tell you about the three cons?" I shook my head, helpless. "Okay. The three cons. We got to *con*tain, *con*fine, and *con*vince. We got to contain the rats in one area of the basement, then we got to confine them to one feeding place, then we got to convince them that this is not a happy place for a rat to be. Move them on to the next building. Where there is *another* basement, just like yours. You can do that. You keep the service, you have me come, and we'll move them along."

Then he showed me some of the darker secrets of his craft. I watched him mix sugar water with poison, and for half an hour we laid out some black plastic trays full of poisoned tuna fish, and then we left the basement.

The problem receded. Soon, I walked out into the bright sunshine and didn't see a thing. The cheap welded-iron net in place on the façade of the building looked awful, but it gave my neighbors confidence. Had the rats gone away, really, because of what Gilbert did? Or is it just that the re-cobblestoning work on the street had moved on to the next block?

Is it even possible, I wonder, that Gilbert's philosophy of containment, which seemed to me at the time to strike some deep, permanent truth about New York, was marked by a little self-interest? He is, after all, the man who is paid to keep the three cons going. All I know for sure is that I no longer listened so intently for sounds in the middle of the night, or scanned the sidewalk quite so jumpily walking home. Life is different after you have seen the basement.

=====

I go back to SoHo often, and try to walk those same streets again. Now Mercer Street is stuffed with mall retailers; there's even a branch of our once-beloved Bloomingdale's. There are no art galleries. The illuminated sidewalks are often paved over. What's there below, Gilbert's open city, has been patched, and the patching has gone on long enough so that it seems permanent, curative. The furtive noises, when they return, are mostly unheard, or bought off.

There is little room to walk amid the shoppers. This is, of course, a universal and not entirely to be mourned truth about New York. What changes is not the city—some twenty-something is even now walking the no longer ample or hilly Brooklyn, and writing it down. No, what changes is us. We start walking outdoors to randomize our experience of the city, and then life comes to randomize us. We decided at the end of the decade to begin to try to have children, and children are the greatest of randomizers: they're like great abstract pictures, in that you know they must mean something, but the meaning takes the form of random-seeming splashes and improvised moments. They make walking unnecessary; we just circle them. Our walking ends as theirs begins.

And then, coming back years later, we know that even our cells have begun to go random on us, producing small failures of replication that mark our surface. We are made for walking, but we are not very good at it; our backs and arches, like querulous Cabinet ministers, at first complain, and then resign. Footsore, we sit down and stay there, until, eventually, we leave the room, feet first, hoping only to be remembered within another head. When you walk in SoHo now, there are still no flowers beneath your feet, and the open basements below the illuminated sidewalks are invisible.

Epilogue

Not long after the last party, Martha decided that she wanted to
leave New York, which had passed from enticement to encum-
brance, and have a child. Since she did, I did, too. We began
to revisit an older dream of going to France. Professionally, life had
become mercifully simple. I had sold a piece to *The New Yorker*. Then
I had sold another, and another, and then they had hired me to write
about the city for the old "Talk of the Town" department, carefully
caricatural reporting on the eccentrics of the city and their hidden
rabbit holes, five years of pure bliss spent in anonymity, learning
that hard craft of exacting wildness. After that, I did go to Paris and
write and then came home and wrote about liberal civilization and
my children, sometimes conflating the two.

And almost forty years after our arrival in New York I look up
and realize I have spent my entire adult life doing exactly what I
wanted to do and it still feels as if I hadn't done it. How this happens
I'm not sure, except that I am sure it is a universal emotion: accom-
plishing something longed for never feels like an accomplishment,
only an accommodation, one that others have made for you and that
you have made for others. The brightest star on Broadway feels herself up there on sufferance and only for now. Certainly, the feelings
that we anticipate will crowd around us once we've accomplished
an ambition are never the feelings we get. (I'm sure that even Maxie's museum was not the unalloyed blessing that he had imagined

it would be.) The feelings we get are the same feelings that got us there.

In me, the feelings remained the same urge to work in order to live. To "live," in the raw sense that pushed me from Frick to MoMA to *GQ* back in the early eighties, the urge to make enough money to pay rent and buy groceries and keep the girl (or keep four people and a dog and a bird now). When Dick Avedon and I took one last trip together in 2004—he would die after a fall a few days later in Texas, taking one more portrait as he did—he said, "We're providing for our families," and for a moment we were just two Jewish gents in a cabana in Margate some lost summer, grunting, providing.

But to live in another way, too. We write in order not to have passed by in vain. We write to offer proof of life, as the G-men say when they demand a photo of the kidnapped holding a newspaper, and as the kidnappers intend when they send an ear or a finger in return. Proof of life is what we traffic in as writers, before we traffic in ideas or even in emotions, even if our body parts get lost or mangled along the way. We like to say that the end of writing is connection, but the starting point is simple affirmation. We have left a trace. The book, shut closed on the tale, but bearing a title and the author's name on its spine, is consoling in itself. I passed this way, and left this here.

At least, the means of life were apparent, even if its meaning was as clouded as ever. I was writing, and it was all I did, all day long and most of the night. The great struggle from *"but"* to *"and,"* from contention to inclusion—an essayist trying to make the shapes of the sentences themselves embody a liberal view of life—went on every day. It still does. The shapes will never be as perfectly pregnant as they ought to be, but they grow shapelier. Writers are sentenced to their sentences, which sometimes set them free.

═══

It was just as the eighties turned into the nineties, when we were already spiritually packing to leave, that I finally got a copy of the complete Rodgers & Hart—a deluxe new edition from Knopf—

with Lorenz Hart's lyrics of "The Blue Room," complete with a long explanatory verse that never gets sung. "Read the little blueprints," the singer urges his bride. "Here's your mother's room. / Here's your brother's room. / On the wall are two prints. / Here's the kiddies' room, / Here's the biddy's room, / Here's a pantry lined with shelves, dear. / Here I've planned for us / Something grand for us, / Where we two can be ourselves, dear." The lyrics run and only *then* comes the familiar words "We'll have a blue room. . . ."

It wasn't a little basement room where two people could live in seclusion! It was a small study off some enormous West Side apartment, the kind of apartment that was stuffed with in-laws and kids, a charming library where you could retreat when stressed! It was a one-percenter's perk, a rich man's luxury, not a starting couple's dream. It was a song of the Strunskys' Manhattan. I had gotten it completely wrong.

And then, not too long after that, I happened upon a biography of Issa, the Japanese poet whose beautiful little haiku I had taken with me on the 5 train when we went to be married. "The world of dew is / a world of dew, / but even so." I had read it as a rueful admission of the possibility of pleasure even as one accepted the transitory nature of existence. . . . In fact, his life was more eventful and more tragic than I had imagined. He had married and had a three-year-old daughter, Sato, who was the light of his life, and who had died of smallpox. It was not a poem of rueful, "mindful" celebration. It was a poem of pure grief: yes, everything passes, but not this, no, this should not have passed for me. The truer translation read: "The world is a dewdrop world. Yes . . . but." There: the shameless little ellipsis, which I offered the *GQ* fragrance editor, put in the service of the unimaginable pain.

Just before we left for Paris, we walked back to the Blue Room, for sentimental reasons, one last look, and noticed what I had never noticed in all the years we lived on East Eighty-seventh Street. The single biggest sign on the street, the single most imposing neighbor directly alongside our basement room at 340 East Eighty-seventh was . . . a funeral home. The Walter B. Cooke funeral home, at 352

East Eighty-seventh. We had lived right beside it for all that time, in the valley of the shadow of death. Mourners must have been going in and out all day—*bodies* must have been going in and out all day! Stiffs, conveyed feet-first inside as we read to each other aloud, and then embalmed as we made toast and coffee and love—and I had never noticed any of it. It was right there, right next door, mortality itself, to remind young lovers as it does the shepherds in Poussin's painting *Et in Arcadia Ego.* . . . The truth is that young lovers are too busy looking at each other to look at the world. The Arcadian shepherds, if they are having fun, never look at the inscription on the tomb, at the signs of mortality, even when they are right next door, under a red awning, in a townhouse with red shutters and a giant sign that says "Funeral Home."

I had managed to get every single important thing wrong: the size and nature of the Blue Room, the meaning of the poem, the sentiment of the song, the purpose of life, the presence of death. It was time to begin.

But meanwhile—no, no "but," not even a "Yes . . . but," as in Issa, just an "and." And meanwhile, at least we were still married, and there were many mornings when, as in the Blue Room, I couldn't see her for seeing her, couldn't tell Martha's face from my eyes upon it. I hope I never shall.

Acknowledgments

Many of the stories in this book I first told onstage for the Moth, the matchless story-telling group that has become such an essential part of my imaginative life, as it has become essential to New York life in general. I thank all of the men and, mostly, women of the Moth, and especially my friend and director Catherine Burns.

Some other stories in this book first appeared, often in very different form, in *The New Yorker*. My editors there, to whom I am forever grateful, included Robert Gottlieb, Tina Brown, David Remnick, Charles McGrath, Ann Goldstein, and Henry Finder. And all of the innumerable fact-checkers who were present to nudge and amend get my thanks, too. George Andreou at Knopf, my old stomping, or barking, grounds, turned these stories into a book. I thank him, yet again, for doing that.

There are too many friends and colleagues from the past and present to name, but I do want to nod, briskly and inadequately, to Alec Wilkinson and Louis Menand. It was Alec who was my first and favorite companion into the mysteries of a wild exactitude, and Luke Menand who, with Emily Abrahams, became the first to encourage me to explore this dubious territory of my life for a book—chiefly I suspect because they had heard the stories of lost pants and keys so often around the table that they wanted to see them permanently retired between covers, as one sends aging parents to Florida. I thank them both.

ACKNOWLEDGMENTS

The Gopniks—Myrna, Irwin, Alison, Morgan, Hilary, Blake, and Melissa—are forever the front line of my consciousness. The Gopnik-Parkers—Luke and Olivia—are forever the front line of my conscience. Martha Parker finally got the dedication for what she has been, hour by hour, to my life; but she also gets my thanks for what she added, sentence by sentence, to this book.

Permissions Acknowledgments

Grateful acknowledgment is made to Alfred Publishing, LLC, and Williamson Music for permission to reprint an excerpt of "The Blue Room" from *The Girl Friend*, words by Lorenz Hart and music by Richard Rodgers. Copyright © 1926 by WB Music Corp. and Williamson Music, copyright renewed. Copyright assigned to Williamson Music and WB Music Corp. for the extended renewal period of copyright in the USA, Canada and BRT Territories. International copyright secured. All rights reserved. Reprinted by permission of Alfred Publishing, LLC, and Williamson Music.

Excerpt of "Epistle to a Godson" from *Collected Poems* by W. H. Auden, copyright © 1969 by W.H. Auden and renewed 1997 by Edward Mendelson. Published by Random House, an imprint and division of Penguin Random House LLC.

A NOTE ON THE TYPE

Pierre Simon Fournier le jeune (1712–1768), who designed the type used in this book, was both an originator and a collector of types. His services to the art of printing were his design of letters, his creation of ornaments and initials, and his standardization of type sizes. His types are old style in character and sharply cut. In 1764 and 1766 he published his *Manuel typographique*, a treatise on the history of French types and printing, on type-founding in all its details, and on what many consider his most important contribution to typography—the measurement of type by the point system.

Typeset by Scribe,
Philadelphia, Pennsylvania

Printed and bound by LSC Communications,
Harrisonburg, Virginia

Designed by Cassandra J. Pappas